STARTING YOUR OWN BUSINESS

THIRD EDITION

Ron Immink
Brian O'Kane

Downloads and additional information available @
www.startingabusinessinireland.com

Researched and written by
Ron Immink and Brian O'Kane.

Published for the
Department of Enterprise, Trade & Employment by
Oak Tree Press
19 Rutland Street, Cork.
http://www.oaktreepress.com
http://www.startingabusinessinireland.com.

ISBN 978-1-904887-35-5

Printed in Ireland by ColourBooks.

Department of
Enterprise, Trade
and Employment

Acknowledgements
Production of first edition of this guide in 1997 was
assisted by the European Commission through the
Community SME Initiative under Measure 4 of the
Small Business Operational Programme.

The authors gratefully acknowledge the assistance
they received from the organisations mentioned in
this guide, the staff of the Department and
the many others who have contributed to the research,
largely carried out by Anne Kennedy for this edition.

Disclaimer
The contents of this guide are believed to be correct at the
time of printing but no responsibility can be taken by the
authors, publisher or Department of Enterprise, Trade &
Employment for any errors herein.
Readers should take professional advice before entering
into any legally binding commitments or investing any
funds.

Business Plan Pro®
— the easiest way to write a business plan.

Producing a business plan can be time consuming and stressful. Instead of staring at a blank Microsoft Word or Excel file, let **Business Plan Pro®** guide you step-by-step through the process helping you create a winning business plan.

- No.1 recommended
- Saves time and money
- 500+ sample plans
- Step-by-step help
- Free product support
- Risk-free (60-day money back guarantee)
- Available as download

To view a demo visit www.paloalto.ie
Palo Alto Software Ltd 021 497 1335

The harsh reality is that too many new businesses fail – many more than ought to. Why? Because of lack of planning. They do not plan to fail, but they certainly fail to plan.

Preparation – in the form of careful and considered planning – is the most important thing you can do to ensure that your fledgling business gets off the ground and continues flying. You can never eliminate **all** risk but you can reduce it significantly – to the point where the odds are weighted in your favour.

This workbook is all about preparation – preparing you for what you will face as an entrepreneur, for the obstacles, hurdles and blockages that will be placed in your way, for the new skills that you will have to learn, for the tasks that you will have to handle, for the rules, regulations and form-filling that may trip you up, right through to the agencies – State and private sector – which can help you make your dream a success.

The first edition of this workbook was developed for the Department of Enterprise, Trade & Employment under Measure 4 of the Government's Operational Programme for Small Business, which was funded by the European Commission. This is now the third edition of what has become a standard text on business planning for start-ups in Ireland.

It was designed to take a potential entrepreneur through the whole process of starting a business, from first thoughts about self-employment to the practicalities of start-up.

The workbook consists of three core chapters:

- **READY** – The first chapter, covering preparation, self-assessment, ideas generation, market research and training for entrepreneurs
- **STEADY** – The bulk of the guide, covering business planning, raising finance, sources of assistance, choosing premises, recruiting staff, marketing, book-keeping and management issues
- **GO** – When everything has been thought through and you are ready, this section provides the remaining information you need to get started.

As you work through the workbook, you will find checklists, flowcharts and questionnaires designed to make you think about your proposed business. The aim is not only to give you the theory behind setting up a business but also to give you the practical tools to actually do it. It all adds up to a turn-key package – a "business in a box".

Each chapter in this workbook is introduced by a number of **KEY QUESTIONS** – searching questions that the entrepreneur needs to consider carefully before moving ahead. Think through your answers to the key questions (but do not write them down yet) before you read the chapter. When you have completed the chapter, read all the sections and worked through all the checklists and questionnaires, you should then come back to the key questions and complete your answers in writing.

In each section of the workbook, you will find clearly-stated **OBJECTIVES** set out beside the section heading. These summarise what you can expect to learn from the section.

Read them before you begin, to decide whether the section is relevant to your needs. And when you have finished the section, go back, read the objectives again and check them off.

And then, when you have reached the end of the workbook, you have filled in and sent out all the forms that are necessary, you have written your business plan, your funding is in place, and all the preparations are made – it's time to rock and roll!

To help you even more, this workbook is linked to a continually-updated web-site, **www.startingabusinessinireland.com**, where you will find spreadsheets and templates to download, as well as updated and additional information and resources.

Good luck.

Ron Immink, Dublin
Brian O'Kane, Cork
October 2009

DUBLIN BUSINESS INNOVATION CENTRE

CONTENTS

INTRODUCTION

CONTENTS

READY?
Introduction   9
What Makes an Entrepreneur?   10
Self-assessment   11
Developing & Testing your Idea   14
Market Research   17
Identifying Future Trends   20
Feasibility Study Grants   21
Training for Entrepreneurs   22
Start-up Alternatives   24

STEADY
Introduction   27
Developing a Mission Statement   28
Developing a Strategy   29
Innovation   32
Competitiveness   34
Using Technology to Advantage   35
Marketing   36
e-Business   49
Products and Production   53
Staff   55
Which Legal Structure?   61
Registering a Business Name   63
Opening a Bank Account   64
Taxation   65
Accounting   71
Insurance   75
Trading Laws   76
Premises   77
Working from Home   78
Finance   79
Operating Budget   87
Cash-flow Planning   91
Assistance – State Agencies   96
Assistance – Other Organisations   104
Reducing Risk   109
Mentors   110
Professional Advisers   111
The Business Plan   112
Presenting & Pitching your Business Plan   136
Smell the Flowers   138

GO
Introduction   139
Completing the Accounts Pages   140
Job Application Form   142
Job Description   143
Employment Contract   144
Safety Statement   146
Advertising Control Sheet   147
Quality   148
Environmental Concerns   150
Health and Safety   151
Intellectual Property   152
Monitoring Performance   154

APPENDICES
1   Addresses   155
2   Further Information   175

I'm a survivor. I'm adaptable. I'm aware and I'm hungry. I'm ready to fight each and every challenge my business is going to face, and now I have over 25,000 fellow businesspeople to turn to for assistance, support and insights. I'm facing the future with renewed confidence.

"MY BUSINESS CAN"

Small businesses and entrepreneurs are coming together in an entirely new way.
To find out how your 'small business can' and to get the right people behind you, visit:
www.smallbusinesscan.com

SMALL BUSINESS
can

powered by ✳ Ulster Bank

INTRODUCTION

- Almost 70% of people who become self-employed do not prepare themselves properly for their new role and responsibilities
- Specifically, almost 90% do not study their market
- As a result, on average about 50% of all businesses in Europe fail within five years of starting.

These statistics should show you the importance of preparation and of carefully considering whether entrepreneurship is right for you – though you should also balance this with Paul Dickson's quote in the page margin.

Chapter structure
This chapter takes you through:
- What makes an entrepreneur?
- Self-assessment (including assessment of your business partners)
- Developing and testing your idea
- Market research
- Identifying future trends
- Feasibility study grants
- Training for entrepreneurs
- Start-up alternatives (buying an existing business, franchising and network marketing).

Key Questions
The Key Questions in the panel are designed to focus your thoughts as you read this chapter.

Think through your answers to these questions before you start to read the chapter. Then come back and write your answers in the spaces provided before moving on to the next chapter.

KEY QUESTIONS

1. Do you have the skills/experience needed to run a business?
   ☐ YES ☐ NO

2. Do you have sufficient motivation to stick with it for as long as it takes?
   ☐ YES ☐ NO

3. Do you have the support of your family? ☐ YES ☐ NO

4. Does your business idea test out?
   ☐ YES ☐ NO

5. Are you eligible for a Feasibility Study Grant? ☐ YES ☐ NO

6. Is your business:
   > A start-up? ☐ YES ☐ NO
   > Buy-in of an existing business? ☐ YES ☐ NO
   > Franchise? ☐ YES ☐ NO
   > Network marketing?
   ☐ YES ☐ NO

7. Do you need further training?
   ☐ YES ☐ NO

8. Are you ready to write your business plan? ☐ YES ☐ NO

OBJECTIVES
o Understand importance of preparation
o Answer Key Questions

Ignore all the statistics that tell you that 95% of all new businesses fail in the first eight years.
Not only are these "statistics" riddled with widely wrong assumptions and false failure rates, but they don't apply to you. Dwelling on the statistics is like staying up to study divorce rates on your wedding night.
PAUL DICKSON

Whatever you think it's gonna take, double it. That applies to money, time, stress.
It's gonna be harder than you think and take longer than you think.
RICHARD A CORTESE, on starting a business

WHAT MAKES AN ENTREPRENEUR?

OBJECTIVES
o Identify the traits of successful entrepreneurs
o Identify success factors

Entrepreneurs are risk-takers, willing to roll the dice with their money or their reputations on the line in support of an idea or enterprise.
They willingly assume responsibility for the success or failure of a venture and are answerable for all its facets.
The buck not only stops at their desk, it starts there too.
VICTOR KIAM

The "entrepreneurial state of mind" is an attitude that says, in short: "I didn't just come to play the game – *I came to win*".
GORDON BATY

Entrepreneurship is the dynamic process of creating wealth, undertaken by people who assume a risk in terms of money, energy, time and/or career commitment of creating value through the provision of some product or service. The product or service may or may not be new or unique but value somehow must be created by the entrepreneur by securing and using the necessary skills and resources.

Why do people become entrepreneurs?
Research suggests four motives:
- Dramatic change in personal situation (unemployment, divorce)
- Availability of resources (idea, money)
- Certain entrepreneurial skills
- Example of another successful entrepreneur.

Typical entrepreneurial traits
The entrepreneur is the key to the successful launch of any business. He/she is the person who perceives the market opportunity and then has the motivation, drive and ability to mobilise resources to meet it.

Although it is difficult to describe a typical entrepreneur, they share certain characteristics or traits:
- **Self-confident all-rounder** – The person who can make the product, market it and count the money
- **The ability to bounce back** – The person who can cope with making mistakes and still has the confidence to try again
- **Innovative skills** – Not necessarily an "inventor" in the traditional sense but one who is able to carve out a new niche in the market-place, often invisible to others
- **Results-orientated** – To make the business successful requires a drive that only comes from setting goals and targets and getting pleasure from achieving them
- **Professional risk-taker** – To succeed means taking measured risks. Often the successful entrepreneur exhibits a step-by-step approach to risk-taking, at each stage exposing him/herself to only a limited, measured amount of personal risk and moving from one

stage to another only as each decision is proved
- **Total commitment** – Hard work, energy and single-mindedness are essential elements in the entrepreneurial profile.

Note that the entrepreneurial characteristics required to launch a business successfully are often not those required for growth and, even more frequently, not those required to manage the business once it grows to any size. The role of the entrepreneur needs to change with the business as it develops and grows. In particular, the management skills of the entrepreneur – in managing staff, managing his/her own time, and in strategic planning – become more important as the business grows.

Success factors
Research suggests that successful entrepreneurs share some common factors. Which of the success factors in the panel below do you have?

SUCCESS & FAILURE FACTORS WHICH DO YOU HAVE?	
1. Hard work	☐
2. Perseverance	☐
3. Motivation	☐
4. Social skills	☐
5. Leadership	☐
6. Good management	☐
7. Integrity	☐
8. Guts	☐
9. Good health	☐
10. Common-sense	☐
11. Luck	☐
12. Support of family	☐
13. Clear initial goals	☐
14. Creativity	☐
15. Ability to accept uncertainty	☐

SELF-ASSESSMENT

Before you decide to start your own business, you should know that:

- The average working week of a self-employed person is 64 hours. In almost half of those businesses, the spouse/partner is also involved for another 21 hours (total, 85 hours)
- Most people do not increase their income by becoming self-employed
- One in five entrepreneurs do not earn anything in the first 18 months
- Support of the spouse/partner is a critical factor in the success or failure of a start-up business.

Running your own business demands a lot of commitment. It is both physically and mentally demanding. Therefore, it is very important to ask yourself why you want to become self-employed. This will take some soul-searching but it is vital to the decision to go ahead. If your motivation is not strong enough, you will not last the race.

You also need to be sure that you have your family's support.

Self-assessment

The questions in the panel below and on the next page will help you assess your own suitability for starting and running a business. Write your answers in the spaces provided.

Copy this page, and the next page, so that your business partners can answer the questions too.

OBJECTIVES

o Need for commitment
o Need for family support
o Self-assessment

Beware of undertaking too much at the start. Be content with quite a little. Allow for accidents. Allow for human nature, especially your own.
ARNOLD BENNETT

Anyone who wants to achieve a dream must stay strong, focused and steady.
ESTEE LAUDER

I do not believe a man can ever leave his business. He ought to think of it by day and dream of it by night.
HENRY FORD

	Is this a Strength or a Weakness?	
	S	W
What personal motivation do you bring to the business?		
What skills do you bring to the business?		
What experience do you bring to the business?		
What training/education do you bring to the business?		

	Is this a Strength or a Weakness?	
	S	W

What supports do you bring to the business?
- Network of useful contacts   ☐ YES ☐ NO
- Support of your partner/spouse   ☐ YES ☐ NO
- Support of your family and friends   ☐ YES ☐ NO
- Finance € _____   ☐ YES ☐ NO
- Other (list)

What personal characteristics do you bring to the business?
- Health   Good/OK/Bad
- Endurance   Good/OK/Bad
- Flexibility   Good/OK/Bad
- Creativity   Good/OK/Bad
- Honesty   Good/OK/Bad
- Confidence   Good/OK/Bad
- Ability to handle stress   Good/OK/Bad
- Other (list)

    Good/OK/Bad
    Good/OK/Bad
    Good/OK/Bad

What time commitments do you bring to the business?
- Social activities   _____ hrs/week
- Family   _____ hrs/week
- Hobbies   _____ hrs/week
- Other (list)

    _____ hrs/week
    _____ hrs/week
    _____ hrs/week

Total time commitment outside the business   _____ hrs/week
How much could you reduce these to make time for the business? _____ hrs/week

What financial commitments do you bring to the business?
- Household expenses   € _____/week
- Loan repayments   € _____/week
- Savings/pension   € _____/week
- Hobbies/holidays   € _____/week
- Other (list)

    € _____/week
    € _____/week
    € _____/week

Total financial commitments   € _____/week
How much could you reduce these to develop the business?   € _____/week

Relationship with family

Your relationship with your family is going to change because of your new business.

You will no longer have a regular income – some months you may have no pay-check at all. Can your family survive on what your spouse/partner earns?

You will be working long hours, through weekends and at times when other people are off. Your working hours will be irregular – nothing to do for periods and then several urgent jobs all to be done at once. You will be under pressure, since you will no longer have a boss to take the final responsibility for everything – you will now be the boss.

You will have more at risk than just your money – your reputation, savings, borrowings, even your ego are also at risk.

All this will affect your relationship with your family. Are you ready?

Why not discuss the situations in the panel with your family? It will help you – and them – understand what lies ahead and how you will react to the choices that may need to be made.

Think positive

Don't be alarmed by this section on Self-assessment. It is merely pointing out the reality of self-employment. If you don't believe it, check with someone you know who has recently started their own business.

And above all – don't let this section put you off. There are positive sides to running your own business:

- You can organise your own working hours
- You can do the tasks you like to do and pay other people to do the things you dislike
- You are in control of your own destiny
- You learn a lot
- You deal with all kinds of different situations
- You deal with a lot of different people
- You get a great sense of achievement
- People respect and admire entrepreneurs.

SITUATIONS TO DISCUSS WITH YOUR FAMILY

1. The kids need new shoes. The business needs a new piece of machinery that costs €100. There is only €100 in the bank. Which comes first?
2. A big order comes in (Congratulations!). For the next two weeks, you need to work at least 14 hours every day (including weekends) in order to meet the order. It is also your turn to look after the kids this weekend. What are you going to do?
3. You promised your spouse/partner a night out. That night a client insists on meeting you. Which comes first?
4. You have booked a holiday and the whole family is really looking forward to it. Suddenly, the person who was supposed to look after the business while you are away cancels. You cannot find another replacement on such short notice. What happens?
5. A deadline needs to be met. You get ill. Who will take over the running of the business while you are out sick?
6. The business is not going as well as expected. Your business needs an extra loan to survive. Your partner/spouse wants you to quit. What happens?
7. Your business has a cash flow problem. As a result, you have not been able to take out a salary for the past two months and some of your household bills (telephone, gas, electricity) are running behind. How long will that be acceptable to your partner/spouse?

Reproduced from LOOK BEFORE YOU LEAP *by permission of the Department of Enterprise, Trade & Employment and the Department of Social, Community & Family Affairs*

ANSWER THESE QUESTIONS BEFORE MOVING TO THE NEXT SECTION

Do you accept the changes the business is going to bring to your life?

Financial insecurity	☐ YES	☐ NO
Long working hours	☐ YES	☐ NO
Irregular working hours	☐ YES	☐ NO
Pressure	☐ YES	☐ NO
Risk	☐ YES	☐ NO
Relationship with family	☐ YES	☐ NO

OBJECTIVES

o Understand thinking processes

o Understand how to develop an idea

> **What kind of business are you thinking about?**
>
> | | | |
> |---|---|---|
> | Are you going to manufacture? | ☐ YES | ☐ NO |
> | Are you starting in retail? | ☐ YES | ☐ NO |
> | Are you starting in wholesale? | ☐ YES | ☐ NO |
> | Are you going into import /export? | ☐ YES | ☐ NO |
> | Are you starting a service? | ☐ YES | ☐ NO |
> | Are you starting in leisure? | ☐ YES | ☐ NO |
> | Are you starting online? | ☐ YES | ☐ NO |
>
> **Describe your idea:**

One sound idea is all you need to achieve success.
NAPOLEON HILL

I work from details outward to the general and I don't stop developing big ideas until I have worked out the minutest detail.
RAY KROC, McDonalds

We haven't got the money, so we've got to think.
LORD RUTHERFORD

Attempt the impossible to improve your work.
BETTE DAVIS

Why should it be done at all?
Why should it be done now?
Why should it be done that way?
HERBERT BAYARD SWOPE

Developing your idea to its fullest potential involves creative thinking.

This section provides an overview of some of the most common creative thinking techniques. They will help you to identify new ideas, develop your existing idea and create new opportunities.

Thinking

We all think in two stages. The first stage is to look, simplify what we see, recognise and name what we see, then filter it through our experience and knowledge. In the second stage, we then judge and conclude. Unfortunately, we spend most of our time thinking in the second stage. With creative thinking, most of the time is spent in the first stage of thinking.

Look below. What do you see?

Your answer is probably: "A black dot".

Yes, there is a black dot, but there is also more text, a numbered list, etc. By jumping straight into second stage thinking, you missed all the surroundings.

You did not take time to sit back, relax and look a little bit longer. You rushed for the obvious answer. But, by taking time to step back, you will see more and, by seeing more, you will also see more possibilities. That is the idea behind creative thinking.

As an entrepreneur, it is important to spend time looking at your idea and trying to come up with new possibilities, extra features, alternatives, etc. This will not only give you an even better understanding of your idea, it will improve it and will make you more competitive. This kind of creative thinking should be an ongoing process to keep your business competitive.

Steps in creative thinking

1. Move away:
• Widen perception
• Question assumptions (Why not? What if?)
• Break the rules
• Make associations.

2. Bring yourself back into the real world:
• Evaluate
• Judge
• Tried before?
• Will it work?

Technique 1: Brainstorming

1. Get a group together (four people is the minimum, preferably more)
2. Define a problem and discuss it
3. Redefine the problem
4. Practice run to warm up the mind – How many uses can you find for a paperclip?
5. Brainstorming
   > Aim to generate as many ideas as possible
   > All ideas are acceptable
   > The crazier the idea the better
6. Select the craziest idea and brainstorm that idea for a while.

Technique 2: Attribute listing

This technique is best used when you are thinking of adapting or developing an existing product or service. Take the particular product and list its attributes: For example, shape, size, design, materials, colour, functions and cost. Then take each attribute and find as many alternatives to it as possible.

Technique 3: Who, what, where, when, why, how

Tease out different perspectives and ideas with any product, service, problem or situation, using the six prompts above.

Technique 4: Assumption-smashing

List the assumptions of the problem or idea, then explore what happens if you drop assumptions. For example, why assume that this product should be made of plastic. What if it were made of something else?

Technique 5: Discontinuity

Disrupt your own patterns:

- Programme interruptions in your day
- Do something you have never done before or read something you would not normally read
- Watch some different TV programmes.

Putting it into practice

Developing an idea is only part of the battle. The idea must also work in practice. Therefore, it is important to ask yourself some critical questions about your business and your product/service. Write your answers below. Copy this page and the next page before answering, so that you can use these pages to develop and test other ideas later.

	Is this a Strength or a Weakness?	
	S	W
1. Why is it a good idea?		
2. On what assumptions is your opinion based?		
3. How can you prove that those assumptions are correct?		
4. What types of customer will be interested in your product/service?		
5. Why?		
6. List four reasons why the idea may **not** work: • • • •		

	Is this a Strength or a Weakness?	
	S	W

7. List four reasons why your idea **will** work:

8. What is different about this idea from others already in the market-place?

9. Why are those differences important?

10. What if ... you changed the product/service in some way?

Make a list of people you know who might be able to help you with the research or whose opinion you trust. Ask their opinion about your idea. Ask them to be critical and honest.

Name   **Opinion**

Marketing is about keeping your customers central in your thinking, behaviour and planning. To do that, you need a combination of information, vision and creativity. One of the techniques to get information is market research, which has three functions:

- **Informing** – Consumer behaviour, market trends, developments abroad
- **Evaluating** – Are goals achieved?
- **Experimenting** – Testing markets or products.

Why do market research?

Market research is the core of your business and business plan. It is important that you:

- Are aware of market developments
- Find out for yourself whether you can approach people at all kinds of levels
- Find out whether you can sell (if not, you will have to find someone to do it for you)
- Find out whether there is a market for your product/service, how big it is, how it can be reached, etc
- Are well-prepared before you commit funds (your own or other people's) to your business
- Are able to show potential financiers that you have taken the trouble to gather the necessary information
- Are able to show that you know your stuff.

But the overwhelming reason for doing market research is to prove the commercial viability of your project - to yourself!

Making your market research practical

Market research is often considered by entrepreneurs to be too theoretical to be bothered with. That's both dangerous and wrong: Dangerous because without market research you may start a business or develop a product/service for which there is no demand; wrong because market research can be very practical.

Practical market research includes things as simple as:

- Counting the cars on your competitors' parking lot (to tell you how many customers they get and how well-off they are)
- Counting the people passing by the premises you are planning to rent (big stores like Marks & Spencer sometimes do this for months before deciding on a location for a new shop)
- Counting the waste bags outside the backdoor of a restaurant (to give you some idea of the volume of their business)
- Checking the number of trucks delivering supplies to competitors (on the basis that level of their purchases gives you an insight into their sales)
- Counting the numbers of customers walking into a competitors' office or shop
- Knocking on every door in a housing estate in which you are planning to open an outlet (to ask whether there is a demand, at what price, etc.)
- Collecting all your competitors' brochures and price lists (to find out what they are offering and at what prices)
- Checking where your competitors advertise and how big an advertisement they take.

Note that market research should be an ongoing process. It should not stop after the business has started (or the product/service has been launched) but should become an integral part of your business.

Sources of information

When you are looking for information as part of your desk research, there is an almost endless list of sources of information, including:

- Your local library
- Central Statistics Office (**www.cso.ie**)
- Enterprise Ireland (**www.enterprise-ireland.com**)
- Government Publications Office
- Government Departments and State agencies (**www.irlgov.ie/www.basis.ie**)
- Business magazines and trade journals
- Newspapers – National and local
- Banks
- Business Innovation Centres
- City & County Enterprise Boards (**www.enterpriseboards.ie**)
- Area Partnership Companies

OBJECTIVES

o Understand market research techniques
o Apply them to own product/service

Three-quarters of all entrepreneurs start up without doing any market testing to establish whether there is demand for their product/service. Only three in ten carry out market research to determine whether a market exists for their business in the first place. Fewer still – one in five – draw up a detailed customer profile to build up knowledge about their prospective customers and their buying habits. Knowing who your customers are and why they will buy from you, rather than from your competitors, should be a crucial part in deciding how a business will fit into the market and whether it is likely to succeed. Those that do not assess their long-term market potential and overall competitive stance may risk early closure or failure. **BARCLAYS**

- LEADER companies
- Professional associations/trade bodies
- Telephone directories
- Trade exhibitions and conferences
- Competitors' catalogues, brochures and price lists
- Professional advisers (accountants, solicitors, consultants)
- Friends
- Chambers of Commerce (**www.chambers.ie**)
- Customers (existing or potential)
- Local authorities
- Internet (use the examples above or the wider range of suggestions on the **www.startingabusinessinireland.com** website).

Many of these sources will give you information free of charge, or at very little cost. Recognise their help where you can – even with just a "Thank You". You'll be amazed at how much it will be appreciated – and how much you will benefit when you go back for more information.

Remember:
- Seek information from a variety of sources, not just from the "experts"
- Get feedback from a variety of sources
- Let people play "the devil's advocate" and argue against you
- Ask "stupid" questions – you will get some very clever answers
- Look around for yourself – don't assume anything.

Doing your own market research

Structure your market research to make sure you collect all the information you need. The structure depends on your product/service, your budget and the time you have available but ought to cover:

1. **Problem definition** – What do you want to find out?
2. **Desk research** – Consulting directories, magazines and newspapers and the Internet
3. **Pre-study field research** – A first test to see whether you are on the right track
4. **Concept questionnaire** – Your initial questions
5. **Testing the questionnaire** – Make sure that the questions can be understood and will give you useful answers
6. **Field research** – Asking the questions
7. **Data processing** – Processing the results
8. **Reporting** – The final stage.

Research techniques

There are many ways of researching your idea, including:
- **Qualitative/quantitative** – Quantitative involves researching figures and percentages; qualitative means researching opinions, reasons why, etc.
- **Consumer/distribution/industrial** – You can research the end user of your product, how the product is brought to the end user, or how the product is made
- **Questionnaires/observation** – You can ask people personally, by mail, by phone, or observe their behaviour (which may be different from what they tell you)
- **Ad hoc/panel** – You can do once-off research, or research a panel for a longer period of time
- **Group/single** – You can interview a group of people or every person in your sample individually
- **Open/half open/closed questions** – You can ask open questions (no control over the answer), half-open questions (give different options), or closed questions (yes or no).

I expect my market research to tell me:

MARKET RESEARCH: A CASE STUDY

A Japanese company had plans to build a paper factory in Georgia, USA. They thought it would be useful to know the production capacity of the local competitors. But these figures were not readily available. So the company started counting the number of train wagons leaving the factories. This gave them the volume of production. Although the wagons were closed, the residue left on the rails after the train had passed told them what the train was carrying. Volume multiplied by content gave them the production capacity of the competitors' plant.

The starting point is to define the problem – What do you want to know? Write it down in the space below.

When you start your desk research, collect information from as many sources as possible. List in the panel opposite the sources of information you intend to use. After you have completed your desk research (and only then), start designing a questionnaire for the target customer groups you have identified. This will need some research in the target groups itself (location, availability, language, level of questioning, perceptions, etc.).

Choose research techniques from the following:
- Group discussion
- Questionnaire by direct mail
- Direct questioning
- Questioning by phone.

Based on the techniques you have chosen, design a questionnaire. Go back to basics. Ask yourself: Who? What? Why? When? Where?

Make a list of questions you want to ask in the second panel. Copy the panel so that you can use it again.

Select only the most relevant questions. Depending on the approach you plan to take, you may need to take the length of the questionnaire into consideration. If it is too long, people won't want to answer it – especially in the case of direct mail or questioning over the phone. Then test it with a small group of people to make sure that it is clear and user-friendly. If you get a poor response here, redesign your questionnaire and test it again.

When the questionnaire is complete, you are ready to do the field research. If your aim is to get quantitative information, the number of people questioned should be sufficient to be statistically valid (minimum between 500 and 1,000). Note that it's quite usual to get a very low response rate to questionnaires.

Reporting results

It is useful to write a report on the results of your desk and field research. When writing the report, it is important to bear in mind who it is written for.

Make sure you include:
- Definition of the problem
- Description of techniques used
- Results of research
- Reliability of the information (sources of information, validity of statistics)
- Copy of the questionnaire.

The more time spent on this market research phase before you start your business, the more it will benefit you by laying the basis for your Business Plan.

POTENTIAL SOURCES OF INFORMATION

QUESTIONNAIRE DESIGN: QUESTIONS TO ASK

MARKET RESEARCH CHECKLIST

Does your market research cover:

Market size	☐ YES	☐ NO
Market structure	☐ YES	☐ NO
Market trends	☐ YES	☐ NO
Market potential	☐ YES	☐ NO
Market share	☐ YES	☐ NO
Competitor activity	☐ YES	☐ NO
Competitor prices	☐ YES	☐ NO
Competitor products/ services	☐ YES	☐ NO
User attitudes/behaviour	☐ YES	☐ NO
Government factors	☐ YES	☐ NO
Economic factors	☐ YES	☐ NO
Demographic factors	☐ YES	☐ NO

OBJECTIVES

o Be aware of existing trends
o Consider future trends

You have to look where the (hockey) puck is going to be, not where it is now.
WAYNE GRETSKY

If you want to be in business for a long time, you need to develop a vision of the future and the place of your business in that future. You need not only to be aware of the trends in your market area (technology, competition, trade regulations, etc.) but also have a sense of the general direction in which the world is developing. Questions to consider are: What will Ireland look like in 2020 – or even in 2050? Where will your business fit? What should you be doing to prepare?

Consider these current trends:

- To protect themselves from crime and hostility, people are retreating into the safe environment of the home
- People want to do exciting things but want to be safe – emotional escape in a risk-free fantasy world. Consider changes in food (exotic meals), shopping (fun shopping), interactive movies and games, etc.
- Luxuries are no longer big purchases but include "rewards" like handmade chocolates, week-end breaks and expensive restaurant meals. Spending patterns are becoming less predictable
- Technology allows products to be focused on very specific needs
- People are less concerned about job security and more willing to change jobs several times during their careers to pursue new opportunities
- Consumers are more health-conscious and critical about the behaviour of companies and the quality of products and services
- People have higher expectations of life. They want to achieve more – often materially
- Time is a major factor in most people's lives. They feel a need to cram activities into the day (reading, movie, theatre, socialising, being a good parent or partner, do a course, make a career, etc.)
- Older people stay healthier much longer and age does not dictate the pace of life any more. Old people act young
- Society and business is more and more influenced by women.

Read science fiction. Much of what was written as science fiction 20 or 30 years ago is now part of our everyday lives.

Train yourself to watch trends. Look for:

- Changes in food, new products, trendy restaurants
- The introduction of new products (failures and successes)
- Changes in family structure
- Changes in demographics
- Changes in work environment
- Changes in environmental behaviour
- Whether there is optimism or pessimism in relation to the economy
- New cultures
- New words (Internet Nanny, search engine, dinky)
- Science fiction becoming real.

Watch for the balancing impact of the Action = Reaction principle. For example:

Action
- Rapid change of technology, increasing role of computers
- Globalisation of markets due to easy access of information and technology
- Re-engineering, jobs replaced or supported by use of new technology
- Multi-cultural influences due to all information available

Reaction
- Back to nature in response to technology
- Back to old values/culture as those things are familiar to us
- Back into our homes to protect us from the outside (hostile) world
- Filters on information (for example, the Internet Nanny)
- Simplifying information
- Escapism in movies, computer games, adventure trips, etc.
- To balance the stress, "perks" to cheer us (massage, fancy dinners, clothes, etc.).

Some other things to think about:
- The use of drugs for specific purposes (memory enhancers, warfare)
- Development of genetic engineering
- The role of computers and telecommunications in our society
- Nano-technology (machines the size of an atom).

What are your predictions for Ireland in 2020 and 2050? Write them down. Where does your business fit within these?

Researching your idea before starting your business may not cost you much in cash terms but during this time you may not be earning anything. However, you may be eligible for a feasibility study grant from your local County or City Enterprise Board, which may cover up to 50% of the agreed cost of the research stage up to a maximum of €6,350 (or €5,100 in South & East). The actual amount is dependent on the needs shown in your business plan or application.

Getting a grant

Your first step should be to check with your local County or City Enterprise Board – you can access a central list of their websites at **www.enterpriseboards.ie**.

Generally, to be eligible for a feasibility grant, you must:

- Be an individual, community group or company
- Be investigating a new manufacturing product or process (CEBs fund services)
- Apply before beginning the study
- Carry out most of the work in the State
- Not repeat work that has previously produced negative results (whether carried out by you or someone else)
- Not seek aid from any other State body for the cost of this project.

If your study is in an area already known to have over-capacity, you are unlikely to be given a grant. Since these areas obviously change from time to time, check before starting work on your application.

Eligible studies currently include:

- Market research
- Preparation of costings and financial projections
- Assessment of manufacturing processes
- Assessment of suitable plant and equipment, etc.
- Sourcing of raw materials
- Negotiation with potential joint-venture partners.

The application process involves providing much of the information that you would include in your business plan (see the next chapter, STEADY), an explanation of the work involved in the feasibility study, and the costs involved. Application forms vary but set out the information required.

Success

If your application is accepted (this can take up to two months during which you cannot proceed with your study), you will receive a letter of offer.

Read this letter carefully. Query any parts of it that you do not understand. It will be against this document, not your original application, that your expenditure will be checked before any grants are paid out to you. Make sure that you know what the terms of the grant-aid are and keep to them. Be sure to sign and return the letter of offer within the time-period indicated – otherwise the grant-aid may lapse.

You can then – **and only then** – start work on the study. You must not start before you get grant approval.

Claiming the grant

When the study is completed, you must submit a report and a summary of your costs, including receipts. Generally, grants from CEBs are conditional on tax clearance. You will be given a form by the CEB, if appropriate. Note that feasibility grants, like other grants from CEBs, are not taxable as income.

Making sure you get a grant

The feasibility study grant is an important tool in developing your business. If you are eligible, it is definitely worth applying, since it reduces some of the costs of the research.

Like all State grants, the feasibility grant scheme is there to help winning projects to achieve success. If your project is badly researched, poorly presented and lacks verifiable evidence that it could be a winner, your grant application is likely to be unsuccessful. Aim at a well-organised application that has as much information as possible. Ensure that the commercial potential of your project is clearly researched and presented. If possible, discuss your application with an adviser before making a formal application.

OBJECTIVES

o Understand purpose of Feasibility Grants

o Identify sources of Feasibility Grants

o Understand method of application

OBJECTIVES

o Be aware of different training needs at different stages

o Be able to prepare a training needs analysis

o Identify sources of training for entrepreneurs

Potential entrepreneurs need (or may need, depending on their circumstances) three kinds of training:

- Training in the specific stages/techniques of starting up a business
- Training in specific skills useful for a start-up, which they lack from previous experience
- Training in specific skills useful once the business is up and running, which they lack from previous experience.

Few people have the first, since training for start-ups is not on many school or college curricula. This guide, and many of the books and websites listed in **Appendix 2, Further Information**, attempt to fill the gap. There are also "Start Your Own Business" courses available from a variety of sources to meet this need.

Training Needs Analysis

Training in other skills, whether pre- or post-start-up, requires a Training Needs Analysis. This simply means that you list your present skills, compare them against the skills you believe that you need and plan to do something about the difference.

Answer the questions on the next page to prepare your own Training Needs Analysis. Your business partners should also complete this analysis – copy the page before you complete it so that they can use it too.

Sources of training

There are many organisations that provide training in specific subject areas – however, only a few provide a general training in entrepreneurship or how to start a business.

Organisations to contact for information on training (especially in relation to start-ups) available to entrepreneurs include:

- FÁS (**www.fas.ie**)
- Your local County/City Enterprise Board or Area Partnership Company
- Enterprise Platform Programmes, including: DIT Hothouse, Dublin; NEEPP, Regional Development

Centre, Dundalk Institute of Technology; SEEPP, Waterford Institute of Technology, M50 EPP, Institute of Technology Blanchardstown; Synergy, ITT Dublin; Carlow, Institute of Technology Carlow; CEIM, Letterkenny Institute of Technology; LEAP, Limerick Institute of Technology; Genesis, Cork Institute of Technology.

Talk to people who have already taken the course you are considering and get their opinions.

Remember also that you cannot know everything. Whatever your own background, you will have to buy in some expertise – from accountants, solicitors, computer experts or consultants. But to give yourself a general understanding of a range of topics, even if the detailed work is done by someone else, attend courses outside your own immediate area of interest.

TRAINING CHECKLIST

Before you commit to a course, check:

- **Time necessary to do the course versus time available** – There is no point starting a course if you don't have the time to do it
- **Entry level** – Have you got the necessary educational background/practical experience to benefit from the course?
- **Background of participants** – Who are the other people on the course? Will their needs be different from yours (and prevent you from achieving your training objectives)?
- **Course programme** – What does it cover? Is this relevant to you?
- **Costs** – How much does the course cost? Are there grants available? Do you qualify for a grant?
- **Available back-up support** – What happens if you have problems during the course? Afterwards?
- **Accreditation** – Is the course officially recognised? Do you get a certificate on completion?

TRAINING NEEDS ANALYSIS

1. List your skills:

    _____

    _____

    _____

    _____

    _____

    Of use to the business?

    ☐ YES ☐ NO

    ☐ YES ☐ NO

    ☐ YES ☐ NO

    ☐ YES ☐ NO

    ☐ YES ☐ NO

2. List your practical experience:

    _____

    _____

    _____

    _____

    _____

    Of use to the business?

    ☐ YES ☐ NO

    ☐ YES ☐ NO

    ☐ YES ☐ NO

    ☐ YES ☐ NO

    ☐ YES ☐ NO

3. What skills do you think you need to start your business?

4. What skills do you think you need to run your business, once it has been started?

5. What skills are you missing?

6. What existing skills would you like to improve?

7. What training do you need?

OBJECTIVES

o Be aware of alternatives to start-up

o Understand risks of buying an existing business

o Understand how to evaluate an existing business for sale

o Understand franchise concept and advantages and disadvantages

o Understand how to evaluate a potential franchise

o Understand network marketing concept

o Understand how to evaluate a potential NM business

Never acquire a business you don't know how to run.
ROBERT W JOHNSON

If you want to run your own business, there are alternatives to starting it yourself. You can buy an existing business, or buy into a franchise or get involved in network marketing.

Buying an existing business

Buying an existing business is a sensible alternative to starting a business from scratch. The main advantage is that you acquire a business with existing products, markets, customers, staff, etc. and do not have to build it all up yourself. The disadvantage is that you have to commit a considerable up-front investment to acquire the business and may have to add to this to develop the business further. You also need to know why the business is being sold – perhaps it is in trouble.

Buying an existing business needs a methodical approach. Insist on both historical figures (preferably three years or more) and future projections. Have the information checked over by a person you trust or hire an expert. Do your own Strengths/Weaknesses/Opportunities/Threats (SWOT) analysis, get feedback from clients, suppliers and competitors. Particular areas to look into are:

- Financial data
- Management and key personnel
- Recent investments (or lack of)
- Product development/improvements (or lack of)
- Innovation (or lack of)
- Use of modern technology (or lack of)
- Hidden liabilities.

You need to know how much more money you will have to put into the business, on top of the purchase price, and how risky is this investment. How long will it take to recover your investment?

When you think you are ready to buy a specific business, take out a sheet of paper and write down your answers to the questions in the checklist. Only buy when you are sure that the business is right for you. Above all, make sure that you take professional advice before committing to buying. Remember, buying the business is only the beginning. You still need to work through the rest of this guide to develop a business plan for your "new" business – while you run it on a day-to-day basis.

BUYING A BUSINESS

1. Why is the business for sale?
2. What is the business of the company?
3. How is it organised?
4. What is its position in the market-place?
5. What are its future prospects?
6. Is there a current business plan? What does it tell me?
7. Does the culture of the company fit my style of working and managing?
8. How dependent is the company on the current owner/managers?

Buying into a franchise

Across the world, there are over 3,000 franchised businesses, covering almost every industry. Some are international brands like McDonald's; others are national brands like The Wine Buff; a few are much smaller, local opportunities.

When you buy a franchise, you are buying the right to use a specific trademark or business concept, which has been tested in practice. The chief benefit is that you are able to capitalise on the business format, trade name, and support system provided by the franchisor.

You pay an initial upfront fee for the rights to open your franchise. This fee may include things like training costs, start-up promotional costs, stock, equipment/fixtures (you may be required to purchase or lease specific equipment and fixtures from the franchisor), and any other costs that are necessary to start your business. Usually, the franchisor helps you during start-up, with selection of premises and equipment, a business plan, raising finance, and publicity. In return, the franchisor supplies a detailed operational manual, which sets out exactly how you should run the franchise.

You also have to pay ongoing fees to maintain the rights to your franchise. Most franchisors charge a royalty fee – typically a percentage of your gross sales, ranging from 1% to as much as 15%. It is also usual for franchisees to pay into a co-operative national advertising and promotional fund that benefits all franchises through increased exposure to the common trade name.

Advantages of buying a franchise are:

BUYING INTO A FRANCHISE CHECKLIST

1. Does the franchisor have a track record of success? ☐ YES ☐ NO

2. What will it cost me?   Once current income? ☐
   Twice current income? ☐
   More? ☐

3. How much can I expect to make?
   Once current income? ☐
   Twice current income? ☐
   More? ☐

4. Will the franchisor give me an exclusive territory for the period of the franchise? ☐ YES ☐ NO

5. Will the franchisor assist me with:
   a) A management training programme? ☐ YES ☐ NO
   b) An employee training programme? ☐ YES ☐ NO
   c) A PR and advertising programme? ☐ YES ☐ NO
   d) Raising capital ☐ YES ☐ NO
   e) Borrowing money? ☐ YES ☐ NO
   f) Merchandising ideas? ☐ YES ☐ NO
   g) Finding a suitable location? ☐ YES ☐ NO

6. How long has the franchisor been operating?   Less than 3 years? ☐
   More than 3 years? ☐

7. Has the franchisor a reputation for fair dealing with its franchisees? ☐ YES ☐ NO

8. Has the franchisor enough finance itself to carry out its plans? ☐ YES ☐ NO

9. What happens when I want to leave/give up? Can I sell the business to anyone I like? ☐ YES ☐ NO

10. Has the franchiser shown me any certified figures indicating exact net profits of one or more franchisees, which I have personally checked with them? ☐ YES ☐ NO

11. Has the franchisor investigated me carefully enough to be sure that I can successfully operate at a profit to both of us? ☐ YES ☐ NO

12. Is my lawyer completely happy with the franchise contract? ☐ YES ☐ NO

Adapted from *Making Money* magazine by permission

- Franchises traditionally have a much lower failure rate than other start-up businesses, since most of the problems have been discovered and solved
- You get a complete package, including trademarks, easy access to an established product, proven marketing method, equipment, stock, etc.
- You have the buying power of the entire network, which can help you against larger competitors
- Many franchisors provide financial and accounting systems, on-going training and support, research and development, sales and marketing assistance, planning and forecasting, stock management, etc.
- Some franchisors help with site selection, making sure that your business is located in an area where it can thrive
- You benefit from national or regional advertising and promotional campaigns by the franchisor.

But, as in anything, there are disadvantages, too. These can include:
- The essence of a franchise - buying and operating a proven concept - can make it seem like you're more of a manager than a boss
- It can take a good deal of cash to open and operate a franchise. Upfront costs can be significant, and ongoing royalty fees may impact on your cash flow
- Just as a franchisor's reputation can benefit you, the franchisor's problems are also your problems
- Your franchise agreement is a binding contract, and can be quite restrictive.

Although you own the business, its operation is governed by the terms of the franchise agreement.

Therefore, you should have your lawyer and/or accountant review the franchise agreement before signing anything.

Before you decide on a franchise, talk to other franchisees. Ask about their experiences. Would they do it again? What would they do differently? Listen carefully to their answers.

Network marketing

As with franchising, everyone is familiar with network marketing, even though they may not know it by that name. Examples of network marketing businesses are:

- **Tupperware** – Household storage items
- **Dorling Kindersley** – Books
- **Amway** – Household products.

Network marketing skips the wholesalers and retailers in the distribution chain and delivers a product directly from the producer to the customer. This means quick delivery, good service and that the product is sold by people who know the product since they use it themselves.

Because there are no intermediaries between producer and customer, a large margin is available to pay the distribution chain. Distributors earn this margin by selling direct to customers and also from a royalty on sales made by other distributors whom they have introduced.

The process is based on the idea that more gets sold by a lot of people each selling a little than by a small number of highly-effective salespeople on their own.

Because all distributors are self-employed and self-motivated, only the successful survive. In the network, back-up is available to provide the members of the network with training, workshops, information materials, manuals, etc.

Unfairly, network marketing has a poor reputation – in part caused by its similarity in a number of respects to the now universally outlawed "pyramid selling". Network marketing, according to one researcher, is not a "get rich quick" scheme – he says it is a "get rich scheme for those prepared to perform consistent, persistent, productive, income-producing activities". Even though it can be done part-time while you work at another job or in the home (and this is one of its key attractions), network marketing needs a lot of time and commitment not only in

selling but also in learning about the products, in training in how to do the presentations, in developing and maintaining a network, delivering the products, book-keeping and administration, etc.

Therefore, it's just as important to write a business plan (see the next chapter, STEADY) for a network marketing business as for any other business idea.

Other alternatives

Other alternatives to the traditional start-up include:

- Inheriting a business from a relative – Nice, but you still have to run it afterwards
- Management or employee buy-outs – Where a group of employees buys the business they work in from the owners.

In every case, there is a need for planning. However you arrive at your chosen business, if it is to be successful, you need to work through this workbook and develop your business plan. That's what the next chapter is all about.

NETWORK MARKETING CHECKLIST

1.	Can I do it part-time?	☐ YES ☐ NO
2.	How good are the products?	Very good? ☐
		Good? ☐
		Just OK? ☐
3.	What customer guarantees does the company give?	No quibble? ☐
		Money back? ☐
		None? ☐
4.	What is the company's track record, history, management, financial standing, etc?	Very good? ☐
		Good? ☐
		Just OK? ☐
5.	What investment must I make at the start? € _____	
6.	How much do I have to sell to break-even? € _____	
7.	How much time do I need to invest? _____	
8.	Am I prepared to do sales presentations for people I know well and recruit them for the network?	☐ YES ☐ NO
9.	Have I met and discussed the scheme with existing distributors?	☐ YES ☐ NO
10.	Do I believe the income figures they quote?	☐ YES ☐ NO

The business plan is the most misunderstood element of starting a business. Too many people believe it needs only to be prepared when you are looking to raise finance. That's not true. Certainly, it is nearly impossible to raise finance without a business plan but the real value of a business plan comes in the thinking about your business that is necessary before you can write down what you plan to do. The business plan is the core of this chapter – and of starting a business.

Chapter structure

This is the longest and most detailed chapter in this guide. Following on from the first chapter, **READY**, it takes you through all the steps involved in starting your own business.

In summary, these are:
- Developing a mission statement
- Developing a strategy
- Marketing
- Products and production
- Staff
- Deciding on a legal structure
- Taxation
- Accounting
- Premises
- Finance
- Operating budget
- Cash-flow planning
- Sources of assistance
- The business plan.

Your mission statement and strategy set the direction for your new business. Putting the strategy into action involves a wide range of topics including marketing, staff, financing, budgeting and cashflow, which are covered in the following sections. Sources of assistance – grants, advice, training, etc – are covered next. Finally, this chapter takes you through the business planning process and helps you complete a business plan that will help you manage your business as well as raise finance.

Everything you have learnt in this chapter is drawn together in your business plan. This is the real aim of the chapter – to help work your way through the thinking you need to do to develop a clear business plan. The thinking is the main thing; writing your business plan is the last 10%. But, unless you go that last 10%, you haven't finished the job.

Some other topics, such as quality, environmental and health and safety issues, are more appropriate to the on-going business and are covered in the next chapter, **GO**.

Key Questions

The Key Questions in the panel below are designed to focus your thoughts as you read this chapter. Think through your answers before you start to read the chapter. Then come back and write your answers in the spaces provided before moving on to the next chapter.

KEY QUESTIONS		
1. Have you developed a strategy for your business?	☐ YES	☐ NO
2. Have you developed a customer profile?	☐ YES	☐ NO
3. Do you know how your business stands in the market-place?	☐ YES	☐ NO
4. Have you developed a promotion strategy?	☐ YES	☐ NO
5. Have you identified the taxes for which you must register?	☐ YES	☐ NO
6. Have you decided how to organise your accounting?	☐ YES	☐ NO
7. Have you decided on a legal structure for your business?	☐ YES	☐ NO
8. Do you know how much money you need to start your business?	☐ YES	☐ NO
9. Have you identified sources of finance to meet this need?	☐ YES	☐ NO
10. Do you know your break-even point?	☐ YES	☐ NO
11. Have you prepared an Operating Budget?	☐ YES	☐ NO
12. Have you prepared a Cash-flow?	☐ YES	☐ NO
13. Have you prepared a Business Plan?	☐ YES	☐ NO

OBJECTIVES
o Understand the steps in a business start-up
o Understand the importance of business planning
o Develop a business plan

Success, as I see it, is a result not a goal.
GUSTAVE FLAUBERT

If we have a formula for growth, it has been:
Start with the best;
Learn from the best;
Expand slowly and solidify our position;
Then horizontally diversify our experience.
MARK McCORMACK, International Management Group

The only place success comes before work is in a dictionary.
ANON

DEVELOPING A MISSION STATEMENT

o Understand the importance of a Mission Statement
o Draft a Mission Statement

A Mission Statement sets out:
- The reason why the business exists
- What the company stands for
- What the company is about.

It is important to think carefully about your mission statement because it defines the core of your business and it strongly influences the direction of the company. It determines the strategy of your business.

For example, your mission statement determines whether your company sees itself as simply selling computer games or as providing entertainment. Selling computer games means that the business will not develop books or videos. But if the mission is broadened to include entertainment, the company can diversify into other activities.

This is not to say that you should make your mission statement very broad – if it is too broad, you have no direction at all. Think of it as a guide to a journey. Unless you have some idea of where you want to go, you may never get there.

Your mission statement should communicate the philosophy of your company in relation to:
- The environment
- Business ethics – The way in which you do business
- People – Staff and customers
- The community in which it is based.

It can be used both internally (your staff and suppliers) and externally (your customers and the community you are working within). Trends show that customers are starting to take mission statements seriously and expect businesses to develop a social conscience. For a clear example of a company that is run according to its mission statement, look at Body Shop, which has built an international business on a very simple and clear set of values.

Developing your own mission
Start developing a mission statement for your own business by answering these questions. Write your answers in the spaces provided.

Ultimately, vision gets translated into sales and profit, growth and return on investment, but the numbers come after the vision. In the old-style companies, the numbers are the vision.
JOHN NAISBITT,
Futurist

Why does your company exist?

What aims (other than profit) does it have?

Draft a mission statement for your business:

Copy this mission statement into your business plan, page 117.

DEVELOPING A STRATEGY

Developing a strategy for your business is as simple (or as complicated) as answering these questions:
- Where are we now?
- Where do we want to go?
- How and when will we get there?

Before deciding on your business' direction and course, you need to analyse the information already available to you and to collect more (see "Market Research" in **READY**). Do a SWOT analysis on the results of your market research, identifying each result as a:
- Strength
- Weakness
- Opportunity
- Threat.

Write your analysis in the panel below. Next, re-read the section "Identifying Future Trends" in **READY**. Start developing a vision of the future and a place for your business in that future.

To begin to develop a strategy, consider :
- **Focus** – On what?
- **Growth, decline, stabilisation** – How is your market developing?
- **Maintain existing markets** – Will this be enough?
- **Life cycle of the product** – What stage are you at?
- **New markets** – Where? At what cost?
- **New products** – How?
- **National or international** – What are your ambitions?
- **Broad market or niche market** – Where are you aiming?
- **Innovation** – What part will it play?
- **Small steps or big steps** – Which are you most comfortable with?
- **Mission Statement** – What is your business' Mission Statement? How does this determine your strategy?

Ask yourself the questions on the next pages. Write the answers in the space provided.

OBJECTIVES
o Understand strategy
o Develop a strategy for your business

Long range planning does not deal with future decisions, but with the future of present decisions.
PETER F DRUCKER, Management author

MARKET RESEARCH RESULTS

- ☐ S ☐ W ☐ O ☐ T
- ☐ S ☐ W ☐ O ☐ T
- ☐ S ☐ W ☐ O ☐ T
- ☐ S ☐ W ☐ O ☐ T
- ☐ S ☐ W ☐ O ☐ T
- ☐ S ☐ W ☐ O ☐ T
- ☐ S ☐ W ☐ O ☐ T
- ☐ S ☐ W ☐ O ☐ T
- ☐ S ☐ W ☐ O ☐ T
- ☐ S ☐ W ☐ O ☐ T
- ☐ S ☐ W ☐ O ☐ T
- ☐ S ☐ W ☐ O ☐ T

What do you want to achieve with your business?
Personal:

Business:

Summarise the trends in relation to your business:
Use of technology:

Customer needs:

Competition:

What are the threats facing your business?

What are the opportunities available to your business?

What are your targets for year 1?

What are your targets for year 5?

What are your targets for year 10?

How are you going to achieve the targets in year 1?

How are you going to achieve the targets for year 5?

How are you going to achieve the targets for year 10?

Copy the answers to these questions into your business plan, page 116.

By answering the questions above, you have actually developed your strategy. You have set yourself targets and found ways of achieving them. You have probably found that you could be very specific about the first year targets, but that 5-year and 10-year targets are more aspirational. But don't be misled by the simplicity of this approach to strategic planning. It looks simple. Maybe you found it simple to do. But it is critical to your business.

Every year, you should set yourself targets for the next year, keeping in mind your 10-year plan, which sets out the direction of your business. Compare it to a road map. The 10-year plan is the destination; the 1-year plans are the turns (right, left, straight, short cut, scenic route, stop-over, break for coffee, etc.). The direction you have decided needs to be checked on a regular basis to see whether your plans need adjustment.

Another way to developing a strategy for your business is to use the simple model below - the Strategic Box.

The shape of the Strategic Box created by your business depends on seven factors:
- Values
- Passion
- Vision
- Mission
- Positioning
- Resourcing
- Targets.

Values are deeply personal. Unlike big businesses, which impose a set of corporate values on their staff in order to achieve uniformity, a start-up begins with the values of its founder - their own personal values. What the founder stands for - and what they won't stand for, too!

Values are about things like integrity and honesty in business, customer service, how you treat staff, and so on. Hard to write down - often only seen clearly when you are faced with difficult choices - but very important.

Passion is what separates successful businesses from the also-rans. Start-ups usually come into being because of the passion of the founder - to do something different, to go beyond existing boundaries, or to make customers' lives easier or better in some way.

Passion is what fuels your determination to succeed - it's what keeps you going through countless refinements of your product or service, until it is just right - like James Dyson, who only got his bag-less cyclone-powered vacuum-cleaner to work on his 5,127th attempt! That's passion at work!

Vision tells you where you are going, where you want to be. It answers the question: "Where do I want to go?".

What is your vision? What do you see in the future? Perhaps not days of wine and roses - but, seriously, what do you expect from your start-up? Why are you doing this? Your Vision must link into your Values and your Passion - there's no point setting out to achieve something that's either not you or that you won't like.

Setting out your Vision for your start-up business helps you to identify the challenges that you will face in achieving it. Don't make the mistake of setting your aim too low - always aim higher than you expect to achieve, you may surprise yourself!

Mission statements (see "Developing a Mission Statement") set out in simple words what you (and your new business) are about and why it's important. If Vision tells you where you want to be, Mission brings people along with you.

Positioning then tells you where other people - your customers and potential customers - think you are. You need to position your start-up in your potential customers' eyes as being suitable and sensible to do business with. That means creating the right image for your business from the beginning.

Resourcing is critical for start-ups, since they have very limited resources - it's their weakest link. But it's an important part of your strategy - knowing what resources you have, what you need and what to do about the difference.

Last, **Targets** make clear your Vision and provide milestones on the way to achieving it. They provide an early warning system to tell you when you are wandering off-course or falling behind - and provide encouragement as you tick them off ahead of schedule.

So strategy is not that difficult after all. Just seven factors.

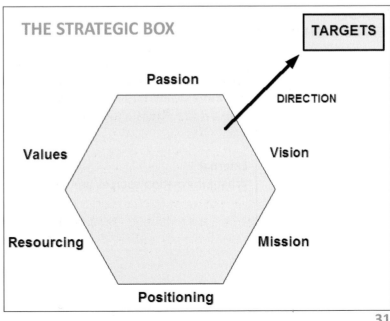

THE STRATEGIC BOX

TARGETS

DIRECTION

Passion

Values

Vision

Resourcing

Mission

Positioning

INNOVATION

OBJECTIVES

o Understand the importance of innovation

o Understand the role of an information system

o Understand how to implement innovation in your business

Business has only two functions: marketing and innovation.
PETER F DRUCKER, Management author

You see how things are, and you ask "Why?"
But I dream of things that do not yet exist, and I ask "Why not?"
GEORGE BERNARD SHAW

Innovation is one of the key success factors in any modern business.

The importance of innovation in the future is going to be even more significant due to constant change in technology, globalisation and the increased availability of information from, and convergence of, the Internet, TV, computer and telephone - not to mention alternative energies, bio-tech and nano-technology.

To keep up with increasing competition, it is essential to be aware of those changes and constantly adjust the business to take account of new developments.

The management guru, Peter Drucker, defined innovation as "the purposeful and systematic search for change and opportunity ".

Thus, the techniques described in "Developing & Testing Your Idea" in **READY** are just as applicable in the management of innovation, to provide structure and continuity.

To manage innovation, it is important to create a constant flow of information through the business.

To do this, you need to set up an innovation information system. This will bring together feedback from within your own business (for example, comments from your staff, clients and suppliers – all of which links with quality management) and combines it with outside sources such as competitors, newspapers, trade magazines, etc. To prevent any restriction of vision, the information sources should be widespread and some should be unrelated to business – to help you keep an open mind.

Answering the following questions in the space provided will help you to develop your information system.

Then go to the next section, "Competitiveness" and complete the "Information System Checklist" for your business.

Internal

How are you going to organise a system of feedback from your staff, clients and suppliers?

What information/comments should you be looking for?

External

What information sources are you going to access to keep informed?

Innovation should be part of the strategic plan (call it your "innovation plan" to get the message across), as well as being part of on-going product development.

Within innovation, there are three main directions:

- **Adjustment** – These are small changes that do not alter the function of the product or service
- **Modification** – Maintaining the technology used but changing the function (from clock to watch)
- **Renovation** – Same function, different technology (from vinyl records to CDs).

You must decide which of these directions (or what combination) is right for your business.

Organising innovation

Innovation does not happen; it must be planned for, organised and managed, through:

- Constant feedback and direct contact with customers (client panel)
- Monthly review of information
- Regular brainstorm sessions with a group of people from different backgrounds
- A budget for innovation
- Appointing someone or making time yourself to search for new ideas (3M allows R&D workers to spend 15% of their time on their own ideas and initiatives and has a rule that 30% of turnover must come from products developed in the last five years)
- Creating an "idea box" (like a suggestions box) with cash prizes if ideas are used by the business
- Creating project teams (made up of both technicians and sales people) to work with clients on particular ideas and giving the team the power and authority to implement changes
- Creating a positive atmosphere in your business towards change.

Innovation does not have to be a "giant leap forward". It can be a small step or, better still, a series of small steps (the "continuous improvement" that is so much a part of Quality Management Systems).

Always be on the look-out for ways to improve your product or service:

- Watch people using your product for a while
- Swap jobs: Let technicians do the selling and let the sales team manage production
- Arrange service contracts with your customers to get constant feedback
- Let clients set the quality criteria.

You will always face resistance when you try to innovate. Don't let it get you down.

Without innovation, your business will stagnate and die. Don't let the excuses in the panel below be heard in your business.

COMMON EXCUSES FOR NOT INNOVATING

1. Tried it before
2. Does not work in our situation
3. Too busy
4. Our company is too small
5. Let's keep our feet on the ground
6. Why change? We are doing fine right now
7. You are right, but …
8. Not practical
9. Impossible
10. We always did it like this.

Which of these excuses apply to YOUR business?

Anything that won't sell, I don't want to invent.
THOMAS EDISON, Inventor

I would think of another fundamental need people have, and I would answer that need by offering a cheaper and more efficient service than anybody else could.
In five years, I'd be a millionaire all over again.
HENRY FORD, Ford Motor Company

Sometimes when you innovate, you make mistakes. It is best to admit them quickly, and get on with improving your other innovations.
STEVE JOBS, Apple

COMPETITIVENESS

OBJECTIVES
o Understand competitiveness
o Identify the competitive success factors in your business

I don't meet competition; I crush it.
CHARLES REVSON, Revlon Cosmetics

Competitive advantage must be gained in one of three areas:
· Operational excellence (production efficiency)
· Product innovation and excellence (premium price)
· Closeness to customer (personal relationship)

You must aim to excel on one, and be at least adequate on the other two.
BRIAN TRACY

Being competitive is very simple: Be better than your competitors. This gives rise to two questions.

The first is how to define "better". This depends on what is important in the market in which the business is operating. In your market, does "better" mean:
o Quicker?
o Friendlier?
o Cheaper?
o Higher quality?
o Technical back-up/after-sales service?
o A wide choice?
o Advice pre-purchase?

Does it mean all of these? Some of these? Something else entirely? You need to know, if you are to be able to achieve it.

Being competitive is closely connected with the overall strategy of the company. Some writers compare it with war, saying that the options are:
• **Deter** – Create barriers through contracts, copyright, licensing, trade agreements, agents; Exploit advantages of contacts, location, economy of scale, flexibility; Seek alliances
• **Attack** – Head on/flank through price, promotion, technology or marketing
• **Defend** – Customer database or network.

Competition forces your business to become a "lean, mean, fighting machine".

The second question is who are your competitors. We'll look more closely at this in "Marketing" a few pages on but, for now, remember than your competition may not just be local but may come from abroad, no matter how "local" your own business may be.

An information system
Part of being competitive is developing a system which constantly collects information about your competitors and about business trends generally. (See "Market Research" in **READY** and the previous section "Innovation".)

Now answer the questions in the checklist panel below about your competitiveness information system.

Benchmarking
To assess how competitive your business is you need a benchmark. The most obvious benchmark is your competitors.

Study them and score how they are performing on criteria which are important to the market and customers (see your earlier research).

Try to identify areas in which:
• Your business is stronger
• Your business is weaker
• You can learn from your competitors
• Your business needs to improve
• Your competitors are developing and which you are ignoring.

Take all these factors into consideration as you write your business plan.

INFORMATION SYSTEM CHECKLIST

1. What types of decisions are you called on to make regularly?

2. What type of information do you need to make these decisions?

3. What type of information do you get regularly?

4. What type of information would you like to get that you are not getting now?

5. On which topics would you like to be kept informed?

6. What do you think would be the four most helpful improvements that could be made to your current information system?

Source: PLATO

USING TECHNOLOGY TO ADVANTAGE

The use of technology can be a success factor for a business. As a start-up, you have a great advantage: You are starting from scratch and can design the technology around the specific needs of your business, subject only to availability of finance. Existing businesses very often have to make do with expensive, but now unsuitable, equipment purchased earlier in their development.

You should consider technology as a means of making your business:

- More competitive
- More efficient
- Better informed
- More family friendly.

Technology for competition

The kind of technology that will give your business a competitive edge depends entirely on the business you are in and is outside the scope of this workbook.

Technology for efficiency

Technology is converging and what were only a few years ago different systems – TV, fax, telephone, E-mail, computer, voice recognition – are now being combined into multi-functional devices that bring cost and time savings.

It is worth your while researching these developments (read any business/technology magazine) and upgrading your skills in using the emerging technology.

You should certainly be considering a computer within your business for efficiency. An obvious area for computerisation is your accounts system. Although sending out invoices using a computer takes probably just as long as doing them manually, computerisation means that, at the press of a button, you can produce a list of outstanding debtors or an up-to-date set of accounts. This can give you valuable information to help you manage your business better. And good computerised accounting systems can be found from under €100 - you can even do your accounting entirely online.

Another use for a computer is to send and receive e-mail – very useful, cost-effective and efficient, especially if you have more than one location, are out of the office a lot, or have international clients.

Technology for information

The world's largest information resource – the Internet – is now available by computer, on mobile phone and TV (WebTV).

Beyond all the hype, Internet access is a valuable tool for many small businesses. The wealth of information on the Internet is literally unimaginable and the ease of access is improving as new software becomes available.

Using search engines (Lycos, Yahoo, etc.) is a cost-effective and fast way of finding your way to the information you need. Use the Internet as part of your information collection process. A number of useful sites for entrepreneurs are included in **Appendix 2, Further Information.**

Family-friendly businesses

A trend among businesses of all sizes is the adoption of family friendly policies, that allow staff to balance between work and home. It's particularly important where there are skills shortages and employers must compete for staff.

Technology can also allow business functions to be carried out independent of location using information and communication technologies.

e-Business

A key part of using technology to advantage is to consider the extent to which your business can become an e-Business. We will consider this in more depth in a later section.

Technology for marketing

Increasingly, it is possible - even essential - to market your business, your products or services online or by mobile phone, using a mix of advertising, referral marketing and social networking.

Check out Twitter, Facebook, LinkedIn and other social media sites. Find out how search engine marketing can boost traffic to your website. Learn about digital marketing - today!

OBJECTIVES
o To understand the importance of technology in gaining competitive advantage
o To evaluate the potential for computerisation in the business

The glory went to the man who discovered electricity but it was the man who invented the electricity meter who made the money.
ANON

Computers are useless.
They only give you answers.
PABLO PICASSO

MARKETING

OBJECTIVES

o Understand principles of marketing
o Understand the importance of constant research feedback
o Be aware of the 4 Ps
o Develop an outline marketing plan

The philosophy behind marketing is to satisfy the needs of every customer as best you can while making a profit. The whole idea is that if you make your clients happy they will buy from you – not just once, but again and again. This section will take you through the stages in developing an outline marketing plan.

MARKET RESEARCH

Your market research should have defined the customers the business is going to target. If not, go back to the "Market Research" section in **READY** and do more research on your potential clients.

Write the answers to each question in the space provided.

> *The central idea of marketing is of a matching between a company's capabilities and the wants of customers in order to achieve the objectives of both parties.*
> **MALCOLM MCDONALD, Marketing author**

> *Business has only two functions: marketing and innovation.*
> **PETER F DRUCKER, Management author**

TOO SMALL FOR A MARKETING DEPARTMENT?

Whether you have a marketing department or not, marketing involves decisions about:
• The product itself
• Price
• Customer service levels
• Physical distribution
• Advertising
• Sales
• The sales force
• Information about markets.

How do **you** decide on these?

Your customers/target groups:
Who are they?

Where are they located?

How do they spend their money?

Where do they spend their money?

Where do they socialise?

Can they be put in a social class and, if so, which class?

What do they read?

What do they watch on TV?

What do they listen to on radio?

Who forms their opinions?

Find out what elements in your service or product are most important to them.

To understand fully your customers' needs, make sure to clarify exactly what the customer means by probing until you are clear what the real needs are.

For example, if customers say they want "Total quality", ask "What do you mean by that?".

When they answer "Quick response", you ask "What do you mean by quick response?".

After asking "What do you mean?" a few times, you will establish the real need.

Write down the five elements of your product/service that are most important to your customers:

1.

2.

3.

4.

5.

If it doesn't exist, it's a market opportunity.
VERN ROBURN

The outcome of any serious research can only be to make two questions grow where only one grew before.
THORSTEIN VEBLEN

I am the world's worst salesman. Therefore I must make it easy for people to buy.
FW WOOLWORTH

Consumers are statistics. Customers are people.
STANLEY MARCUS

COMPETITION

A competitor is a business that provides the same goods or services as yours or an alternative. Your competition can be local, national or, increasingly, international. Use the questions in the panel below to identify and assess your competitors.

	Is this a Threat or an Opportunity?	
	T	O

Your competitors:

What are the alternatives for your products or services?

Who makes/sells these alternatives?

What range of products or services do they have?

What kind of choices do they offer customers?

How broad is their range?

What are their target groups?

What are their future prospects?

What are they good at and what are they not so good at?

IMAGE

As markets are becoming more competitive and businesses have the same access to technology and information, image is increasingly important as a way to distinguish your business from the competition.

You should now decide what image you want your business to convey to your customers. For example, you may want your business/office/practice/shop to appear:

☐ Practical, simple and objective
☐ Exclusive, high value and durable
☐ Modern, new and trend-setting
☐ Personal, multi-faceted and results-oriented.

Once you have chosen an image, make sure it is expressed in all aspects of your business. Think about your business' image in these areas. Tick the ones you will use:

☐ Interior
☐ Accommodation
☐ Pricing
☐ Name
☐ Business stationery
☐ Brochures
☐ Packaging
☐ Quality
☐ Business plan
☐ Advertising
☐ Correspondence
☐ Service
☐ Telephone answering
☐ Presentation
☐ Promotion
☐ Selling
☐ Employees.

Once you have chosen the image you want to present to your customers, you should remain committed to it in the long term. See it as an investment in the future of your business.

Image needs to be maintained and should be checked on a regular basis with the reputation the company actually has. What perception do you want to project (= image)? And what is the image of your company with your customers (= reputation)? Reputation is more important than image.

THE 4Ps OF THE MARKETING MIX

To market your product and project your image, you use a mix of techniques and tools to get the best effect, depending on your product/service and the customers you are targeting.

IMAGE CHECKLIST

What image do you want to present?

Why? How does this link back to your customers/target group?

How do you plan to achieve this image?

If you sell physical products, you should use the classic 4Ps of the marketing:

• Product
• Price
• Place
• Promotion.

Recognising that selling services was different from selling products, marketing theorists extended the marketing mix to include the 3Ps of service:

• People
• Physical evidence
• Process.

Increasingly, the lines between product selling and services selling is blurring.

Within Promotion, we will look closely at Advertising, Personal selling, Public Relations, the Internet and Customer Service.

PRODUCT

For most customers, a product is not only the product itself (the core), but also the services and intangibles that surround it (the product surround). For example, a pub sells pints (core) and quick service and atmosphere (surround); a clothes shop sells clothing and appearance or personal image, a flower shop sells plants and flowers and ambience in the house. What do you sell?

The customer also wants a choice. What you have to offer consists of a range, a selection of choices, products that complement each other and make it attractive for the customer to come and buy. A pub also sells meals, a clothes shop also sells accessories, a flower shop also sells earthenware. What range of choices do you give your customers? Customers also want to know what extras come with your product. What do you do that the others do not do? Think about packaging, service, personal attention, brand articles, originality, creativity and so on. What extras do you offer?

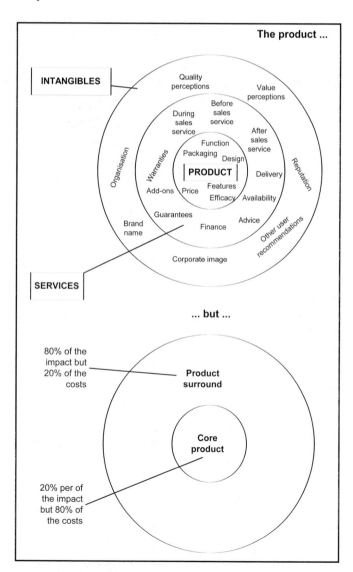

Your product:

Describe briefly the product(s) you want to launch:

Describe your product's core:

Describe your product's surround:

What choices do you offer your customers?

What extras do you offer compared to the competition?

PRICE

Pricing is important for several reasons:

- The price you charge will determine your margins and, in the end, your own salary
- Price is also closely associated with the quality and credibility of your product or service
- Once you have established your price, it is very difficult to increase it without losing customers.

To establish your price, it is important to know what your customers are used to paying, and what they are prepared to pay (see the panel below). (At this stage, price has nothing to do with cost – that comes later!)

You need to be well informed about competitors' prices. Sometimes prices are prescribed or recommended by industry organisations or professional associations. You can always deviate from established prices by means of special offers, discounts, reductions in rates, etc.

But be careful when researching price. You need to listen VERY carefully to what people say and how they say it. If your pricing is way off line, people will tell you quickly. But, if it's a little dear, and they don't want to suggest that they can't afford it, they may say the price is fine. You will only find out that it's not when you can't sell the product/service. You must also bear in mind that anyone who intends buying a product or service is unlikely to tell you if it is too cheap. Tread carefully!

When you sell a product, you have something tangible to show the customer. With services, you have nothing to show until you have done the work – and sometimes not even then. If you offer a service, when you agree a price it is a good idea to write down exactly what your customer can expect – for example:

- Details of your service
- The time to complete the service
- The time when the service will start
- The price
- The agreed method (and time) of payment
- Whether the cost of materials is included
- Whether other expenses (travel to the customer's location, for example) are included.

You also need to look at price in the context of cost. There is no point selling lots of a product if you are losing money on it! Work through the questions below to determine your pricing strategy.

Note the impact of e-Business: If your customers are on-line, they can easily compare prices with other suppliers. How will this affect your pricing strategy?

> Get the confidence of the public and you will have no difficulty getting their patronage ... Remember always that the recollection of quality remains long after the price is forgotten.
> **H GEORGE SELFRIDGE,** retailer

> Price: Value plus a reasonable sum for the wear and tear on conscience in demanding it.
> **AMBROSE BIERCE, US Humorist**

> Almost anything on earth can be manufactured a little less well and be sold for a little less money. And those who are only interested in price are the main victims of this rule.
> **JOHN RUSKIN, Philosopher**

Your price:

What are customers accustomed to paying already?	€ _____
What are your competitors' prices (average)?	€ _____
What is your price?	€ _____
How is your price made up?	
• Materials	€ _____
• Time	€ _____
• Machine cost	€ _____
• Other	€ _____
• Total costs	€ _____
• Profit margin	€ _____
• Selling price	€ _____
Will you offer discounts?	☐ YES ☐ NO
If yes, what kind of discount?	
Will you give special offers?	☐ YES ☐ NO
If yes, what will they be?	

PLACE

Place means the location where your business will be established.

In some cases, a customer will never come near your place of business – for example, if you run a window cleaning or mail order business. In such cases, we only use the P for place to mean distribution (that is, getting the product or service to the customer).

In retail businesses, place can be the most important part of the marketing mix. Important questions to ask, particularly for retail businesses, include:

- What will the customer see and experience when he or she visits your business?
- How easy is it to find you?
- Where are you situated (shopping area, a hotel or restaurant district, an office centre, in the centre or in the outskirts of town, etc.)?
- What does the area look like?
- What draws customers to your location?
- Do you provide a location map for your customers? Do you need to?
- Why did you choose this location?

Channels of distribution

You need to understand the channels of distribution that you will be using for your product. Each industry is different and fortunes have been made (and lost) on changes to the channels of distribution. Look at how Dell has changed the way people buy computers - and how slow other companies have been to catch up.

The diagram above summarises the main channels and the stages within them. The fewer stages, the lower the distribution cost – which is why lots of businesses try to cut out the middleman. On the other hand, the middleman provides a useful service – holding stock, sourcing customers, advising on market conditions – and cannot always be dispensed with. You need to balance distribution costs with promotion costs. Very often, sales channels with low distribution costs have high promotion costs.

Consider also alternatives to the traditional channels above that are making huge changes in the way people buy. How will they impact your business?

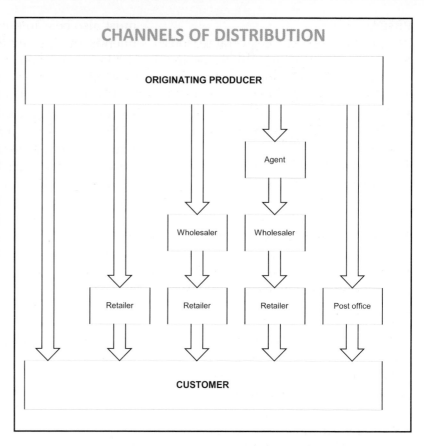

CHANNELS OF DISTRIBUTION

ORIGINATING PRODUCER

Agent

Wholesaler | Wholesaler

Retailer | Retailer | Retailer | Post office

CUSTOMER

DISTRIBUTION CHECKLIST

What distribution system are you considering?

Why?

What do your competitors do?

Where are the weaknesses in your system?

How can they be corrected?

PROMOTION

This is the stage when you begin to develop your entire marketing policy. It is a mistake to think that marketing begins and ends with advertising. Advertising is just a part of the promotion policy, and it is therefore only one of the means of promotion. The vehicles of your promotion policy include:

- Direct mail
- Personal selling
- Public relations
- Publicity and advertising
- The Internet – see the section on "e-Business".

Each will be covered in more detail later, but below is a brief summary to set the context.

Direct mail

Use a database of the names and addresses of the customers within your target groups to send a sales letter or brochure. Make it easy for the customer to respond. Where you can, follow up by phonel.

Personal selling

The final target is selling your product. In most cases, you are the one who is going to sell. So, you must:

- Prepare your sales talk well
- Write down your customers' buying motives of and also the reasons why they might not buy
- Think of reasons to counter those objections.

Public relations (PR)

PR embraces all the activities you undertake to get positive attention for your business among the public in general. Good PR creates a positive image for your business and helps to ensure that people recognise and remember your business. Good PR is also useful for your contacts with your suppliers. If you need a quick delivery, a special order or a credit, try to make sure that your supplier will go out of their way to help you. The same applies for your neighbours, local authority, etc. Good PR will also lead to free publicity.

Advertising and publicity

The key steps in advertising are:

- Use the image you choose as the basis for ads
- Look for an aspect of the image that can be represented graphically
- Always emphasise the advantages for the customer
- Remain credible and trustworthy
- Gain attention with a headline and give sufficient information
- Raise interest with a special offer

- Motivate your public to come and buy
- Stimulate action by including something that has to be returned, an invitation, an opening, special sales days, discount coupon valid until (date).

Methods of promotion

There are hundreds of ways of promoting your business and the products/services you offer. Try some of these:

- ☐ Advertise in a regional newspaper – in the classified advertising section; in Sunday papers; in a monthly magazine aimed at your target group
- ☐ Advertisement or entry in the Golden Pages (a basic line entry is free of charge)
- ☐ Design and print brochures that can be delivered house-to-house with the newspaper delivery or deliver them yourself; distribute brochures during large meetings or conferences, at markets, in the street, to customers, etc.
- ☐ Have posters made and hang them strategically
- ☐ Direct mail – Send sales letters directly to potential customers and your existing customers for whom you have an address
- ☐ Participation in trade exhibitions, markets, hiring a stand at a conference. You will gain the opportunity here to demonstrate your products. Remember you will need brochures to distribute. You can also make a special exhibition offer
- ☐ Make up your front window display according to a special theme.

In practice, you will probably choose a combination of methods to make up your promotion mix.

TYPES OF PROMOTIONAL ACTIVITY UNDERTAKEN RANKED IN ORDER OF POPULARITY	
Word-of-mouth	60%
Advertising in business directories	30%
Advertising in local press	30%
Advertising in trade/business press	12%
Direct mail	11%
Brochures, leaflets, point-of-sale material	5%
Telephone contact/personal visits	5%
Local radio	4%
Posters, vehicle sides, branding	4%
Seminars/conferences/exhibitions	4%
National press	3%
Sponsorship	2%
Public relations	1%

The codfish lays
ten thousand eggs,
The humble hen
just one.
The codfish never
cackles
To tell you when
she's done.
And so we scorn
the codfish
While the humble
hen we prize
Which only goes to
show you
That it pays to
advertise.
ANON

Doing business
without advertising
is like winking at a
girl across a
darkened room:
You know what you
are doing but no
one else does.
ANON

Give them quality.
That's the best
kind of advertising.
**MILTON
HERSHEY**

When business is
good, it pays to
advertise;
When business is
bad, you've got to
advertise.
ANON

Advertising:
The education of
the public as to
who you are, where
you are, and what
you have to offer
in the way of skill,
talent or
commodity.
**FRANK
MCKINNEY
HUBBARD
US Humorist**

ADVERTISING

Advertising is a way of communicating your product or service. Based on your market research, you know who your target groups are and how to reach them. What do you want your advertising to achieve?

☐ Sales
☐ Awareness
☐ Image
☐ Name recognition
☐ Introduce new product
☐ Introduce new service

Go back to your market research. Remind yourself of your customers' buying motives. Then decide which of your product's/service's features meet these motives and should be emphasised in your advertising.

Next begin to consider where you might advertise. You want to use an advertising vehicle (newspaper, magazine, radio, TV) that reaches your target group as economically as possible. Therefore, advertising in a national Sunday paper or on prime-time TV (even if you could afford either!) makes no sense if your market is made up of customers in your own locality. But there are now lots of local papers and radio stations, which might suit your needs much better.

Take control!

Ask for a "media pack". This will tell you not only the rates, but who the readers/listeners/viewers are, how many they are, what income groups they are in, etc. You need this information in order to decide whether a vehicle is suitable. Use the Advertising Control Sheet (see **GO** for an example) to help you place your advertising.

Don't be pressurised into advertising, either in the wrong place or at the wrong time. Most ad salespeople are on commission. They want you to buy NOW! and will give you "special discounts" – if you decide today. Don't do it until you are ready.

Don't be fooled by price either. Yes, one magazine costs €500 for a half-page against €300 for a full page somewhere else – but it goes to 20,000 of your core customers whereas the other really doesn't cover your market at all. Which is better value?

When you have placed your ads, measure the response. Unless you do this, you will never know whether your advertising works. There is a famous advertising story of an American car manufacturer which advertised for a year in a well-respected national magazine. At the end of the year, they found that people who had not read the magazine bought more of their cars than did readers of the magazine. Their advertising was UN-selling the cars!

If it is appropriate, place a coupon (order form) or response mechanism ("Call us now for special offer details") on your advertisement. Record the number of responses you get from each ad. When people phone or call to place an order, ask them where they heard about you. This builds up invaluable information and will save you from advertising in the wrong places in future.

Writing advertisements

Writing advertisements is an art. It looks simple but it is, in fact, very hard. Keep these words by David Ogilvy, founder of Ogilvy & Mather, one of the world's largest advertising agencies, in mind:

"I do not regard advertising as entertainment or as an art form, but as a medium of information. When I write an advertisement, I don't want you to tell me you find it 'creative'. I want you to find it so interesting that *you buy the product*."

The secret is to keep it simple. Be direct. Explain what you are selling, its benefits to the customer, and where they can get it.

Use your logo

If your business has a strong visual appeal, design a logo. Use it as widely as you can. Use it on envelopes, T-shirts, posters, pens, van signs, lighters/matchboxes or umbrellas.

Make sure that wherever they go, your target customers are always aware that your business exists.

PERSONAL SELLING

For lots of people, selling still has a negative connotation – the image of the slick sales person pushing products down someone's neck.

Not any more. Modern-day selling is about partnership and communication. It is important to build a relationship with your customers. The customer has to trust and respect you.

Try to build a database with the names and addresses of your customers. Try to memorise the names of your customers, remember what they bought the last time, or what they asked about last time. Again, get as much information as you can about your customers' hobbies, family situation, job, etc. Use that information when you next talk to them.

The following checklists may be helpful to you in developing your personal selling techniques.

WHEN SELLING

1. Are you prepared?
2. Do you know your customers' needs (ask lots of questions)?
3. Do you listen?
4. Are you clear in your language (no jargon!)?
5. Do you talk about benefits instead of the product?
6. Do you have answers to your customers' objections (What are they?)?
7. Do you know when to close the sale?
8. Are you persistent (do not give up)?

THINGS TO ASK YOURSELF BEFORE YOU START SELLING

1. Do you know enough about the product?
2. What is the product core?
3. What is the product surround?
4. Are you talking to the right person?
5. Who are:
   - The recommenders?
   - The influencers?
   - The supporters?
   - The deciders?
6. Do you know what the customer wants?
7. Does what he wants fit with what he needs?
8. Why does the customer want it?
9. Have you had any previous experience with the customer?
10. Has the customer had experience with your competition?
11. Who is the end user of your product?
12. How will your product be used?
13. How will the customer's life be better or easier after he/she uses your product?

All of the above is wasted if you do not get sales appointments. Realise that nine out of 10 appointments result in a "No". But if you get nine Nos, you also get one "Yes". Therefore self-motivation is critical. Selling – day in, day out, year in, year out – is the most underestimated element in business.

To sell
no matter what,
no matter how,
to no matter whom;
behold in these
words the whole
diplomacy of the
peasant at the fair.
**JOSEPH ROUX
(1834-1905)**

The average
salesperson
spends less than
25% of their time
face-to-face with
their clients.
Personally,
I spend 90%.
That's the only way
to make money in
sales.
EDNA LARSEN

To open a shop is
easy, to keep it
open is an art.
CONFUCIUS

PUBLIC RELATIONS

Public relations (PR) is not just about getting your business in the papers. Public relations is exactly what it says: Building a relationship with the public.

Let's first define public. From the perspective of where your business is located, it includes:

- Neighbours
- The neighbourhood
- The local community.

Internally, it includes staff and suppliers.

In a wider context, public includes:

- Colleagues
- Unions
- Government (local, regional, national)
- Politicians
- Consumer groups
- Financial institutions
- Trade organisations.

PR builds and maintains a good reputation. If your business is well-regarded, your marketing mix will be strengthened and it will be easier to influence people or get things done (planning permission, recruiting staff, word-of-mouth sales, etc.)

It goes back to your mission statement and what social profile you want to project. You have to decide which groups you want to maintain a positive relationship with and how you plan to do this. Keep it practical and within your means (both money and time).

Local newspapers are always looking for news. If you have good news about your business, make sure you let them know. Build a profile for yourself and your business through your local paper.

And while the relationship you build will not protect you totally when bad news has to be reported, it means the reporter knows and trusts you already and may go out of their way to check facts with you before going to print.

CUSTOMER SERVICE

Businesses spend a lot of money on attracting new customers. But it is cheaper to keep your existing customers than to find new ones.

Loyal customers:

- Spend more money with you than other customers
- Bring in new customers (through word-of-mouth recommendations)

Public relations is the management function which evaluates public attitudes, identifies the policies and procedures of an individual or organisation with the public interest, and executes a programme of action to earn public understanding and acceptance.
ANON

Get someone else to blow your horn and the sound will carry twice as far.
WILL ROGERS, US humorist

If you mean to profit, learn to please.
CHARLES CHURCHILL

Good service isn't a mystery – employ nice people.
KEN McCULLOCK, One Devonshire Gardens Hotel, Glasgow

PUBLIC RELATIONS CHECKLIST

Which groups are important for your company?
- ☐ Neighbours – Who are they?
- ☐ Local banks
- ☐ Local politicians
- ☐ Local authority
- ☐ Local press
- ☐ Trade organisations
- ☐ Unions
- ☐ State agencies
- ☐ Other

How will you reach them?
- ☐ Sponsorship
- ☐ Press releases
- ☐ Visits/Open Days
- ☐ Information/newsletter
- ☐ Profile in local newspapers
- ☐ Donate your services for a worthy cause

THE IMPORTANCE OF CUSTOMER LOYALTY – CALCULATE THE LIFETIME VALUE OF A CUSTOMER

Average sale value per customer	€ _____
multiplied by	
Number of sales per year per customer	_____
Total sales value per year per customer	€ _____
multiplied by	
Number of years customer buys from you	_____
Gross lifetime sales value per customer	€ _____

Plus, if every satisfied customer tells one or two other people and they become customers, look how fast your sales will grow!

- Cost less than acquiring new customers.

Use the panel on the previous page to calculate the lifetime value of one of your customers.

What steps will you take to keep your customers loyal to your business:

☐ Regular visits?

☐ Regular telephone contact?

☐ Regular direct mail contact?

☐ Regular evaluation of your business' performance in meeting their needs?

☐ Interviews with customers whose business you have lost to find out why this happened?

One way of creating and keeping loyal customers is through customer service – not just any old customer service but through superb world-class customer service. World-class? Why not? Where's the competition? When did you last get service from any business that was so good that you would recommend someone else to use them? When did you last get service so good that you noticed?

The fact that you have only a small business makes no difference – in fact, it makes it easier for you to be close to the customer.

Customer service involves:

- Doing what you promised the customer
- Willingness to help
- Providing prompt service
- Well-trained staff
- Individual attention
- Little things which make the difference.

Research shows that businesses that provide top class customer service experience:

- Improvements in morale (reducing staff costs)
- Lower staff turnover (reducing recruitment costs)
- Longer customer retention (up to 50% longer)
- More repeat business (20-40% lower selling costs)
- More referrals (20-40% lower promotional costs)
- Higher prices (7-12% higher)
- Increased margins (7-17% more profit).

Calculate the difference this would make to your profits. Then decide how you are going to put customer service into action in your business.

EXPORT

It may appear strange to be considering exporting when you haven't yet got your business up and running but many Irish businesses have to consider exporting at an earlier stage in their development than is usual in other countries. Use the checklist below to help you plan your export strategy.

EXPORT CHECKLIST

1. How specific are your plans? Are they an integral part of your business plan and strategy for the business?
2. Which products or services do you want to export?
3. Which countries do you want to export to and in which order of priority?
4. What is your target market/segments within the market?
5. Have you done desk research on your export markets?
6. Have you actually visited the countries involved?
7. Do you have sales experience in your proposed export markets?
8. Do you have the language skills needed?
9. Have you organised your administration for foreign payments and customs/excise regulations?
10. Are you familiar with the regulations relating to your products/services in your export markets?
11. Does your product or service need adjustment? For safety, environment, quality, packaging, taste, fashion, culture or language?
12. Is your price, after calculation of the extra costs involved in exporting, still competitive?
13. What are your turnover targets: per country, per market, per segment?
14. Do you have enough time available to build and develop the export market?
15. Who will be responsible for marketing and sales abroad?
16. Is your organisation, from telephonist to after sales, ready and prepared for export and dealing internationally?
17. Can your business cope with the demands of foreign markets: Delivery times, transport, quantities?
18. Which channels are you planning to use in your export markets?
19. Do you have the right promotion and instruction materials?
20. Are your term and conditions, contracts, quotes, etc. translated and adjusted to your export markets?

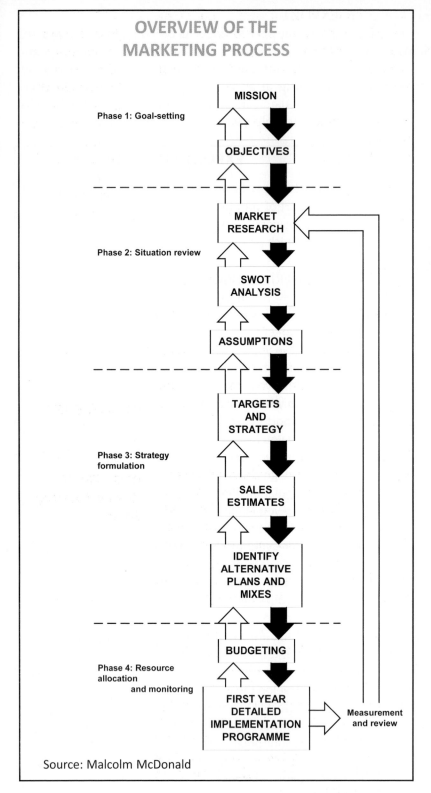

OVERVIEW OF THE MARKETING PROCESS

Phase 1: Goal-setting

MISSION

OBJECTIVES

Phase 2: Situation review

MARKET RESEARCH

SWOT ANALYSIS

ASSUMPTIONS

Phase 3: Strategy formulation

TARGETS AND STRATEGY

SALES ESTIMATES

IDENTIFY ALTERNATIVE PLANS AND MIXES

Phase 4: Resource allocation and monitoring

BUDGETING

FIRST YEAR DETAILED IMPLEMENTATION PROGRAMME

Measurement and review

Source: Malcolm McDonald

OUTLINE PLAN

At this stage, you should have enough information to be able to develop an outline marketing plan. Just as marketing is the heart of your business, so your marketing plan is the heart of your business plan – which is what this chapter of the workbook is about.

As shown in the diagram, your plan should start with the mission statement, include your business and personal objectives and then summarise the results of your market research. The SWOT analysis, based on the market research, leads to assumptions, which in turn lead to the definition of targets and strategies.

Sales estimates may not be acceptable first time around, so alternatives may need to be considered.

Sales estimates can be difficult for a start-up, since you have no track-record or experience to base them on. Try to support your sales estimates with as much hard evidence – forward orders, etc – as you can.

Once sales estimates have been agreed, the budgeting process can begin – and then work begins in earnest on putting the plan into action.

Note that the diagram also includes a measurement and review loop. Marketing is a constant process.

E-Business and the power of the Internet have significant benefits to offer small businesses. For example, the Internet lowers the barriers to entry for many markets, allowing small businesses to compete in wider geographic areas than would otherwise be possible.

Use of the Internet also facilitates a reduction in transaction costs. Some estimates suggest that the use of a B2B exchange could cut transaction costs by 90% for some businesses. Even allowing for exaggeration, there is clearly an enormous potential for cost reductions in many areas of business, which will bring benefits to the economy, individual businesses and ultimately to the consumer.

Last, all public organisations, and some bigger companies, have plans to move their purchasing on-line, so it is good to be prepared.

Some of the hype about the Internet and e-Business has been extremely positive, some very negative. As with all things, the truth is probably somewhere in the middle. What the Internet will not do is make you a millionaire overnight. It is not a magic wand. You need a good understanding of your business model and where e-commerce might fit.

Where do you want to use the Internet? For:

☐ Communicating with your customers?
☐ Promotion on-line?
☐ Selling on-line?
☐ Communicating with your suppliers?

and to what effect:

☐ Quicker?
☐ Easier?
☐ Cheaper?
☐ Promotion?
☐ Sales?

and at what cost in terms of:

☐ Up-front investment?
☐ On-going costs?
☐ Time commitment?

The Internet and e-business can fit within your business model in three key areas:

• Marketing
• Production
• Administration.

Don't get bogged down with, or put off by, the technology. As any good techie will tell you, it is not the technology that is the key to success, but how you use the available technology.

Getting started

To get started, you need:

• A computer
• A modem
• A telephone line
• A connection to the Internet via an Internet Service provider (ISP)
• Browser and e-mail software.

Most modern computers come with a modem and browser/e-mail software installed. In choosing an ISP, you need to decide between a "free" service that may provide a restricted service and/or charge for support, or one where you pay for the services you require – your usage of the Internet usually will determine which is better value.

E-mail

Most businesses use the Internet first for e-mail. It's a handy and cheap way of sending information all over the world for little more than the price of a local phone call. It means you can deal with queries outside normal working hours or over long distances. E-mail is also increasingly useful for marketing.

Why should you have a web-site?

A web-site offers a window onto a global networked market-place, making it easy for you to reach customers whom you would probably never have considered targeting. For example, Oak Tree Press, publisher of this workbook, has a web-site (**www.oaktreepress.com**), which reaches customers around the world, through an on-line catalogue.

Software companies provide updates and new releases of software for downloading from their web-sites. Newspapers and magazines have discovered a treasure trove in their archives of material from back issues, which they can sell on-line to people looking for specific information.

Sales is one reason for establishing a web-site – and probably the best, since it

OBJECTIVES

o To understand the importance of e-Business

o To evaluate the potential for e-Business in the business

o To understand how to implement e-Business

In Internet business, profitability is for wimps. It means your business plan wasn't aggressive enough.
DOONESBURY

It's working if it makes the till ring.
DES KENNY,
Kenny's Bookshop, Galway

The golden rule of complying with e-commerce law is: Be transparent! By being completely and fully transparent about who you are, what you are doing and how you will serve your customer, you will find that you are not only staying on the right side of the law but you are also keeping your customers happy.
CORINNA SCHULZE and JEFFREY BAUMGARTNER,
Don't Panic: Do E-commerce

THE JARGON EXPLAINED

HTML: Hyper-text mark-up language allows you to bring text, images, audio and video together so they can be viewed over the web.

ISP: Internet Service Provider, providing you with access to the Internet over your telephone connection. ISPs provide e-mail and web-site hosting.

Domain name: This identifies your web-site on the Internet – www.yourcompanyname.com or www.yourcompanyname.ie, for example.

Web server: A computer linked to the Internet 24 hours a day. Your site must be hosted on a Web server to allow people to access it.

Virtual server: Owning and maintaining your own Web server is expensive and complicated. Most small web-sites are hosted on shared servers maintained by ISPs – these are called "virtual servers".

Web host: A specialist company that provides hosting services (virtual servers). It may also be an ISP but need not be.

Front end: The part of the web-site that a user sees on screen: the text, graphics, forms and overall design.

Back end: The part the user doesn't see, which handles communications between the user's computer and the web server. The more complex your site, the more complex the back end needed.

Shopping cart: Software that keeps track of your purchases on-line, allowing you to accumulate them until you are ready to complete the transaction.

Payment solutions: At present, these are credit card-based, allowing you to accept payment by credit card for user's purchases. Electronic wallets and digital cash are under experiment.

Adapted from Taking Your Business On-line, Enterprise Ireland

PLANNING YOUR E-BUSINESS

Consider:

- **Purpose:** Why develop as an e-business?
- **Budget:** How much will it cost?
- **Expected return:** What do you expect to get back? And when?
- **Staff:** Will all staff have access to the Internet/e-mail? What training do they need? Who is responsible for keeping the site up-to-date?
- **Marketing:** Who are your customers on-line? What impact will on-line selling have on your traditional markets?
- **Process:** Can you use the Internet to reduce costs?

most clearly recovers your investment – but there are others.

A web-site can act as an on-line brochure, attracting potential customers to contact you about doing business. It can also establish your credibility in a certain field, if your site is full of authoritative information on a specific topic. Last (though not a good reason for incurring the expense) is that it can act as a symbol of "corporate up-to-dateness".

The stages are:

- Typically, web-sites begin as an on-line brochure, simply moving the business' corporate "message" into a new medium
- The next step is to list the products and services on-line – a "catalogue" site
- Next, the business decides to allow customers buy these products or services on-line and provides some form of payment mechanism, ideally with on-line credit card clearance
- Once customers have bought from the site, it's good marketing to encourage repeat buying – so the site develops "customer retention" features, like free updates or support for registered customers
- **The final step is to integrate the web-site into the business so that it becomes the business, reducing costs by using the Internet itself.**

There are many examples of the first three types – brochure, catalogue and on-line sales. Software companies, probably because they have a digital product and are tuned into the medium, have some of the best customer retention-type sites. Most integrated sites are found in the Business-to-Business (B2B) arena, where industry-specific sites for buying and selling deliver economies of scale.

Some sites combine more than one stage of development. For example, courier companies like DHL and FEDEX allow customers track shipments on-line, giving customers more "power" but also reducing their own costs since they no longer have to field telephone enquiries.

Some of the so-called "dot-coms" are fully-integrated web-sites, where there is no business apart from the web-site. In other cases, for example, the Ryanair site, the site provides benefits to customers in terms of speed and ease of booking flights while significantly reducing Ryanair's costs, both in commission to travel agents and in handling phone bookings.

Setting up a web-site

Before you rush into setting up your own Web-site, stop and think. Ask yourself:

- **Is your business suitable?** – Are you providing

goods or services that can be delivered easily world-wide (or, at least, remotely from your present location)? Or, if not, can you attract customers to come to you (hotel, tourist resort)?

- **Are your customers (and potential customers) connected to the Internet?** – Think carefully about what you need to invest, simple e-mail may be sufficient.
- **Are you clear about what you are trying to do?** – A web-site can be used for a number of purposes (often simultaneously), including providing product support to existing customers, providing product information to potential customers, selling on-line, identifying prospects, receiving feedback from customers, advertising your business' existence, capability and excellence. Which are you doing?
- **Can you afford it – time-wise?** – Establishing a site is only the first step. You must then update it regularly. How often depends on your business and the web traffic you generate. Once a month is a good target to aim for. But it all takes time
- **Can you afford it – money-wise?** – Setting up a web-site costs money. Not a lot, to be sure, but it all adds up.

On-line sales

On-line sales can be made from a "catalogue" site, where you list or display your products and invite interested purchasers to order products by conventional means: letter, telephone, fax or email. You then handle the sale in your normal way.

The next step is to add "shopping cart" software that tracks users' purchases until they are ready to complete the transaction. This software is usually bundled with on-line credit card processing (including a merchant Internet account with a bank) as an "online shop". Adding a shopping cart and online credit card processing gives you an "e-commerce" site.

Security

Issues in relation to security on the web include:

- **Safety:** Whether sensitive information (credit card details, for example) is protected while it is being sent from the user's computer to the web server and onwards (if applicable)
- **Trust:** Whether commitments made on the web will be honoured (for example, will goods bought and paid for on-line be dispatched?)
- **Privacy:** Whether there are restrictions on the access to, and use of, personal information (for example, age or financial status) provided by a user as part of a web transaction.

Secure payments solutions for credit cards involve:

TEN RULES FOR A SUCCESSFUL B2C E-COMMERCE SITE

1 Keep it simple.
2 Make it fast.
3 Build trust.
4 Give directions.
5 Welcome the shopper.
6 Create communities.
7 Service the customer.
8 Think globally.
9 Shipping must be easy.
10 Let the world know.

Source: Marco Argenti & Efrim Boritz

- A bank that provides an Internet merchant account (even if you already have a merchant account with a bank, you need an Internet merchant account)
- Software that encrypts credit card details while they are being sent form the user's computer to the bank
- A secure certificate for data encryption.

There are a number of schemes – ChamberSeal and eTrust, for example – that vet applicants before allowing them to use a logo on their web-sites signifying that they are trust-worthy.

The EU Data Protection Directive says that personal information must be:
- Obtained fairly and lawfully
- Used only for the original specified purpose
- Adequate, relevant and not excessive to purpose
- Accurate and up-to-date
- Accessible to the subject of the information
- Kept secure and destroyed after its purpose is completed.

Legislation

The Electronic Commerce Act 2000 introduced the EU's Electronic Signatures Directive into Irish law. Among other things, this means that electronic signatures and contracts have the same force as their hand-written or typed equivalents.

As a general rule, content on a website must be cleared for copyright and must avoid defamation.

Strictly, terms of trade must comply with legislation in each country in which you do business, though this may be difficult since there are few standards internationally, especially in consumer protection. The best protection is to make your terms of trade fair and clear – the "golden rule" is to be transparent. For example:

- Give your physical address
- Make it easy for people to do business with you
- Show the full price of items, including VAT and delivery costs if any
- Give a contact point where people can complain.

VAT

Under present legislation, VAT is charged (if applicable) on online transactions in the country in which the transactions originate. However, if your sales to other EU countries exceed certain limits, you may need to register for VAT in those countries. This area is still developing and new EU rulings are expected.

Domain names

A domain name identifies your business on the Internet. This is why it's important to have a name in the form www.yourcompany.com rather than www.webhost.com/~yourcompanyname. The latter is like putting "We're not a very important company" on your letterhead!

The suffix (.com or .ie) is determined by where your name is registered. Names registered with US agencies get a .com address. The reason there are so many of these (and why so many non-US web-sites have them) is that they are easy to get, with little formality beyond payment. The downside of this is that many names have already been acquired – some by people who plan to use them for their business, others by people who hope to sell them on to someone else at a profit (cyber-squatting). You can register a .com domain name at, for example, **www.godaddy.com**.

Irish domain names, distinguished by the .ie suffix, are registered through the IE Domain Registry (**www.domainregistry.ie**). To prevent cyber-squatting, IEDR requires proof that you have an entitlement to use the name you ask for – for example, it is the name of a limited company or registered business name that you own. Since IEDR also requires hosting information, it is often easier to let your ISP register your domain name.

Just like a company name, a domain name must be distinctive and memorable. Ideally, it should be your business name but it could be a brand name or some other more general descriptive name.

On-line marketing

On-line marketing is something of a misnomer, since some of it takes place off-line. Primarily, it consists of attracting people to your web-site. You can do this by:

- Publicising your web-site address (your domain name) as widely as possible – on your letterheads, compliment slips, brochures, vans, etc
- Achieving high positions in search engine results
- "Viral" marketing – the on-line equivalent of "word-of-mouth" and the most effective (and cheapest) form of on-line marketing
- Advertising on-line on other web-sites – many sites accept advertising, though the value of online advertising is increasingly in question.

Increasingly, online marketing involves or uses social networking - websites or systems that allow users to connect electronically - for example, Twitter, Facebook or LinkedIn. Many businesses have found this form of marketing very effective - explore it to see how it can help you.

Other issues

Other e-business issues include:

- **Currency:** Good marketing practice suggests you offer products for sale in your customers' currency (usually US $ on the Web). This raises issues because of fluctuating exchange rates/differing price points.
- **Delivery:** Can you meet customers' expectations for delivery? After all, if they can find your product and order it in a few minutes, why must they wait for several weeks while it travels to them?
- **Shipping costs:** Who bears shipping costs? You will find that postage of bulky items overseas is expensive – and express couriers are not cheap.

The future

For many businesses (not all), the Web is the future. For some, it will be their business; for others, it will simply be another channel through which to reach their markets. But, for most businesses, there will be no escaping its impact. Think about it as part of your business planning.

Production is deliberately placed AFTER marketing in this guide because, too often, in the real world, production comes before marketing – to the detriment of the business.

This section will help you think through what you should be doing.

Start by writing down the answers to the questions below.

Products

Product/service   *Description*   *Price*

A _____   _____   € _____
B _____   _____   € _____
C _____   _____   € _____
D _____   _____   € _____
E _____   _____   € _____
F _____   _____   € _____

Copy this section into your business plan, pages 116 and 123.

Describe your production process. Draw a flowchart on a separate page, if necessary.

What experience do you have with this process?

Are you involved with (or will you be using) new techniques or new products in your production processes?   ☐ YES ☐ NO
If yes, are you receiving assistance from experts?   ☐ YES ☐ NO
If yes, who are they and how are they engaged?

Develop Standards

To ensure efficient production, it might be worthwhile developing procedures and measuring your activities so that you can standardise your approach. Standards should enable you to:

1. Do the job the easiest (and safest) way
2. Prevent errors from (re-)occuring
3. Have a benchmark to measure and improve against
4. Have objectives to work against
5. Provide a basis to train your future staff
6. Preserve the knowledge and experience you are developing as you go along.

In the same way as you analysed your idea in the **READY** chapter, you should now put your production process under the microscope. Use the panel below to help you.

Then read widely on production and manufacturing techniques, according to your needs.

PRODUCTION – OTHER ISSUES

The panel on the previous page records your production process. Look at it closely. Ask yourself:

Where are there gaps?

Where are there inefficiencies?

Where is there duplication of work?

Where is there work that could be sub-contracted out more effectively?

How could the process be improved?

Are there any capacity constraints or bottle-necks?

How can these be overcome?

How do you propose to keep your product up-to-date?

What parts of your product can be recycled?

Could it be re-designed so that more could be recycled?

At what cost?

Is your product protected by patent?

What quality assurance systems have you in place?

How do they operate?

Have the systems been certified by an external body?

HOW MANY STAFF?

At an early stage, you need to begin to estimate how many staff you may need and how this number will grow – and where you will recruit staff from. There's not much point planning expansion if you can't get the people to do the work.

Use the panel below to estimate your initial staff numbers and how you see this developing within the first 12 months and within the first three years. These figures will help you in developing your Operational Budget (see page 87) and in making applications for employment grants, if you are eligible.

Remember that salary is not the only cost in employing someone. PRSI must be paid on their earnings (see "Taxation"); they may be entitled to bonuses, commissions, etc.; they will need training – and there will be other costs you have not thought of.

DELEGATING

Delegating is difficult for entrepreneurs. Their whole business, their way of life, is built on their own vision. What should be done, when and how are all determined by the entrepreneur. And now parts of the business, even decisions, are to be handed over to someone else. Ouch!

This is very often the way that entrepreneurs see delegating – in a negative light, as giving up control. But that's not delegating – that's giving up control!

Delegating is a specific sequence of techniques that empowers one person (the person to whom work is delegated) while freeing up the time of another (the person delegating). Delegation involves:

- **Define the task** – In terms of resources available and outcome required, not in terms of method
- **Transfer a clear understanding** – To the person who is to do the work
- **Stand back and let them do the work, while being available to help** – But only when asked
- **Careful, shared evaluation of the outcome**.

It is critical that achievement of the task is judged only in terms of the outcome – not the methods used to achieve it. You want a store-room tidied and products placed on shelves in alphabetical order. Does it matter whether the person starts by finding all the most popular items first and putting them aside? Or that the alphabetical sequence starts left of the door and not right? Or that he begins tidying at Z and not A? Just because it isn't done the way you would have done it does not make it wrong.

The important points in delegation

OBJECTIVES

o Be aware of recruitment sources and techniques
o Be aware of employment legislation
o Be aware of staff management techniques

We wanted people who were intelligent, knowledgeable and experienced but, in choosing among candidates who had these attributes, I wanted men around me who shared my enthusiasm for work.
HAROLD GENEEN

All commercial operations can, in the final analysis, be summed up in three words: personnel, products, profits. Personnel comes first. Without a good team, it is impossible to expect anything from the other two.
LEE IACOCCA

The person who figures out how to harness the collective genius of his or her organisation is going to blow the competition away.
WALTER WRISTON

STAFFING PLAN

Initially, how will your staffing be organised?

• You alone, while holding another wage-earning position	☐
• You alone, full-time	☐
• You and your partner: Full-time	☐
• You and your partner: Part-time	☐
• You and your business partner(s)	☐
• You and your business partner(s) with employees at a wage	☐
• How many employees full-time?	_____
• How many employees part-time?	_____

Copy this section to your business plan, page 118.

How do you see this expanding?	+12 months	+ 3 years
Management	_____	_____
Production	_____	_____
Sales	_____	_____
Marketing	_____	_____
Administration	_____	_____
Other (specify)	_____	_____

DELEGATION

How much does your time cost?　　€ _____
(the standard calculation is 3 times salary,
divided by 200 days,
divided again by 8 hours in a day
 = € per hour)

Do you **really** want to take work home
in the evenings and weekends?　　☐ YES ☐ NO

What areas do you think you must deal with
yourself?

What areas are most critical to the business?

What areas are you comfortable delegating to
another person?

Delegate what to whom?

Develop a profile of the right person for each task
you want to delegate and match your staff to the
profiles.

---

are the task definition and the evaluation. You must sit down with the person after the task is complete and talk through what they achieved. Because you have more experience, you may know faster, better, cheaper ways of doing the task – but you should let the person identify these for themself. If you tell them, they will never learn. Worse still, they will give up, saying to themselves "I did the job. Got the right result. But all the boss was concerned about was doing it his way".

The other difficulty that entrepreneurs have with delegation is a lack of recognition that their own drive differs from that of their employees. You will quite happily stay at work late into the night, work through weekends and bank holidays, but you cannot expect that your staff will always want to do the same. Good staff will be prepared to work on to get the job done – but not just for the sake of doing. You need to learn to motivate – and be reasonable in your demands.

RECRUITING

Recruiting staff is a major stumbling block for many small businesses. It takes time and effort. But the results can have an enormous impact on your bottom line. Hire the right people, and you will have a strong staff who will move your company forward. But the wrong person will pull down morale, waste your time, and cost you more than just an extra salary.

The key steps are:
- Know what you're looking for
- Finding applicants
- Interviews.

Know what you're looking for

Before you begin looking for someone to fill a vacancy, you need to know what you're looking for. You should:
- **Create a detailed job description** – Write down the specific tasks you expect this employee to perform. Think about every detail. Then summarise and put the tasks in order of priority
- **Develop a list of skills required** – What skills are essential? What skills are merely desirable?
- **Decide whether there are other things you want?** – Specific educational background? Experience in a particular industry? What else is necessary for the person to develop in your company?
- **Think about personality** – You need people who share your vision and your standards.
- **Take a reality check** – Look at what you have written down. Which areas are priorities? Where are you willing to compromise? Will you get the person you want for the salary you are offering?

Finding applicants

Requirements defined, you now need to find people to meet them. Here are some suggestions:
- **Look in your files** – A visible and successful company will have people writing in looking for jobs, even though no vacancies are being advertised. If any of these people look promising, make time to meet and find out more about them. Then, when you need a particular mix of skills, you may find the perfect candidate in your files already
- **Ask your staff** – Your own staff may know someone with the right skills whom they would be happy to recommend (for a bonus, perhaps). And they will come with a built-in guarantee, since they won't want to let down the staff-member who sponsored them
- **Ask around** – Ask everyone you know (including customers and suppliers) whether they know anyone they would recommend. Have some background information available on the job ready to give out
- **Advertising** – Make it clear what you are looking for and write the ad to attract candidates. But make sure you have the time to handle a deluge of responses
- **Use a recruitment agency** – A sensible route if

you do not have the time or ability to screen applicants, but it can be expensive. Through their contacts, agencies can often find people whom you would otherwise not reach with an advertisement

- **Look on-line** – The Internet has opened up a new set of places to post your job vacancy. These are best used for high-tech vacancies
- **Contact University/IT career offices** – They are always looking for jobs for their graduates and will usually circulate your listing free of charge
- **Job fairs** – An opportunity to give your company some visibility and talk to a variety of candidates in an unpressured environment
- **Non-traditional workers** – Don't overlook older or part-time workers or those with disabilities – they can be very capable and committed
- **Recruit overseas** – May be necessary where you face skills shortages (see below for more information).

Whatever route you choose, it is a good idea to insist that every candidate completes a standard application (see next chapter, **GO**). Keep the form simple but make sure that you get all the information you need to decide whether a candidate has the skills you require for the specific position. Use the candidate's CV as a back-up.

Make a shortlist

Before you start looking at CVs or application forms, write out again a summary of the main points you are looking for in a candidate. Screen quickly looking for these – and only these. Put all applications that do not meet these criteria into a separate bundle. If you want, review them later to see whether they include any candidates you might want to keep for your files. Otherwise, remove them from consideration immediately. Write to them to say that you will not be calling them to interview – from the candidate's point of view, it's better to get bad news than not to hear at all.

Concentrate on the ones that meet your criteria. Read them again more carefully. Look for little things: gaps in employment, jobs that don't quite fit a career path, hobbies that don't sit well with the personality type you are looking for, inconsistencies and even, if the job involves written communication, misspellings and poor grammar.

Make a shortlist. Decide which candidates you want to interview and contact them to arrange dates and times. Although interview candidates should do their own research on your business before coming for interview, it is helpful to include some background information on your business with the letter

INTERVIEW CHECKLIST		
Candidate name	_____	
Meets educational criteria?	☐ YES	☐ NO
Meets experience criteria?	☐ YES	☐ NO
Passed competence test?	☐ YES	☐ NO
Has essential skills?	☐ YES	☐ NO
Has desirable skills?	☐ YES	☐ NO
Has additional skills?	☐ YES	☐ NO
Good oral communication skills?	☐ YES	☐ NO
Good written comm. skills?	☐ YES	☐ NO
Has foreign language skills?	☐ YES	☐ NO
Good personality?	☐ YES	☐ NO
Would fit in well with other staff?	☐ YES	☐ NO
Currently employed?	☐ YES	☐ NO
Notice period needed?	_____	
Clean driving licence?	☐ YES	☐ NO
Smoker?	☐ YES	☐ NO
Good health record?	☐ YES	☐ NO
Days off in past year?	_____	
Permission to contact referees?	☐ YES	☐ NO

confirming the interview.

Overseas recruitment

Before deciding to recruit foreign workers, consider whether you can source staff locally, since overseas recruitment is usually more expensive when all costs are considered than local recruitment.

If it's necessary, you should know that:
- Workers from outside the EU or EEA (EU plus Norway, Liechtenstein and Iceland) require work permits
- Work permits are issued by the Department of Enterprise, Trade and Employment to the **employer**, not the employee
- Visas may be required by some non-EU nationals
- All non-EU nationals resident in Ireland for more than 90 days must register with the Gardai.

INTERVIEWING

When interviewing, you only have a short time to find out all you need to make an informed decision about investing in someone who should become an asset to your business. Therefore:

- **Use an interview checklist** (above) – Develop a list of points that you want to cover during the interview
- **Ask open-ended questions** – Avoid questions that can be answered "yes" or "no"; use questions like "Why did you like working in sales?", "What are your strengths and weaknesses?" or "Why are you leaving your current job?"
- **Ask unconventional questions** – See how candidates think (and how fast) by asking them questions they may not have prepared for. For example, "Why shouldn't all staff be paid the same?", "If you didn't have to work, what would you do with your time?"
- **Find out what's important to the candidate** – What is he/she looking for: growth opportunities, regular hours, training, new responsibilities? Will he/she finish the job or just clock-watch?
- **Listen** – Spend 20% of the time talking and 80% listening. The purpose of the interview is to help you learn about the candidates, not to talk about yourself or your business
- **Interview more than once** – Use the first interview to find the top two or three candidates; use the second to make sure you choose the best
- **Involve other staff** – If you are particularly pleased with a candidate, let them meet some of your existing staff with whom they will be working. Get these staff-members' opinion
- **Check references** — Ask what the relationship between candidate and referee is. Confirm previous positions, responsibilities and achievements. Ask about working habits, ability to get along with others, problems, etc.

Be open with candidates. Tell them that you are interviewing others. Give them a date by which they can expect to hear from you – one way or the other. Be fair - keep to it.

The job offer

You have already discussed the job offer with your ideal candidate at interview, before writing to offer the job – in some cases, you may make the offer at the interview and shake hands on a deal. Either way, you should write to the selected candidate and set out clearly:

- The job title and description
- The salary; how it is to be paid; and whether it includes overtime, bonuses, etc
- The normal hours of work

- Holidays
- Period of notice required on resignation/dismissal
- Grievance procedures
- Any other "house" rules.

Send two copies of this letter, both signed by you, and ask for one back, signed by the new appointee to signify their acceptance of the position on the terms offered.

EMPLOYMENT LEGISLATION

Note that there is a clear distinction, particularly for tax purposes, between employees and self-employed contractors. Check with the Department of Social, Community and Family Affairs or the Revenue Commissioners.

By law, full-time employees are entitled to:

- A written contract of employment
- Minimum wages
- Equal pay for equal work
- Protection against discrimination
- Holidays and rest periods
- Maternity, adoptive and parental leave
- Trade union membership
- Minimum notice on termination of employment
- Protection against unfair dismissal
- Protection against redundancy, and minimum payments if it should occur.

A written contract of employment

Employees are entitled to a written statement of the terms of employment, within one month of requesting it (see sample in GO). This must set out:

- Details of the employment
- The dismisal procedure the employer will use
- Salary
- Deductions from salary.

Minimum wages

The National Minimum Wages Act requires employers to pay experienced adult workers (those over 18, more than two years employed and not a trainee) a minimum average hourly rate.

Equal pay for equal work

Where men and women perform similar work, under similar conditions, or requiring similar skills, or work of similar value or responsibility, they must be paid the same.

Equality Officers of the Labour Court have the right to enter premises, examine records and seek information where an equality claim is made.

Protection against discrimination

The Employment Equality Act bans discrimination on the basis of sex or marital status in:
- Recruitment
- Conditions of employment other than pay or pension (covered by equality legislation)
- Training and work experience
- Opportunities for promotions.

Holidays

Most employees are entitled to a minimum of 20 days annual leave, plus public holidays (8 each year). The "holiday year" runs from 1 April to 31 March and pro-rata entitlements apply for periods of less than a year.

The Organisation of Working Time Act, 1997 also requires that employees:
- Work no more than a 48-hour week, averaged over a 4, 6 or 12 month period as appropriate
- Have rest breaks while at work
- Have 11 hours rest in each 24-hour period
- Have one period of 24 hours rest per week, preceded by a daily rest period of 11 hours.

The Act applies to all workers, except Gardai and the Defence Forces. Its general provisions may be varied by collective agreement.

Maternity leave

Regardless of length of service, a pregnant employee has the right to:
- Take up to 26 weeks paid and 16 weeks unpaid maternity leave
- Return to work, to her previous job or one of similar status, afterwards
- Reasonable time off for ante and post-natal care.

The Department of Social, Community and Family Affairs pays her a pay-related Maternity Allowance for 26 weeks. The remaining 16 weeks maternity leave are unpaid. There is no obligation on the employer to pay any salary during maternity leave.

The employee must give her employer four weeks written notice of her intention to take maternity leave and the dates of her leave. She must also give her employer four weeks written notice of her intention to return to work after maternity leave.

Adoptive leave

A women employee is entitled to 24 weeks paid and 16 weeks unpaid adoptive leave under much the same terms as maternity leave above. Similar leave is available to sole male adopters.

Parental leave

Both parents are entitled to up to 14 weeks unpaid leave to take care of a child up to eight years of age.

This leave can be taken in a single block, weekly blocks, days or even hours, though the employer must be informed in writing six weeks in advance.

The Parental Leave Act, 1998, as amended by the Parental Leave (Amendment) Act, 2006, provides for paid "force majeure" leave of up to three days in a year or five days over three years on the sudden illness/injury of an immediate family member.

Trade union membership

The Irish Constitution is an employee's ultimate assurance of the right to form or to join a trade union. Union activities, in particular, disputes and their conduct, are covered by the Industrial Relations Act, 1990, which also established the Labour Relations Commission.

Minimum notice on termination of employment

The Minimum Notice to Terminate Employment Act, 1973, applies to employees in continuous service for 13 weeks.

Protection against unfair dismissal

Where an employee has been employed for more than 12 months, he/she is deemed to have been unfairly dismissed unless the criteria for a fair dismissal laid down in the Unfair Dismissals Act, 1977 have been met. Inter alias, the Act requires that:
- The procedures for dismissal laid down by the employer be fair
- The procedures be operated fairly.

A short-term contract must be signed by both employeee and employer and clearly state that the provisions of the 1977 Act do not apply, in order to be considered a valid reason for dismissal at the expiry of the contract term.

Protection against redundancy

Where redundancy is unavoidable, an employee is entitled to payment by the employer (or failing this, from the State). The amounts of the payments are set by law and vary according to age and length of service.

Where the employee meets certain criteria, the employer may recover 60% of the statutory redundancy payments from the Redundancy and Employers Insolvency Fund, administered by the Minister for Enterprise, Trade and Employment.

Part-time employees

Part-time workers do not have the same rights as

full-time workers, although the Worker Protection (Regular Part-time Employee) Act, 1991 extended some benefits of full-time working to "regular" part-time employees, defined as those in continuous service for at least 13 weeks and normally expected to work at least eight hours per week.

MANAGING STAFF

Businesses go through different stages of development and the management style appropriate to one stage may not be right for another. For example, a person who runs a one-man business does not need to worry about delegating – but when he/she has a dozen employees delegating becomes more important than doing. You should be thinking about managing long before you have anyone to manage. The starting point is your own strengths and weaknesses as an entrepreneur. Go back to the "Self-assessment" and "Training for Entrepreneurs" section in the chapter, **READY**. Look again at your skills and training needs.

Consider whether a partner or key employee could supply some of the skills you are missing. Use the panel below to identify critical areas in your business and those where a partner or key manager could make a difference. Could your business bear the financial impact of another salary? One that would make a critical difference to the speed at which your business develops? Could you reduce your own salary for a while to compensate?

If you are to build a strong team, you need to become a good manager yourself. There are lots of books and courses available to help you here. You need to build skills in delegation, time management, coaching, appraisal and communications to name but a few. But one of the most important points to make is that successful managers show, in lots of little but important ways, that they care for their staff, that they trust them and that they are willing to allow them to use their initiative (and to make mistakes!).

Good managers listen, they are interested in people in and outside work, they share information and knowledge, they are open to new ideas, they are enthusiastic and have a sense of humour. Check your own management style by writing the answers to the questions below in the panel below.

STAFF RETENTION

It may seem strange to consider staff retention before you have even recruited your first employee but, as in many things, forward planning pays off.

Staff are a key success factor in any business. Managing staff has implications in every part of the business as very often your staff will be responsible for implementing all the bright ideas you come up with. They can make or break your ideas. And, properly encouraged, they can produce bright ideas of their own. Therefore, a lot of time and thought should be given not only to considering whom you want to recruit but also how to keep your staff happy and productive. To see why this is important, consider the costs of staff turnover:

- **Loss of capacity:** There's no one there to do the work, until you find a replacement
- **Loss of knowledge:** All that the person has learnt, before joining and in your business, is gone
- **Loss of experience:** All the experience the person had is gone
- **Loss of network:** All the contacts that the person had are gone – some other employer has these now (are they a competitor of yours?)
- **Loss of training**: All the training you gave the person is gone
- **Cost of recruitment:** You will have to spend time and money recruiting a replacement and may have to pay the new person more than the person who left
- **Cost of induction:** The new person will take a little while to settle in, during which time they are producing below expected output and a drain on the time of other staff
- **Cost of new training:** You may have to train the new person.

All this makes it worth minimising staff turnover.

CRITICAL BUSINESS AREAS

Which of these areas are most critical to the development of your business? Where would a partner or key manager make the most difference? Rank them 1, 2, 3, etc.

	Critical	Difference
Marketing	____	____
Sales	____	____
Financial control	____	____
Production	____	____
Management	____	____

YOUR MANAGEMENT STYLE

Are you a good listener?	☐ YES ☐ NO
Do you like people?	☐ YES ☐ NO
Do you mind sharing?	☐ YES ☐ NO
Do you have an open mind?	☐ YES ☐ NO
Are you enthusiastic?	☐ YES ☐ NO
Do you have a sense of humour?	☐ YES ☐ NO
Do you have clear job descriptions?	☐ YES ☐ NO
Do you know what you expect from your staff?	☐ YES ☐ NO
Are you personally willing to improve?	☐ YES ☐ NO

When starting in business, you have a choice of four main types of business entity through which to conduct your enterprise. They are: Sole trader, Partnership, Limited liability company and Co-operative. Four things will decide which you choose:

- **The kind of business you are starting** – Some professional firms can only be formed as sole traders or partnerships
- **The expectations of those with whom you plan to do business** – Many business people expect to deal with limited companies and are wary of other forms of business entities as trading partners
- **Your attitude to risk** – In particular, to risking those of your assets that you are not planning to commit to the business. A limited liability company limits the risk of losing your capital if your enterprise is not successful.
- **How you wish to organise your tax affairs** – Certain kinds of favourable tax treatment are only available to limited liability companies.

You are taking a risk in starting an enterprise. You are risking your money, time and reputation. You are entitled to protect those of your assets that you do not wish to commit. For this reason, you are strongly advised to form a limited liability company. However, because of the tax and other implications of doing so, you should take professional help and advice before making your decision.

Sole Trader
You automatically become a sole trader by starting up a business on your own. Setting up as a sole trader needs almost nothing by way of legal formality, apart from registering with the Registrar of Business Names at the Companies Registration Office (**www.cro.ie**), which is optional.

An advantage of being a sole trader is that apart from normal tax returns, which every taxable person must make, a sole trader is not required to make public any information about the business. The downside of being a sole trader is that you have no protection if your business fails. All your assets become available to pay off your creditors.

Partnership
A partnership, essentially, is an agreement between two or more people to go into business together. It may be no more formal than a handshake or may run to a multi-page legal document. Whichever route you take, build the following points into your planning:

- In a partnership, **each** partner is liable for **all** the liabilities of the business. If the business fails, and your partner(s) abandon(s) you, you could be left to pay for everything out of your own pocket. Before entering a partnership, decide whether you trust your partner(s)-to-be with everything you own — because that's what you will be doing.
- If you write down nothing else, write down and have all the partners sign a partnership agreement setting out how the business is to be financed, how profits and losses are to be shared, and what will happen if one of the partners decides to leave. These are important points. Failure to agree on them at an early stage can lead to difficulty later.

A limited liability company
A limited liability company is a legal entity separate from its shareholders. The shareholders are only liable, in the event of the business becoming unable to pay its debts, for any amount outstanding on their subscribed shareholdings.

Some limited companies are limited by guarantee – the guarantee being the amount that the members agree to pay in the event of the company going into liquidation. This form of company is more suitable for clubs and associations than for trading businesses.

The advantages of a limited company over a sole trader or partnership are:
- Limited liability status
- The possibility of obtaining credit more easily
- The only income taxable on the owners of the business is any salaries

or dividends taken from the business
- Business Expansion Scheme relief for a qualifying company
- Scope for tax planning.

The disadvantages include:
- The cost of formation expenses
- The requirement for an annual audit (in some circumstances not required for companies limited by shares)
- The public filing of information with the Companies Registration Office
- The need for accounts to comply with Companies Acts and accounting standards
- Business losses may not be set against personal income
- Possibility of further taxation on capital gains if appreciating assets are taken from the business.

EU regulations now allow the formation of private limited companies with only one member (as against the normal requirement for two members), although two directors are still required.

Registration and other forms are available for download from **www.cro.ie**

A co-operative

A worker co-operative is where a team comes together to form and run a business according to a set of values that include self-help, self-responsibility, democracy, equality, equity and solidarity. The business is jointly owned and democratically controlled, unlike other more hierarchical business structures. Co-operative members believe in the ethical values of honesty, openness, social responsibility and caring for others. The Co-operative Principles, which provide guidelines setting out how the business should conduct itself, are:
- **Voluntary and open membership:** Co-operatives do not permit gender, social, racial, political or religious discrimination and are open to all willing to accept the responsibilities of membership
- **Democratic member control:** Co-operatives are democratically controlled by their members, who actively participate in setting policies and in decision-making
- **Member economic participation:** Members contribute equitably to the capital of their business. Surpluses are used to develop the business, benefiting members in proportion to their transactions with the co-operative and supporting activities approved by the membership
- **Autonomy and independence:** In all contracts with external bodies, co-operatives ensure that members retain democratic control and their co-operative autonomy
- **Education, training and information:** Co-operatives provide education and training for their members and employees to ensure their effective contribution
- **Co-operation among co-operatives:** Co-operatives work together through local, regional, national and international structures
- **Concern for community:** Co-operatives work for sustainable development through policies approved by their members.

Formation of co-operatives is by Model Rules. Co-operatives can be formed as limited companies.

Directors' responsibilities

If you are a director of a limited liability company, you take on responsibilities – and the enforcement regime for these is becoming increasingly strict – including:
- Responsibilities given under the company's Articles of Association
- Responsibilities imposed by company law
- A fiduciary duty under common law.

This last point means that directors act on behalf of all shareholders, not just some, and requires directors to consider the long-term implications of their actions, since they have a duty to future shareholders as well as present. Directors owe a duty to exercise skill and diligence in their work, in line with their knowledge and experience, though they cannot be held responsible in law for errors of judgement. In certain circumstances, directors may become personally liable for the debts of a company – for example, where it can be shown that they are guilty of reckless or fraudulent trading, or where the company has failed to keep "proper books of account".

On a day-to-day basis, the Companies Acts impose requirements on directors (strictly on the company but the directors are responsible for ensuring compliance) in relation to returns of information – for example, an Annual Return each year following the AGM. Following many years of non-compliance (or, at best, lax compliance, even among sizeable companies), the Companies Registration Office, backed by the Director of Corporate Enforcement, is now taking a harsher view and imposing penalties and "striking off" companies for late returns. The impact of this is that, where a company continues to trade after it has been struck off, the directors become personally liable for its debts. In company secretarial work and your responsibilities as a director, take advice from your accountant.

The name of a business is one of its most important assets, even though it does not appear in the balance sheet with the other assets. Choose the name of your business carefully.

The right name will be:
- Unique
- Easy to remember, pronounce and spell
- Informative
- Image-creating.

If your business is going to trade as a limited company, there are some restrictions on the name you choose (see panel).

Even if your business is not going to trade as a limited company, there are still some rules to be followed. You still cannot use the name of an existing business, or one that will be confused with the name of an existing business. However, a partnership can use the same name as an existing partnership, provided the name consists only of the names of the partners. In general, follow the rules for companies above.

Registering a business name

If, trading as a limited company, you wish to trade under a name other than the company's registered name (for example as *West Cork Forest Advisory Services*, even though the company is registered as *Frank Kelly Limited*), you must register the business name.

If you are trading in one of the other business structures, it is advisable to register the name of the business.

However, note that registration of a business name does not:
- Give protection against duplication of the name (since others may be entitled to use it, though you can prevent them from "passing off" – pretending to be you)
- Imply that the name will prove acceptable as a company name (it may already be registered, or become registered later, as a company name)
- Authorise the use of the name, if its use could be prohibited for other reasons — for example, because the name proposed is the trade mark of another person.

Because of this last point, it is important to check whether someone else might have rights in the proposed name before spending money on stationery, signs etc. Check on the Companies Registration Office website.

To register a business name, you must:
- Complete Form RBN1B (available for download from the Companies Registration Office web-site)
- Send it with the prescribed fee, to The Registrar of Companies, Companies Registration Office, O'Brien Road, Carlow.

You can do this when you are sending in the documentation for the formation of the company.

On registration of your business name, you will be issued with a Certificate of Business Name. This must be displayed prominently at the company's registered or principal office and in every branch or premises.

Internet names

Because of abuse of the facility to register Internet "domain" names, you may now be required by the IE Domain Registry (**www.domainregistry.ie**) to provide evidence that you have some entitlement to an .ie domain name that you wish to register. A registered business name may help provide this evidence.

CHOOSING A COMPANY NAME

You may not use as a name for a limited company any name which:
- Is identical to the name of an existing company
- Is identical to, or could be confused with, the name of a foreign company which conducts business in Ireland
- Is identical to a well-known trade mark
- Could be confused with the name of an existing company, because it is phonetically identical or the difference in spelling is such as to be immaterial
- In the opinion of the Minister for Enterprise, Trade and Employment, is undesirable
- Implies State sponsorship
- Uses certain restricted words, such as "Bank", "Banker", or "Banking", "Society", "Co-op", "Co-operative" or "Insurance".

OBJECTIVES

o Understand the steps involved in opening a business bank account

At least one bank account is essential for any business, however small. Don't be tempted to run your business through your own personal bank account "until it gets off the ground". That is a recipe for disaster. Open a separate bank account for your business as soon as you begin to trade.

A limited company needs to pass a resolution of the Board of Directors to open a bank account. The steps are:

- Ask your bank manager for a bank mandate form. This authorises the bank to carry out the instructions of the directors regarding the operation of the account
- Decide what instructions you want to give the bank regarding who is authorised to sign cheques on behalf of the company, and how often you want to receive statements
- Hold a meeting of the directors of the company
- Propose the resolution at the meeting in the form required by the bank – see the mandate form for the wording – and have it adopted by the directors
- Complete the mandate form
- Get sample signatures from each of the people authorised to sign cheques on behalf of the company
- Return the mandate form and sample signatures to your bank manager
- Give the bank manager a copy of each of your company's Memorandum and Articles of Association. These will be kept for the manager's files
- Show the original of the company's Certificate of Incorporation to your bank manager. A copy of this will be taken for the manager's files and on the copy will be marked the fact that the original has been seen by the manager. You will not be asked for, and you should not give the bank manager, the original Certificate of Incorporation (except in the larger city branches where the documents to open your bank account go to the Securities department for checking. In this case, your bank manager should give you a receipt for the certificate and give you a date when you can return to collect it - better still to get your local manager to sgn that he / shee has seen the original certifcate and take a copy for the bank's file, allowing you to take your original certificate home with you immediately)
- Have available some money to lodge to the new account
- Decide the name in which you want the account to be opened. You can use only the registered name of the company, unless you are trading under a registered business name. In this case, you will also need to show the bank manager the Certificate of Registration of Business Name for the company
- Depending on the bank and branch, it may take a few days or a few weeks to clear all the paperwork associated with opening your company's bank account. Allow for this in your planning
- If you need immediate access to the money you are lodging, your bank manager can usually arrange for temporary cheques to be made available while a chequebook is being printed.

OPENING A BANK ACCOUNT – CHECKLIST

When you go to the bank to open your bank account, make sure that you have:

- A completed bank mandate form ☐
- Sample signatures for all those who will sign cheques on the company's bank account ☐
- A copy of the Memorandum and Articles of Association (limited company only) ☐
- Certificate of Incorporation (limited company only) ☐
- Certificate of Business Name (if you are trading under any name other than the company's registered name) ☐
- Cash or cheques to lodge to your new account. ☐

Businesses in Ireland are subject to:
- **Income tax** – Sole traders and partnerships on their profits
- **Corporation tax** – Limited companies on their profits
- **Value added tax (VAT)** – All businesses with turnover in excess of €75,000 (goods) or €37,500 (services)
- **PAYE/PRSI** – All businesses with employees (including owner/directors).

Registration for tax

It is your obligation to notify the Revenue Commissioners through your local tax office of the establishment of your business and to provide them with the information required to register your business for the relevant taxes.

You must complete one of two forms, depending on your circumstances:
- Form TR1, if you are a sole trader or partnership
- Form TR2, if your business is a limited company.

Each of these forms gets you registered for all applicable taxes. They are available for download on the Revenue's web-site.

Shortly after registration, you will receive a "new Business Visit" from a Revenue official who will go through the requirements to ensure that you have proper systems in place.

CORPORATION TAX

Limited companies pay Corporation Tax. This tax is charged on the company's profits which include both income and chargeable gains.

A company's income for tax purposes is calculated in accordance with Income Tax rules. Chargeable gains are calculated in accordance with Capital Gains Tax rules. If an individual is trading through a company, any losses arising cannot be offset against any other personal income earned. The losses can only be offset against trading income of the company or against future or past profits, subject to certain restrictions.

Self-assessment

The self-assessment system applies to companies. Preliminary Tax is payable within six months of the end of the accounting period, which is generally the period for which the company makes up its accounts. To avoid an interest charge of 1.25% per month, Preliminary Tax paid must be 90% of the final liability for the period. A company must submit a return (Form CT1) no later than 9 months from the end of the accounting period to which the return relates. If the Preliminary Tax paid was sufficient, the balance of tax is payable within one month of the issue of the assessment by the Inspector of Taxes.

There are also restrictions on the use the company can make of certain reliefs and allowances if the return is not submitted on time.

There are two rates of Corporation Tax:
- 12.5% on trading income
- 25% on non-trading income.

INCOME TAX

Income tax is payable by individuals on income earned in the tax year – that is, on annual profits or gains from an individual's trade, profession or vocation and on other income, such as investment income, rental income etc.

A tax assessment is usually based on actual income earned in the tax year – from 1 January to 31 December. It is up to the individual/business to decide the date to which the accounts are prepared, usually to the same date each year.

A self-employed person will be taxed under the Self-Assessment system.

Preliminary Tax is an estimate of the income tax payable for the year. It includes PRSI and Health Contribution (and any additional levies) as well as income tax. The duty lies on the individual to calculate their own Preliminary Tax. If Preliminary Tax is not paid by the due date, or if the amount is too low, interest will be charged at a rate of 1.25% per month or part of month on the balance of tax outstanding. Failure to submit a tax return by the tax return filing date will result in a surcharge being added to the final tax bill.

Where a new business is set up, the surcharge will not be imposed if the return for the first year is made by the return filing date for the following year.

OBJECTIVES
o Understand system of taxation
o Understand basics of individual taxes

REVENUE COMMISSIONERS' MISSION
To serve the community by fairly and efficiently collecting taxes and duties and implementing import and export controls.

There's nothing so hard to understand as the income tax.
ALBERT EINSTEIN

The trick is to stop thinking of it as "your" money.
UK REVENUE AUDITOR

An explanatory booklet (IT10) on *A Guide to Self-Assessment* is available from the Revenue web-site.

Calculating taxable profits

Taxable profits are calculated by deducting allowable business expenses from turnover. Turnover is the gross amount of income earned by a business before deducting any business expenses – the total amounts from sale of goods or provision of services. If a business is registered for VAT, the turnover figure should exclude VAT.

If a business makes a loss, it is either offset against other taxable income or carried forward against the future profits of the business.

Business expenses are normally referred to as revenue expenditure, which covers day-to-day running costs (exclusive of VAT, if the business is registered for VAT), including:

- Purchase of goods for resale
- Wages, rent, rates, repairs, lighting, heating etc
- Running costs of vehicles or machinery used in the business
- Accountancy and audit fees
- Interest paid on any monies borrowed to finance business expenses/items
- Lease payments on vehicles or machinery used in the business.

Some expenses cannot be claimed as revenue expenditure, including:

- Any expense, not wholly and exclusively paid for the purposes of the trade or profession
- Any private or domestic expenditure
- Business entertainment expenditure – the provision of accommodation, food, drink or any other form of hospitality
- Expenditure of a capital nature.

For expenditure relating to both business and private use, only that part relating to the business will be allowed.

A deduction for the running expenses of a vehicle used for business purposes can also be claimed. To calculate the split of capital allowances (wear and tear) and running expenses, total mileage for the year and the total number of miles travelled for business purposes must be recorded. Journeys between home and a regular place of work are treated as private and not business mileage.

Expenditure is regarded as "capital" if it has been spent on acquiring or altering assets which are of lasting use in the business – for example, the purchase or alteration of business premises. Capital expenditure cannot be deducted in arriving at the taxable profit. However, capital allowances may be claimed on capital expenditure incurred on items such as office equipment, business plant and machinery, taking account of wear and tear on these items.

To arrive at the correct taxable income, the net profit should be calculated and any allowances and relief entitlements should be deducted.

TAXPAYERS' CHARTER OF RIGHTS

In your dealings with the Revenue Commissioners, you are entitled to:

- **Courtesy and Consideration** – To expect that Revenue staff will at all times carry out their duties courteously and considerately.
- **Presumption of Honesty** – To be presumed to have dealt with your tax affairs honestly unless there is reason to believe to the contrary and subject to the Revenue Commissioners' responsibility for ensuring compliance with the law.
- **Information** – To expect that every reasonable effort will be made to give you access to full, accurate and timely information about Revenue law and your entitlements and obligations under it. So that they can do this, Revenue staff are entitled to expect that you will give them all the facts and the full co-operation which they need to deal with your affairs.
- **Impartiality** – To have your affairs dealt with in an impartial manner by Revenue staff who seek only to collect the correct amount of tax or duty, no more and no less.
- **Privacy and Confidentiality** – To expect that personal and business information provided by you will be treated in strict confidence and used only for purposes allowed by law.
- **Independent Review** – To object to a charge to tax or duty if you think the law has been applied incorrectly and to ask that your case be reviewed. If the matter cannot be resolved to your satisfaction by Revenue officials, you have rights in law to independent review.
- **Compliance Costs** – To expect that the Revenue Commissioners and their staff recognise the need to keep to the minimum necessary the costs you incur in complying with Revenue law, subject to their responsibility to carry out their functions efficiently and economically.
- **Consistent Administration** – To expect that the Revenue Commissioners will administer the law consistently and apply it firmly to those who try to evade paying their lawful share.

Sub-contractors

Sub-contractors in the construction, forestry or meat-processing industries will have tax deducted at 35% on all payments to them by principal contractors unless they have a certificate of authorisation (C2).

The decision as to whether a person is an employee or sub-contractor is matter of fact determined by guidelines set out in an explanatory guide for sub-contractors (IT64), which is available on the Revenue's web-site.

When starting a job as a sub-contractor, you must produce your C2 and sign a Form RCT1, which the principal contractor keeps. All payments to you then will be gross. Otherwise, at the end of the job, the principal contractor will issue you with a Form RCTDC, a deduction certificate, which shows how much tax has been deducted.

Whether you are paid gross, or with tax deducted, you are still liable to complete tax returns under the Self-Assessment system and pay any balance of tax due.

You can apply for a C2 at your local tax office.

PAYE/PRSI

The Pay As You Earn (PAYE) system operates on the basis that an employer deducts tax at a specified rate from an employee's pay. The system is designed so that, as far as is possible, the correct amount of tax is deducted from an employee's pay to meet his/her tax liability for the year. To achieve this, PAYE is normally computed on a cumulative basis, from the beginning of the tax year to the date on which a payment is being made.

In certain situations, it is not appropriate to operate PAYE on a cumulative basis and, therefore, tax is deducted on a "Week 1" basis.

In addition to deducting PAYE, employers are also obliged to deduct Pay Related Social Insurance (PRSI) from employees on behalf of the Department of Social, Community and Family Affairs. The employee's PRSI contribution is made up of:

- Social Insurance, which varies according to the earnings of the employee and the benefits for which the person is insured
- 2% Health Contribution.

From 6 April 2001, the old system of tax free allowances was changed in favour of a "tax credit" system, which operates as follows:

- An employee pays tax at the standard rate (20%) on all his/her taxable earnings for a pay period up to the standard rate cut-off point for that period
- He/she pays tax at the higher rate (41%) on all

COMPLETING FORMS TR1 AND TR2

Both forms register businesses for Corporation Tax, Employer's PAYE/PRSI and/or VAT, in one operation. Use Form TR1 for sole traders or partnerships, and Form TR2 for limited companies.

For either form:
- To register for Income Tax/Corporation Tax only, complete Parts A, B and C
- To register for Employer's PAYE/PRSI only, complete Parts A, B and D
- To register for VAT only, complete Parts A, B and E
- To register for ALL taxes, complete Parts A, B, C, D + E.

Whatever sections of the form have been completed, the Declaration in Part A **MUST** be signed before a company may be registered for any tax.

Make sure you give:
- The full name of the company as registered under the Companies' Acts (not the trading name)
- The name of your accountant, who will prepare the accounts and tax returns for the company
- Where a different person handles matters relating to Employer's PAYE/PRSI and/or VAT, give their name(s) and address(es).

Check with your accountant about:
- Election for registration for VAT if you are not obliged by law to register
- Election for registration for VAT in respect of certain lettings of premises where the services provided are normally exempt from VAT
- Election for cash receipts basis of accounting for VAT.

These forms are available on the Revenue's web-site.

earnings for the pay period above this point
- The total of the tax due by the employee for the pay period is reduced by tax credits due to the employee in respect of the pay period.

The amounts of the standard rate cut-off point and tax credits due to the employee are determined by the tax office and advised on a Certificate of Tax Credits and Standard Rate Cut-Off Point issued to the employee.

Employers' PAYE/PRSI
When starting in business, you must register for PAYE/PRSI if you pay:
- €8 per week (€36 a month), or more, to an employee who has only one employment
- €2 per week (€9 a month), or more, to an employee who has more than one employment.

A company must register as an employer and operate PAYE/PRSI on the pay of directors even if there are no other employees.

It is important to distinguish whether a payment, benefit, expense etc. should be regarded as "pay" and taxed under the PAYE system. There are particular areas of benefits/perks (car, medical insurance, etc.) which have different tax implications.

Expenses incurred by employees while carrying out the duties of the job and for which receipts can be produced are not generally regarded as pay.

Registration as an employer
To register for PAYE/PRSI, employers must complete form TR1 (sole trader or partnership) or TR2 (limited company). You will receive confirmation of your registration as an employer, including a registered number for PAYE purposes and detailed information regarding the operation of PAYE/PRSI.

If you become an employer and fail to register for PAYE/PRSI purposes, the Revenue Commissioners will compulsorily register you. You will have to pay the PAYE and PRSI due and interest will be charged at 1.25% per month from the date on which it should have been paid.

Payments and returns
PAYE and PRSI payments must be paid to the Collector-General within 14 days from the end of the income tax month during which the deductions were made.

A form P30 Bank Giro/Payslip is issued to the employer each month on which the figures for total tax and total PRSI contributions should be entered, together with the gross total which will equal the amount of the payment. The form P30 should be returned marked "Nil" if there is no PAYE/PRSI liability for a particular month.

Employers can arrange to pay PAYE/PRSI through a direct debit scheme and make an annual return/declaration of liability. At the end of the tax year, the employer must complete end-of-year forms P35, P35L and P35/T which are sent by the Collector-General. These forms must be returned by the due date.

Employers must also issue a Form P60 to each employee who was in employment at 31 December. This form shows total pay, tax and PRSI contributions for the year ended 31 December.

VALUE ADDED TAX
Value Added Tax (VAT) is a consumer tax collected by VAT-registered traders on their supplies of taxable goods and services in the course of business and by Customs & Excise on imports from outside the EU. Each registered trader pays VAT on goods and services acquired for the business and charges VAT on goods and services supplied by the business. The amount by which VAT charged exceeds VAT paid must be paid to the Collector-General.

If the amount of VAT paid exceeds the VAT charged, the Collector-General will pay over the excess to the trader. This ensures that VAT is paid by the ultimate customer and not by the business.

Taxable persons
A taxable person for VAT purposes is an individual (other than an employee), a partnership, company etc, who supplies taxable goods and services in the course of or in the furtherance of the business.

Taxable persons are obliged to register for VAT where the amount of their annual turnover (the amount of receipts excluding VAT) exceeds or is likely to exceed €75,000 – goods or €37,500 – services.

Traders whose turnover is below these limits are not generally obliged to register for VAT but may do so if they wish.

The current rates of VAT are:
- **21.5% (standard rate)** – all goods and services that are not exempt or are taxable at the zero or reduced rates
- **13.5%** – certain fuels (coal and domestic gas), building and building services, newspapers, certain other goods and services
- **4.8%** – livestock, live greyhounds and the hire of horses
- **Zero** – exports, certain food and drink (bread

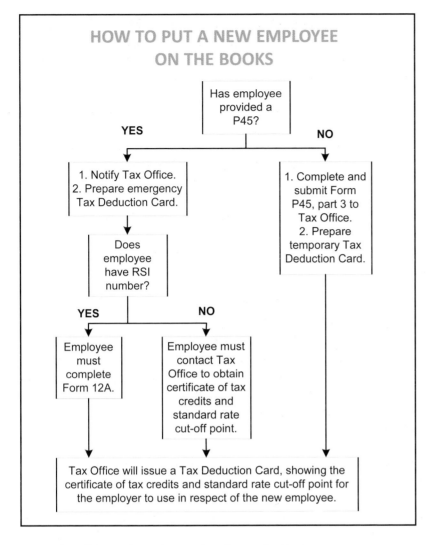

HOW TO PUT A NEW EMPLOYEE ON THE BOOKS

- VAT due to Revenue or repayable to you
- Goods supplied to/received from other EU member states.

You are required to make a VAT return even if you do not owe any VAT for the period.

An annual return of trading details is also required. This return can be prepared for any period of 12 months that best suits your accounting arrangements.

VAT may be paid through the Revenue's direct debit scheme. Any excess VAT will be repaid automatically by electronic transmission to your nominated bank or building society.

GENERAL
Record-keeping
The Revenue Commissioners have certain requirements regarding record-keeping and accounts (see "Accounting", page 71) which you must comply with.

Returns
For each of the taxes, you are required to supply the Revenue Commissioners with specific information on or by specific dates. These are called "returns" and there are severe penalties for late submission or not submitting returns at all.

Information and assistance
Comprehensive guides to all aspects of business taxation, including a "Starting in Business" guide, may be obtained from any tax office, the Revenue Forms & Leaflets Service at (01) 878 0100, or the Revenue's web-site (**www.revenue.ie**). Your accountant will also provide advice.

Revenue audits
A revenue audit is a cross-check of the information and figures shown in tax returns against those shown in a business's records, covering:
- Income Tax, Corporation Tax or Capital Gains Tax and/or
- The returns submitted for VAT, PAYE/PRSI or Relevant Contacts Tax (RCT).

and milk), oral medicine, books excluding newspapers, brochures
- **Exempt** – financial, medical and educational activities.

Registration
To register for VAT, complete form TR1 (TR2 for a limited company).

Cash basis of accounting
Any registered person whose annual turnover is less than €635,000, and 95% of whose customers are non-VAT-regsitered, may account for VAT on receipt of payment rather than on the issue of an invoice. This gives a significant cash-flow benefit. Applications to use the cash basis of accounting should be made to your local tax office, after discussing the matter with your accountant.

Returns
When you register for VAT, the Collector-General will send you a form VAT3 every two months (less often at the discretion of the Collector-General). You must complete this form and return it to the Collector-General before the 19th day following the end of the two monthly period giving details of:
- VAT charged by you for the period
- VAT paid by you for the period

The Revenue Commissioners use three methods of selection for audit:

- Screening tax returns
- Projects on particular business sectors
- Random selection.

Generally, 14 days' advance notice in writing is given, stating the name of the person who will carry out the audit, the date and time of the audit and the year(s), accounting period(s) or VAT period(s) which are to be audited.

The auditor will examine a business' books and records to verify that the figures have been correctly calculated and that the tax returns and/or declarations for the different taxes are correct. If adjustments are required, the auditor will quantify these, discuss them with you/the appropriate person, seek agreement to the total settlement figure and issue written notification. Interest will be charged at 15% on tax underpaid where a taxpayer makes an incomplete or incorrect return and publication of an audit settlement may occur.

An explanatory booklet, *Revenue Audit – Guide for Small Business* is available from any tax office.

Taxpayers' Charter

It's not all one way, however. The Revenue Commissioners have issued a "Taxpayers' Charter" (see panel earlier), which sets out your rights as a taxpayer.

Tax clearance

Generally, grant offers from State agencies or the County/City Enterprise Boards are conditional on tax clearance. If you receive grants between €600 and €6,000, you must submit the following information:

- The tax district dealing with your tax affairs
- Your tax reference number

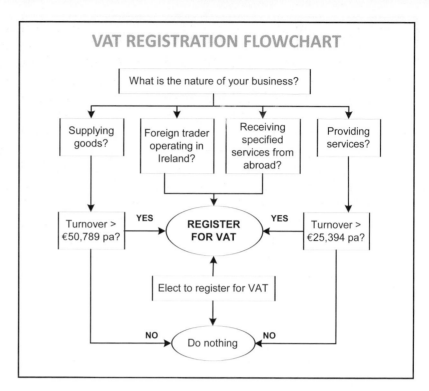

- A signed statement indicating that, to the best of your knowledge, your tax affairs are in order.

If you receive grants of €6,000 or more, you must submit with your claim a Tax Clearance Certificate from the Revenue Commissioners confirming that your tax affairs are in order. Form TC1 should be completed when applying to the Revenue Commissioners for a Tax Clearance Certificate. You will be given a TC1 application form by the agency or CEB.

Tax clearance will also be required in respect of each contractor, where sub-contractors are employed on a construction project.

Revenue On-line Services

The Revenue Commissioners are increasingly moving on-line. Not only are all forms and publications available on their web-site but Revenue On-line Services (www.ros.ie) allows registered users to:

- View current employer taxes position on-line
- File and pay certain forms and returns on-line.

Talk to an accountant

Because tax regulations are becoming increasingly complicated, it is worth talking to an accountant about your specific situation and needs.

ACCOUNTING

Accounting – anything to do with financial matters – is the part of being in business that most small business owners like least. So they neglect it, saying that it is more important to be "out there selling". Or they hand over responsibility for it to someone else – and forget about it. But you wouldn't do that with any other part of your business. You wouldn't hand over responsibility for marketing, for product development or for recruiting staff to anyone else. Why do it for something as critical to your business as accounting?

Accounting consists of three steps:
- Recording transactions
- Analysing them so that they provide information
- Interpreting them so that they are useful for decision-making.

Recording transactions

First, identify what transactions you need to record. Most businesses have:
- Purchases on credit
- Sales for credit
- Receipts – Cash into the bank account
- Payments – Cash out of the bank account
- Petty cash.

Let's start with these. For each transaction, you need to record:
- The date
- The type of transaction
- The other person involved
- The amount involved.

If you use a separate page for each type of transaction, you do not need to record the type of transaction – the page it is recorded on will tell you what type it is.

So you now have five pages for each of the transaction types with a limited amount of information recorded on each - the next chapter, GO, shows examples of each of these.

Analysing transactions

Next, begin to analyse the transactions to provide information.

Take purchases on credit. You might analyse the transactions under the following headings:

- **Fixed assets** – Items not for resale
- **Stock** – Items for resale
- **Overheads** – Expenses incurred in running the business (analyse these further into categories – Staff, Production, Premises, Transport, Sales and promotion, General expenses and Finance – these can be further subdivided if necessary to show the detail you need)
- **Miscellaneous/Sundry** – Items for which we can find no other obvious category or which happen so seldom that it's not worth setting up a separate analysis of them.

Sales on credit might be analysed by product/service type.

Cash into the bank account might be analysed by source, one of which will be debtors paying for goods/services bought earlier on credit. Other sources will include cash from cash sales (which should tie up on a daily basis), loans to the business, VAT and miscellaneous items.

Cash out of the bank account might be analysed by destination, one of which will be creditors from whom we bought goods/services on credit earlier. We might also have bought goods and services and paid by cheque, so we need to analyse these. We also need to include overheads, using the categories above.

Small items of expenditure are recorded as Petty cash expenses.

Value Added Tax

If your business is registered for it, recording VAT is the next step.

With certain exceptions (see the previous section, "Taxation"), VAT paid on purchases is recoverable, while you must account to the Revenue Commissioners for VAT you charge on sales. This means that, if the amount you pay for purchases includes VAT, you can reduce the cost to your business by the VAT amount. Similarly, you must deduct VAT from your sales before accounting for them in your business.

The "books"

The next chapter, GO, shows the very basic "books" that you must keep.

OBJECTIVES
o Understand basics of book-keeping
o Appreciate need for records and regular accounts

A Tradesman's Books, like a Christian's Conscience, should always be kept clean and clear; and he that is not careful of both will give but a sad account of himself either to God or Man.
DANIEL DEFOE (1660-1731)

Of course, you don't need to buy expensive accounting analysis books. Ordinary paper with ruled columns will do perfectly well to start with. Keep your sheets in a folder, with dividers for each type of page.

Use an extra column – perhaps one right in at the margin – to write the number of the transactions. Keep a sequence going from the day you start. And write the transaction number onto the receipt or invoice. File all the receipts and invoices away safely in transaction number order. Then, if there are ever any queries, you will be able to find the answers quickly and easily.

These "books" are available as Excel spreadsheets to download from the website **www.startingabusinessinireland.com**.

Bank balance book

Your bank balance is one of the most important pieces of information in your business. You need to know what it is on a daily basis. To save time ringing the bank every day, since you have all the information you need to calculate it yourself, keep a Bank Balance Book. This is a simple ledger book (you'll find cheap versions in any stationery shop), with columns for:

- Date
- Transaction details
- Cash into the bank account
- Cash out of the bank account
- Balance.

An example of a Bank balance book appears in the next chapter, **GO**.

Record every transaction that goes through your bank account in this book, and you will always know what your balance is. Get into the habit of checking the balance before you write cheques (even if they are essential) and you will avoid unpleasant surprises. If your Bank balance book shows that writing a particular cheque will make your account overdrawn and you have no permission to do so, you have two choices:

- **Don't write the cheque** – Strictly, it's against the law to write a cheque when there isn't enough money in your account to meet it
- **Get permission** – However bad the news, it's always better to break it to your bank manager in advance than after the event, when he is in trouble with his bosses over your unauthorised overdraft.

Yes, you are duplicating some of the information on your "Cash into the bank account" and "Cash out of the bank account" pages but your Bank balance book can be written in summary form ("Cheque" will do under "Transaction details") to save time.

Transactions that originate with the bank (bank charges, interest and fees) should always be notified to you before they are charged to your account. As soon as you receive details of these amounts from your bank, write them into your Bank balance book.

Then you will be able to sleep easy at night, without worrying that the bank manager might call querying an unauthorised overdrawn situation.

Get into the habit of checking your bank statements when they arrive each month. Check to see that:

- All lodgements have been made
- All cheques cashed – You should deduct any cheques that you have written but which have not yet been cashed from the balance shown on the bank statement
- No charges or fees have been charged to your account without your knowledge.

If you find anything that you do not understand, however small the amount, check with the bank immediately.

"Still due" file

In addition to your bank balance, you also need to know who owes you money and how much. A simple way of doing this is to set up a "Still due" file – a folder into which you place a copy of every invoice you send out for sales on credit. As you get paid, take out the relevant invoice and tear it up. Adding up all the invoices in the file tells you how much you are owed. And the thickness of the file provides a quick visual check of the effectiveness of your credit control procedures (see below).

"Still to be paid" file

Another piece of essential information is the amount of money you owe – particularly to suppliers, who may stop supplying you if they don't get paid on time.

Open a file, into which you put a copy of every invoice you receive from your suppliers for goods or services you buy on credit from them. As you pay your suppliers, take out the relevant copy invoices and staple them to the cheque you are sending. Whatever is in your "Still to be paid" file at any point is the total of what you owe. In addition, your suppliers know exactly which invoices you are paying, since you have sent them a copy. Management information in two businesses, no less!

An information system

You can begin to combine, adapt and expand the

"books" and files above to provide you with an information system, following your accountant's advice.

For example, if you have very few transactions, you might put all the "books" onto a single sheet of paper which you use to record all transactions for a day or week, whatever period is appropriate. Instead of filing away the receipts and invoices, staple them onto the sheet. In this way, the sheet becomes your "books" and provides you with an immediate overview of what's going on in your business.

As you become more familiar with the financial side of your business, you will identify figures that help you understand what is happening – sales each day/week/month, for example. Organise a system to extract and report these regularly.

Interpreting the figures

What we have done so far covers recording and analysing. The next step is interpretation.

Most of this is common-sense:

- If your bank balance is always overdrawn, you are spending more than you are bringing in – and you will need to schedule another meeting with your bank manager
- If your purchases are high, and sales are low, stocks will begin to build up – and worse, you may not be able to sell the stock because it might be perishable, go out of fashion or become damaged
- If your overheads are high, you may be spending money on unnecessary items, like fancy office stationery and equipment, instead of on more productive items.

Talk to an accountant about the kind of information you need to manage your business and make sure that your system of recording and analysis provides it for you. And, of course, extracting the figures is only the starting point – you also need to do something about them.

Regular accounts

Every business effectively is required to prepare formal accounts once a year – some because they are limited companies and are required to do so by law, others because the tax authorities will need them to determine how much tax the business should be paying. But annual accounts are not much help in running and managing a business because:

- They are too infrequent – A year is a long time not to know what is happening to the finances of your business
- They are prepared to a different format – One

that often is not helpful for decision-making.

So you need to consider preparing more regular accounts. Monthly accounts may be too much of a burden on your time and may not repay you with enough useful information but quarterly accounts are essential.

In preparing accounts, all you are doing is summarising the information you have recorded and analysed – the analysis helps you with the summary. You don't need anything fancy. A simple profit and loss account to tie in with your Operating Budget (see page 87) will do. Talk to your accountant, if you need help.

Spreadsheets

If you are a computer user, you will have noted that the "books" are ideal for conversion to spreadsheets. Simply replicate the format on your spreadsheet and use its functionality to provide totals, summaries, etc.

But, if you decide to go the spreadsheet route, take some simple precautions:

- **Include a date/time on every printout** – So that you can determine which version you are looking at
- **Make back-up copies of everything** – You do not want to have to recreate your files from scratch at the end of the year or when the taxman comes calling
- **Consider locking cells** – To prevent them being overwritten by accident.

Accounting software

There are lots of accounting software packages that will do all this work for you – except the inputting of data, of course.

Some are very expensive and more suitable for larger businesses. But there are others – Big Red Book, Sage, TAS Books and MYOB – that have versions suitable for small businesses. Some of these cost as little as €100 so, if you have a computer, they may be worth considering.

A computerised accounting system provides information literally at your fingertips when you need it (if you have kept your inputting up-to-date!). Talk to your accountant before spending any money, to make sure you buy the right system for your needs.

Credit control

Your "still due" file is the second element in your credit control procedures – the first is sending out accurate invoices on time. If you do not send out accurate invoices, customers will complain and delay paying you.

Equally, if you do not bother to invoice customers as soon as a job is done, it suggests that you are not in a great hurry to get paid – and customers again will delay paying you.

Build a simple credit control system like this:

- Always invoice as soon as a job is done. Don't wait for the month-end
- Make sure the invoice clearly states the date on which it is due to be paid
- File invoices in your "Still due" file in the order in which they are due to be paid, so that you can see at a glance which invoices are overdue
- Check your "Still due" file every week for overdue invoices. Telephone the customer to ask when you can expect a cheque. Get the name of the person who you are speaking to and ask for them the next time you phone
- After three or four phone calls, write. Say that you will have to put the account into the hands of your solicitors and/or cut off supplies. Only threaten to cut off supplies when you really mean it.

Some customers only pay when they receive a "Statement of Account", a listing of all invoices due which is usually sent to them at the end of each month. Find out which customers need this and make sure you send them a statement.

Also find out your customers' paying habits. Some businesses pay all invoices received up to the 27th day of the month in the first week of the next month. In this case, make sure your invoices are in their hands by the 27th! Fax copies, with the originals following by post.

Cash registers

If yours is a cash business with over-the-counter takings, use a cash register. Most registers will allow you to record total sales for the day, receipts for the day and an analysis of sales for the day. These daily figures can be entered directly into your books, without having to record every individual transaction.

KEEPING BOOKS AND RECORDS FOR TAX PURPOSES

You must keep full and accurate records of your business sufficient to enable you to make a proper return of income for tax purposes. These records must be kept for six years. Failure to keep proper records or to keep them for the necessary six years, where you are chargeable to tax, is a Revenue offence, punishable by fines and/or imprisonment.

The records kept must include books of account in which all purchases and sales of goods and services and all amounts received and all amounts paid out are recorded in a manner that will clearly show the amounts involved and the matters to which they relate. All supporting records such as invoices, bank and building society statements, cheque stubs, receipts etc., should also be retained.

You need to be able to account for:

- Your business takings
- All items of expenditure incurred, such as purchases, rent, lighting, heating, telephone, insurance, motor expenses, repairs, wages, etc.
- Any money introduced into the business and its source
- Any cash withdrawn from the business or any cheques drawn on the business bank account, for your own or your family's private use (drawings)
- Amounts owed to you by customers, showing the total amount owed by each debtor
- Amounts owed by you to suppliers, showing the total amount you owe to each creditor
- Stocks and raw materials on hand.

You will need to submit the following with your Tax Return:

- A **Trading Account** showing details of goods sold during the period and the cost of those goods, the difference being the gross profit/loss for the period
- A **Profit and Loss Account** showing details of gross profit and the various expenses of the trade during the period, the difference being the net profit/loss for the business for the period
- A **Capital Account** showing details of opening and closing capital, net profit/loss for the period, cash introduced and drawings (not required from a limited company)
- A **Balance Sheet** setting out details of the business' assets and liabilities at the end of the period.

Small businesses may use the Business Profile (Form BPI) which includes a simplified form of accounts. This form is available from your local tax office, from the Revenue Forms & Leaflets Service at (01) 878 0100 [24 hours a day], or www.revenue.ie.

INSURANCE

When you start in business, you need to consider both business and personal insurance.

Business insurance
The main kinds of business insurance are:
- **Fire** – To cover rebuilding costs, etc following a fire
- **Burglary/theft** – To replace stolen or damaged assets
- **All risks** – Coverage against loss of assets, however caused
- **Public liability** – Coverage against claims by members of the public
- **Product liability** – Coverage against loss relating to defective or dangerous products
- **Employer's liability** – Coverage against claims from staff
- **Motor insurance** – Coverage against driving accidents.

Most insurance companies offer these (or some combination) in a single "Office" or "Business" policy, which is more cost-effective than separate policies for each.

Other areas for which you might consider the protection of insurance include:
- Legal fees protection
- Credit insurance
- Bad debt insurance
- Computer equipement and data
- Travel
- Goods in transit
- Patents
- Business interruption.

Since insurance companies rate risks differently, it is worth talking to an insurance broker, whose job is to find you the widest coverage at the lowest price. Ask whether you can reduce the premiums by paying an excess (just like motor insurance). Ask also whether the premiums can be paid over the year rather than all at the start.

People-related insurance
If the business is dependent on yourself, or one or two key staff, it is also a good idea to take out "keyman insurance" on these people. Then, if they die or are unable to work, the insurance company will pay a lump sum to help overcome the difficulty.

You may also want to look at life assurance (to provide "death-in-service" benefits), critical illness, permanent health insurance or medical expenses insurance for your staff. Here cost, and whether staff value the insurance, will be major factors.

Your own insurance
What insurance you take out on yourself depends on the risk you are willing to take, your budget and your family situation. You may already have some insurance in place, in which case taking out more through the business would be duplication.

Look at the key risks:
- **You could get sick and not be able to work** – You need insurance to provide a replacement income (permanent health insurance)
- **You could get sick or die and have no one to take over the running of the business for you** – You need a replacement income plus enough extra to pay someone else to run your business (permanent health/critical illness/life assurance).

Talk to a life assurance broker about coverage against these risks. Talk to him/her also about pensions. A pension can be a tax-effective way of transferring cash from your business to yourself.

OBJECTIVES
o Understand the different types of insurance
o Assess your need for insurance

CALCULATE YOUR MONTHLY INSURANCE PREMIUMS

Business insurance

Fire	€ _____
Burglary/theft	€ _____
All risks	€ _____
Public liability	€ _____
Product liability	€ _____
Employer's liability	€ _____
Motor insurance	€ _____
	€ _____

Personal insurance

Health	€ _____
Disability	€ _____
Life assurance	€ _____
Pension	€ _____

TRADING LAWS

OBJECTIVES

o Be aware of key trading legislation

Don't learn the tricks of the trade.
Learn the trade.
ANON

The Single European Market removed "technical" barriers to trade and thus opened opportunities for Irish businesses to export into Europe on a scale not possible before. However, selling in Europe means meeting European product standards – increasingly, selling at home in Ireland means the same.

EU Directives set out requirements for the manufacture of a wide and growing range of products. Compliance with these Directives is shown by the CE Marking, subject to assessment by the National Standards Authority of Ireland (NSAI).

Food labelling

The labelling of foodstuffs, in order to give accurate information to consumers, has become very important and increasingly regulated.

The basic rule is that labelling of pre-packaged goods must be "clear, legible, indelible and not obscured by pictorial or written matter". It must be "in a language easily understood by the consumer" and "not mislead".

Specifically, you are required to show:
- Name of food
- Net quantity in metric
- Date of minimum durability ("Best before"/"Use by")
- List of ingredients
- Special storage instructions
- Name or business name and address of the manufacturer or packager (or seller in the EU)
- Country of origin (only where absence would mislead)
- Instructions for use
- Alcoholic strength (beverages 1.2%+ alcohol by volume)
- If irradiated, a declaration
- If packaged in a modified atmosphere, a declaration.

Certain products – jams and jellies, fruit juices, mineral waters and quick frozen foods – have additional labelling requirements.

Food labelling regulations are enforced by both Environmental Health Officers and officers of the Director of Consumer Affairs, who can enter premises where food is kept, manufactured, sold or transported, take samples, inspect documentation and take copies and examine, test and inspect products.

Most businesses involved in food preparation will have to be registered with the local Health Board and comply with the requirements of the Food Hygiene Regulations; the Environmental Health officer of your local Health Board will be able to give you details.

Licenses and registration

Most businesses can be started immediately but, in some cases, a license or registration is required.

Examples include:
- Public houses and off-licences
- Driving instructors
- Employment agencies
- Taxi drivers
- Providing credit services.

Other trading regulations

You should check with a solicitor to make sure that you are not breaking any regulations, that you are operating in line with best practices and that you are up-to-date on the latest requirements.

Websites/emails

EU law requires businesses to show on all websites, blogs and emails details of the business, including:
- Name (and trading name , if relevant)
- Address (not just a PO box)
- Email address
- Company registration number, place of registration and registered office
- Licensing information
- VAT registration number, if VAT-registered (even not selling online).

If you are selling online, you must display prices that make clear whether VAT is included, as well as the cost of shipping.

In "Marketing", we saw how important place is as part of the marketing mix (4 Ps). In the property business, they say that only three things matter: Location, location, location. For certain kinds of business – shops, hotels, restaurants – location can make or break the business. But in all cases, the right working environment is important.

Choosing the right location

If you are looking for offices, consider somewhere that offers administrative support (for example, telephone answering, message taking, fax, photocopying, reception, etc.) It will save you hiring admin staff until the workload justifies it. And you save buying equipment.

For workshops and factories, you need to check lay-out, logistics, transport, weight of machinery, health and safety regulations, environmental issues, availability of three-phase electricity, etc. Draw out your ideal space before looking for accommodation.

Picking the right location for a shop or restaurant needs lots of market research. Major retail chains like Marks & Spencer are known to spend months monitoring pedestrian traffic outside possible locations before coming to a decision. Be prepared to spend several days standing outside what you think might be a suitable premises to check:

- Traffic flow (vehicles and pedestrians)
- Types of customers in the area
- Their spending patterns in other premises close by
- The timing of any rushes
- What other traders in the area think about the location
- What development is proposed for the area that might have an effect (positive or negative) on your plans.

Buy or rent?

This depends on how much money you have. But consider whether you are in the product/service business or in the property business. It's very easy to get involved – and get your business' cash-flow involved – in improving a property you have bought, instead of getting on with making your business a success.

Leases for rented properties should be checked very carefully. They may not always include all the terms the letting agent told you about – and, by the same token, will probably include some clauses he didn't mention at all. Have the lease checked by a solicitor. And don't be rushed to sign anything until you have completed your business planning, made sure of your financing and know what you are signing.

Other issues

Wherever you locate, consider insurance premiums, compliance with food hygiene and health/safety regulations, planning permission (for signs, usage, extensions, etc), lighting, heating, alarms, signs, locks, insurance, toilets, interior decor, fittings.

OBJECTIVES
o Understand the importance of location
o Be aware of issues relating to premises

PREMISES CHECKLIST

1. How important is location for your business?
   Very ☐
   Reasonably ☐
   Not at all ☐

2. What is your budget for premises?
   Purchase € _____
   Rent (annual) € _____
   Renovations € _____
   Fixtures & fittings € _____

3. How much space do you need? _____ m^2

4. How is this to be divided between:
   Administration _____ m^2
   Storage _____ m^2
   Sales _____ m^2
   Production _____ m^2
   Other _____ m^2

5. Will your customers visit your premises? ☐ YES ☐ NO
   Do those visitors need to be impressed? ☐ YES ☐ NO
   Is parking an issue? ☐ YES ☐ NO
   Will you need space for deliveries? ☐ YES ☐ NO

6. Could your work be done from home? ☐ YES ☐ NO
   Have you a suitable space? ☐ YES ☐ NO
   Have you planning permission? ☐ YES ☐ NO

7. If renting, are you and your solicitor happy with the lease, as regards:
   Period of the lease? ☐ YES ☐ NO
   Rent (+ other charges)? ☐ YES ☐ NO
   Your responsibilities? ☐ YES ☐ NO
   The landlord's responsibilities? ☐ YES ☐ NO
   Terms for renewal/termination? ☐ YES ☐ NO

WORKING FROM HOME

OBJECTIVES
o Understand the benefits and drawbacks of working from home
o Be aware of legal and other requirements

Working from home is the simplest, and often the cheapest, choice in relation to premises for your business.

It suits certain kinds of business and does not suit others. Think about combining working from home with serviced offices, where you will have a professional telephone answering/ message-taking service, a "business" address and access to meeting rooms for times when your customers want to come and talk to you.

Planning permission

The use of a private residence for business purposes is usually subject to planning permission. In most cases, local authorities will not require planning permission (or deny it, if it is applied for) where there is no impact on neighbouring properties. For example, a financial consultant who does his/her paperwork at home but meets clients on their own premises would expect little difficulty in relation to planning permission. But opening a garage to tune performance cars might bring complaints from your neighbours – and a refusal of planning permission.

Conditions for planning permission to work from home vary around the country. Check with your local authority's planning department before making any decision.

A dedicated workspace

If you work from home, you need to set aside a clearly-defined "workspace". In this area – and in this area only – you work. When you leave it, you are "at home". If you do not do this, you will never get a break from your business, and will burn out.

Make your workspace a "Do not disturb" zone. If you are to work properly, you must be able to put aside the distractions of home life (telephone calls, children, visitors, chores) while you are in your workspace (just as you would in a "proper" office).

But it's MY home!

Bear in mind that working from home becomes complicated when you have employees. It may suit you to get up late and work in your dressing-gown, but what example do you set for your staff? And what happens when you want a day off – do you have to leave home in order to get away from calls?

Other issues

Your insurers will need to be informed if you are working from home. If you have business visitors, you may need public liability cover. You are also responsible for health and safety (your own and any visitors') in your home office.

WORKING FROM HOME – ISSUES TO CONSIDER

How much space do you need and where is that space available in your home?

How will you separate home and work (think about telephone, use of computers, use of space, home duties, etc.)?

What does your family think?

What image do you want to present (meetings, telephone answering, address, etc.)?

What are the costs and cost savings (both time and money)?

Use of technology?

What happens when you are on holiday?

What about the children (holidays, after school, when they are sick, etc.)?

Can you switch off or will the home office become a constant distraction?

Do you need planning permission?

It is said that there are only three occasions when you must pay attention to the way in which your business is financed:

- At start-up
- When you need additional finance for expansion
- All the time in between.

At start-up, you need to raise as much finance as possible in order to ensure that your business has enough money to get going yet, perversely, this is the time when it is most difficult.

The need to raise additional finance to expand a business suggests a successful business, which should have little difficulty in attracting the necessary funding – though not always.

In between start-up and second-stage fund-raising, and all along the way, your business will have a financing need that must be met day-to-day and planned in advance.

Start-up finance

There are basically only two types of finance:

- **Equity** – Capital invested in the business, usually not repayable until the business closes down finally
- **Debt** – Capital lent to the business, usually repayable at a specified date.

There are also only two sources:

- Your own money
- Someone else's money.

OWNERS' EQUITY

If you are putting equity into the business (and you MUST – if you won't, who else will!), recognise that this investment will be at risk. Decide whether there are assets you want to keep in your personal name or which you are not prepared to put up as security or to mortgage. Identify these and then look at everything else you own:

- How easily could they be sold and what would they fetch?
- Are they mortgagable assets?
- Will they be acceptable as collateral?

Before you mortgage your family home,

obtain professional advice. Consider:

- Ownership of the property
- The impact of the Family Home Protection Act
- What would happen to the family home and your family if the business fails
- The approach that the banks and the courts take in such circumstances.

It is important that you raise as much as you can from your own resources, since most financiers work on a "matching funds" basis – they will invest no more than you are investing. This may mean being creative and including as part of your investment some items that would have been available to the business on an informal basis anyway. For example, if you plan to start a software business, you probably have your own PC and peripherals and probably intended using these in the business until it could afford to buy newer (and faster) machines. Put a value on them and include them as part of your investment, which might now be made up of €3,000 cash and €5,000 equipment – which looks better than just €3,000 cash!

If you can raise all the money you need from your own resources, then you can count yourself lucky and move further on in this section. Everyone else, keep reading!

OUTSIDE EQUITY

Before you raise outside equity, you need to be prepared to allow other people to own part of your business. This sounds logical, but many entrepreneurs forget it and react badly when their investors begin to want some involvement in the business in return for their investment.

If you are looking for outside equity, there are three types to consider:

- **Seed capital** – Less than €250,000, for start-ups
- **Venture capital** – Between €250,000 and €600,000, for businesses at an early stage of development
- **Development capital** – €1,000,000+, for companies ready to expand.

Seed capital is the one you probably want. Unfortunately, it is also the hardest

OBJECTIVES

o Understand the different types and sources of finance
o Calculate initial investment
o Identify possible sources of funding
o Calculate personal expenses

Small debts are like small shot: they are rattling on every side, and can scarcely be escaped without a wound;
great debts are like cannon: of loud noise, but little danger.
SAMUEL JOHNSON (1709-1784)

I am convinced that the more money a new business needs to begin with, the less chance it has of success.
MARK McCORMACK, International Management Group

to get, although the recent success of Irish technology companies means that there is funding available, sometimes linked to incubation facilities.

Sources of equity

The first sources you should try are:

- **Family and friends** – Depending on your personal circumstances, this can be a fruitful source. But make sure they understand the risks involved and can afford to lose an investment. Put agreements in writing
- **Business contacts** – It's worth checking to see whether someone you know in business will help you get started with a small investment
- **Business angels** – Professional investors who may take an active role in managing the business as well as providing finance. Enterprise Ireland, Shannon Development and Dublin Business Innovation Centre all have investor registers.

Then turn to the professionals:

- **ACT Venture Capital** – ACT operates its own fund and the ACT Enterprise Fund, aimed at the technology sector, jointly funded by Enterprise Ireland. ACT invests upwards of €600,000.
- **AIB Seed Capital Fund** – This fund has €30 million under management, with AIB and Enterprise Ireland both committing €15 million. It is managed by experienced managers, at Enterprise Equity and Dublin BIC, who are empowered to make seed investments of up to €500,000.
- **Bank of Ireland Kernel Capital Partners Private Equity Fund II** – A €70 million fund that targets equity investment opportunities in the €2 to €10 million range, across all industry sectors and all stages of a company's development. Investments larger than €10 illionm are syndicated with others, while investments below €2 million are considered where appropriate.
- **Bank of Scotland** – Provides equity investment through a corporate finance unit and venture capital funds.

- **Business Expansion Scheme (BES)** – Properly called "Relief for Investment in Corporate Trades" (RICT), BES is intended to help smaller businesses. Fund-raising companies must be incorporated and resident in Ireland, must not be quoted on the Stock Exchange (except for the Irish Enterprise Exchange), and must be engaged in a "qualifying trade". It is up to the business to find potential investors (usually through a broker or accountant) and, when it does, to obtain Revenue approval. The maxmum amount that can be raised by a company is €2 million, with a maximum of €1.5 million in any 12-month period.
- **Cross Atlantic Capital Partners** – Cross Atlantic Capital Partners (XACP) manages four venture funds with over $500 million under management.
- **Delta Partners** – The €105m Delta Equity Fund III began investing in summer 2007, focused on start-up and early stage technology investments in communications technologies, software and life sciences, typically investing €500,000 to €3,000,000.
- **Enterprise Equity** – Established by the International Fund for Ireland, Enterprise Equity provides venture capital of between €250,000 and €1.5 million to new and expanding businesses in all areas outside of Dublin and all sectors other than property, retail and hotels.
- **Fountain Healthcare Partners** – A life science-focused venture capital fund headquartered in Dublin, with an office in New York. Fountain specialises in in biotechnology, medical device, specialty pharma and diagnostic companies and will invest between €500,000 and €7 million over the life of the investment.
- **Growcorp Innovation Centre** – Growcorp develops businesses with leading-edge platform technologies in ICT and biosciences, through an incubation process.

Before you borrow money from a friend, decide which you need more.
ANON

Seed capital is a race against insolvency.
KARL SCHUTTE, Business Innovation Fund, Dublin

You never lose money by making a profit.
ANON

The average cost of setting up in business is €11,000, one-third of which is funded externally.
The average time taken to raise external funding is one month, with 45% receiving funding within a week.
Banks are the main providers of external finance, with family and friends an important secondary source.
BARCLAYS BANK

- **Irish Venture Capital Association** - The IVCA represents the VC industry in Ireland. Its website provides a list of VC funds and their interests.
- **NCB Ventures** – This fund backs management teams undertaking MBOs, MBIs, implementing 'buy and build' strategies, effecting recapitalisations and spin outs. The Fund invests in the range of €1 million to €5 million and aims to realise those investments within a five-year time horizon. The Fund aims to build businesses from low entry values to values of €50 million to €100 million.
- **Seed Capital Scheme** – Operated by the Revenue Commissioners, the scheme repays income tax to people leaving employment to start their own businesses (only companies qualify, not sole traders or partnerships). In the year of starting their business, qualifying individuals may claim back the tax paid in respect of up to €100,000 of income in each of the previous six tax years.
- **Seroba Bioventures** - Seroba provides support to promising start-up and early-stage lifescience and medical technology companies arising from leading Irish research institutes, universities, research hospitals and existing companies.
- **Shannon Development** – Shannon Development delivers specific support packages for businesses in the Shannon Free Zone, in the eareas of international services, medical, engineering, electronic and aerospace and software / ICT.
- **TVC Holdings** – Following flotation on AIM in London and on the IEX in Dublin, under the name TVC Holdings plc, TVC continues to actively support and invest in its portfolio companies, and to seek new investment opportunities in all business sectors in the €10 million to €25 million funding range.
- **Ulster Bank Diageo Venture Fund** – A €75m fund, managed by NCB Ventures, that invests in companies at early and expansion stages of development across a broad range of industrial sectors.

OWNERS' DEBT

This is not a major source of finance for start-ups, since other investors prefer to see the owners' investment in the form of equity (more permanent than loans). However, it may be appropriate to put some part of your investment in the business as a loan (and thus repayable). Take your accountant's advice here.

OTHER DEBT

Debt comes in a variety of forms, from a simple loan from a friend with few conditions attached, through overdrafts, term loans, long-term loans, mortgages, etc.

Debt finance available to start-ups includes:
- **Overdraft** – The simplest form of bank finance. Basically, this is no more than permission to have a minus balance on your bank account. However, overdrafts must be cleared (and stay cleared for at least 30 days during the year, though not necessarily consecutive days) on an annual basis and the overdraft is repayable on demand
- **Term loan** – A loan for a fixed period, usually at a variable rate. Repayments include interest and capital
- **Long-term loans** – Often subsidised by Government or EU schemes, these aim to provide businesses with capital for 7 to 10 years
- **Mortgages** – Loans to buy business property, secured on the property itself, with fixed or variable rate options
- **Leasing** – A way of acquiring the use of fixed assets (for example, plant and machinery, cars, office equipment) by paying a regular monthly or quarterly payment, which is usually allowable for tax purposes. At the end of the lease, depending on the terms, you may have the option to continue using the asset for a small continuing payment or to buy it outright from the lessor
- **Invoice discounting** – A facility linked directly to sales, which maximises the cash value of current assets. The bank will pay you, say, 80% of the face value of an invoice when it is issued. The balance, less charges, will be paid to you when the invoice is paid. Useful for the company that is expanding and in danger of being choked for lack of cash.

When considering financing your business with debt, you must consider:
- Fixed or floating
- Long-term or short-term.

Fixed debt is a loan that is secured on a specific asset – for example, on premises. Floating debt is secured on assets that change regularly – for example, debtors.

"Secured" means that, in the event that the loan is not repaid, the lender can appoint a "receiver" to sell the asset on which the loan is secured in order to recover the amount due. Thus, giving security for a loan is not something to be done lightly.

Because you have to pay interest on debt, you should try to manage with as little as possible. However, few businesses get off the ground without putting some form of debt on the balance sheet. The issues are usually:

- What is the cheapest form of debt available?
- What is the right balance between debt and equity?
- How to reduce the amount of borrowing required?
- Will borrowing be backed by personal assets?

It is a good idea to try to match the term of the loan to the type of asset that you are acquiring:

- To avoid constant renewing/restructuring problems
- To ensure that each loan is covered by the break-up value of the assets in case of disaster.

For example, a loan to buy premises should be a long-term loan, unless you can see clearly that you will have enough money within a short space of time to repay it. Taking out a short-term loan or overdraft to buy premises is a recipe for disaster. You will have to renegotiate it time and again – and, if your business runs into temporary difficulties, you run the risk of losing everything if the bank calls in the loan.

Short-term loans, or even overdrafts, are more suited to funding stock or debtors because you should be able to repay the loan once you have sold the goods or got the money in. Short-term finance is also used to fund other forms of working capital and cash flow. It should always be repaid within the year – even if, at the end of the period, you still need to borrow more to fund future cash flow. If you have to borrow the same sum of money against the same asset for longer than a year at a time, you should be considering longer-term finance.

If disaster strikes and you have to repay the loan suddenly, it will be much easier to do so if the value of the assets it was used to fund is roughly equivalent to the value of the loan. Thus, for instance, you would hope to sell your premises for at least as much as you borrowed to buy them. Machinery may be more difficult, as the resale price is rarely comparable with the purchase price. For this reason, unless the equipment you need is very specialised, consider buying second-hand for your start-up (although this may lose you grant aid).

If you can, you should arrange your loans so that unrealisable (or slow to realise) assets are purchased out of your own equity, using borrowing only for realisable assets. If an asset is easily realisable, the bank is much more likely to accept it as security.

Sources of debt
Sources of debt you should try first include:

- **Family and friends** – Depending on your own circumstances, this can be a fruitful source. But make sure your family and/or friends understand the risks involved and can afford to lose their investment. Put any deal in writing, with professional advice on both sides
- **Business contacts** – It's worth looking to see whether someone you know in business will help you get started with a small investment
- **Banks** – The main source of start-up borrowing
- **Credit cards** – If you have a credit card with a high credit limit (and a low balance!), this may provide a source of funding (though more expensive than most). However, once your business is up and running, a company credit card not only provides an additional credit line but can cut purchasing costs and simplify administration
- **Credit unions** – Willing to help members start businesses, especially co-operatives, although loans tend to be to the individual who then lends/invests the money in the business
- **Finance companies** – Sometimes more willing to lend than a bank, as long as they can secure the loan with assets or personal guarantees. Rarely cheaper than banks, but may sometimes be prepared to lend when banks refuse.

When looking for finance, beware of "specialists" who claim that they can find you money at favourable rates of interest if only you pay an up-front fee. Don't pay **anything** until you have the money.

Often, if you only need a small amount of money, the best way to raise it is to approach a bank with which you have already built up some relationship, whether on a personal basis or in a business capacity. The larger borrower may feel it worthwhile to seek professional help to put together a more sophisticated fund-raising package. Your accountant is the best person to give you advice in this area and may have contacts that will ease your path.

Bank finance
The following banks provide loans to start-ups:

- **AIB Bank** – AIB offers a range of banking facilities, including overdrafts, loans, leasing, hire purchase, invoice discounting, business insurance, credit cards and electronic banking, with special offers for start-ups, and a team of SME specialists available across its branch network.
- **Bank of Ireland** – In addition to the full range of banking facilities, Bank of Ireland also offers

a special start-up package with free current account banking for two years and a range of offers from it partners. It also offers an online start-up training course.

- **Bank of Scotland (Ireland)** – Services include commercial lending and SME banking, asset finance, treasury and trade finance.
- **PermanentTSB** – Though geared towards the personal banking market, it offers current accounts and deposits to business customers.
- **Rabobank** – A broadly-based commercial bank.
- **Ulster Bank** – Ulster Bank's nationwide branch and business centre network provides sector-specific expertise and a wide range of products and capabilities, including working capital support, invoice finance, business start-up loans, Lombard Asset Finance, access to venture capital and European Investment Bank funds, and business community support with smallbusinesscan.com and the Ulster Bank Business Achievers Awards.

Other sources of start-up finance include:
- **Credit Unions** – Members of credit unions or businesses structured as co-operatives may qualify for a credit union loan. Each application is treated in confidence and will be considered on its own merits. In deciding whether to grant the loan, the member's record of saving and repayments, as well as ability to repay, and need will be taken into account. Usually loans are to individuals, who can then lend the money into their business.
- **First Step** – First-Step Microfinance provides loans of up to €25,000 to start up or expanding new businesses. First-Step receives funding from Enterprise Ireland through the EU Seed and Venture Capital Fund and the Social Finance Foundation and is the beneficiary of an SME Guarantee Facility created within the framework of the Competitiveness and Innovation Framework Programme (CIP) of the European Community.

INITIAL INVESTMENT

The rule for funding a new business is: "As little as possible, as cheaply as possible". Do not put money into the unnecessary. It is better to start your business from an attic without a loan than in a glossy, but unnecessary, high-profile office with heavy bank borrowings.

On the other hand, do adopt a realistic position on the amount of money that you need to get going. Your financing will have to be sufficient to carry the business for a reasonable period before it reaches some kind of balance, when money coming in equals money going out.

In addition to capital investment in plant, equipment and premises, your financing may have to supply most of the working capital until sales begin to generate sufficient income to give you an adequate cash flow.

Try this technique:
- **Close your eyes** – Pretend to be in your new business. Look around you. What do you see? Make a list – from carpets to lamps, from computers to phones, from equipment to signs, from stock to the van for deliveries. Make the list as long as possible
- **Put a value on each item** – How much would it cost to buy new? Could you buy it second-hand?
- **Look at the list again** – Mark off the items you already have (chair, telephone, desk, lamp)
- **Calculate the difference** – This is your initial investment in starting your business
- **Take it a stage further** – You need to buy all the items you do not have at present, but do you need to buy them all at the beginning or could some wait a few weeks or even months? What could wait?

Use the Initial Investment panel on page 85 to calculate and record what you need to start your business.

Then go back through the list and take out what is not absolutely necessary. Be hard – take out anything that you don't REALLY need. But don't cut back so far that you will be unable to get the business off the ground.

What you are doing is what an investor or banker who reads your business plan will be doing – challenging everything to make sure that you have done your homework. Do it yourself before it's done to you and you will find raising finance for your start-up much easier.

Next, you need to put your initial investment into a format suitable for your business plan by identifying:
- **Fixed assets** – Property, renovations, fixtures and fittings, transport, machines and equipment, etc
- **Current assets** – Stocks, debtors
- **Cash**
- **Start-up expenses** – Expenses paid before the business begins, promotion and opening costs, etc.
- **Margin for unforeseen costs** – There will always be something you have forgotten or that could not have been expected when you did your planning. Allow for it here.

CALCULATING YOUR INITIAL INVESTMENT

	Need?	How many?	Have now	Need to buy	Cost new €	Cost 2hand €	Total cost €	Now €	Mth 1 €	Mth 2 €	Mth 3 €	Mth 4-6 €
										Timing of purchase		

Office:

_____	Y/N	____	Y/N	Y/N
_____	Y/N	____	Y/N	Y/N
_____	Y/N	____	Y/N	Y/N
_____	Y/N	____	Y/N	Y/N
_____	Y/N	____	Y/N	Y/N
_____	Y/N	____	Y/N	Y/N
_____	Y/N	____	Y/N	Y/N
_____	Y/N	____	Y/N	Y/N
_____	Y/N	____	Y/N	Y/N
_____	Y/N	____	Y/N	Y/N

Factory/Workshop:

_____	Y/N	____	Y/N	Y/N
_____	Y/N	____	Y/N	Y/N
_____	Y/N	____	Y/N	Y/N
_____	Y/N	____	Y/N	Y/N
_____	Y/N	____	Y/N	Y/N
_____	Y/N	____	Y/N	Y/N
_____	Y/N	____	Y/N	Y/N
_____	Y/N	____	Y/N	Y/N
_____	Y/N	____	Y/N	Y/N
_____	Y/N	____	Y/N	Y/N

Shop:

_____	Y/N	____	Y/N	Y/N
_____	Y/N	____	Y/N	Y/N
_____	Y/N	____	Y/N	Y/N
_____	Y/N	____	Y/N	Y/N
_____	Y/N	____	Y/N	Y/N
_____	Y/N	____	Y/N	Y/N
_____	Y/N	____	Y/N	Y/N
_____	Y/N	____	Y/N	Y/N
_____	Y/N	____	Y/N	Y/N
_____	Y/N	____	Y/N	Y/N

Transport:

_____	Y/N	____	Y/N	Y/N
_____	Y/N	____	Y/N	Y/N

Other:

_____	Y/N	____	Y/N	Y/N
_____	Y/N	____	Y/N	Y/N
_____	Y/N	____	Y/N	Y/N
_____	Y/N	____	Y/N	Y/N
_____	Y/N	____	Y/N	Y/N
_____	Y/N	____	Y/N	Y/N

TOTAL

INITIAL INVESTMENT
ANALYSIS FOR BUSINESS PLAN

Copy this panel into your Business Plan, page 127.

1. Fixed assets

Property	€ _____
Renovations	€ _____
Fixtures and fittings	€ _____
Transport	€ _____
Machines and equipment	€ _____
Goodwill, security deposits	€ _____
Other	€ _____
Total fixed assets	**€** _____

2. Current assets

Stock of raw material	€ _____
Stock of finished goods	€ _____
Work in progress	€ _____
Debtors	€ _____
Other	€ _____
Total current assets	**€** _____

3. Liquid assets

Cash	€ _____
Bank	€ _____
Other	€ _____
Total liquid assets	**€** _____

4. Start-up costs

Prepaid expenses	€ _____
Promotion, opening	€ _____
Other	€ _____
Total start-up costs	**€** _____

5. Margin for unforeseen costs   **€** _____

Total investment   **€** _____

INITIAL INVESTMENT
PROPOSED SOURCES OF FUNDING

Copy this panel into your Business Plan, page 128.

Personal assets available

Fixed assets	€ _____
Car	€ _____
Additional private mortgage	€ _____
Savings	€ _____
Deferred loans (family)	€ _____
Other	€ _____
Total personal assets	**€** _____

Introduced as:

Equity	€ _____
Loans	€ _____

External equity   *Agreed?*

Source	€ _____	Y/N

External debt

	Term	Amount	Agreed?
Long/medium-term			
Mortgage	_____ years	€ _____	Y/N
Loan	_____ years	€ _____	Y/N
Leasing	_____ years	€ _____	Y/N
Other	_____ years	€ _____	Y/N
	_____ years	€ _____	Y/N
Total		**€** _____	

Short-term finance

	Amount	Agreed?
Overdraft	€ _____	Y/N
Suppliers' credit	€ _____	Y/N
Payments received in advance	€ _____	Y/N
Other	€ _____	Y/N
	€ _____	Y/N
Total	**€** _____	

Subsidies/grants

	Amount	Agreed?
Agency	€ _____	Y/N
Enterprise Board	€ _____	Y/N
Area Partnership Company	€ _____	Y/N
Other	€ _____	Y/N
	€ _____	Y/N
Total subsidies/grants	**€** _____	

Total available finance   **€** _____

CHECKLIST FOR INITIAL INVESTMENT

1. Can you support the required investment in fixed assets with quotations from suppliers? ☐ YES ☐ NO

2. How did you estimate your stock levels?

3. How did you estimate the value of your debtors?

4. Do you have sufficient cash to fund on-going operational costs until sales begin to realise cash? ☐ YES ☐ NO

5. Do you have sufficient cash, or assets that can be quickly turned into cash, to cope with disappointments, delays and unexpected expenses? ☐ YES ☐ NO

Use the panel to help you to complete the checklist.

Sourcing your initial investment

Now that you know how much you need (and what for), you need to find appropriate sources of finance. Re-read this section. Then decide how you will raise the money you need. Complete the panel on page 85, showing your sources of funding. If you have some sources already agreed, indicate this in the panel.

Personal expenses

Just because you are starting a business does not mean that the real world will go away. You and your family still need to be fed, to buy clothes, to pay for food, clothing, heating, bus fares, mortgages, etc. You need to allow for this. Complete the panel on this page to calculate your personal expenses. This is not a target – it is what you need. It must be factored into your Operating Budget and Business Plan.

Downloads and updates for this section available @
www.startingabusinessinireland.com

CALCULATE YOUR PERSONAL EXPENSES

Expenses	Week	Month	Year
Rent/mortgage	€ _____	€ _____	€ _____
Gas, water, ESB	€ _____	€ _____	€ _____
Food	€ _____	€ _____	€ _____
House expenses	€ _____	€ _____	€ _____
Clothing/footwear	€ _____	€ _____	€ _____
Telephone	€ _____	€ _____	€ _____
Insurance	€ _____	€ _____	€ _____
Study expenses	€ _____	€ _____	€ _____
Memberships	€ _____	€ _____	€ _____
TV licence	€ _____	€ _____	€ _____
Transport	€ _____	€ _____	€ _____
Loan repayments	€ _____	€ _____	€ _____
Holidays	€ _____	€ _____	€ _____
Replacing fridge, etc	€ _____	€ _____	€ _____
Luxuries	€ _____	€ _____	€ _____
Other expenses			
_____	€ _____	€ _____	€ _____
_____	€ _____	€ _____	€ _____
Sub-total (A)	€ _____	€ _____	€ _____

Deductions	Week	Month	Year
Children's allowances	€ _____	€ _____	€ _____
Government benefits	€ _____	€ _____	€ _____
Rent/lease subsidies	€ _____	€ _____	€ _____
Spouse/partner's income	€ _____	€ _____	€ _____
Other income	€ _____	€ _____	€ _____
Subtotal (B)	€ < __ >	€ < __ >	€ < __ >

	Week	Month	Year
Personal expenses (NET OF TAX) (A) less (B)	€ _____	€ _____	€ _____
Allowance for tax	€ _____	€ _____	€ _____
Gross taxable income needed	€ _____	€ _____	€ _____

Budgeting is the process of estimating costs in advance, in order to:
- Ensure adequate finance for the business to achieve what it has planned
- Provide a control mechanism over subsequent spending.

With the exception of "zero-base budgeting", most budgets begin with the previous year's actual figures and make assumptions about the future:
- Adding a percentage for inflation
- Adding new costs and activities
- Deleting old costs and activities.

However, as a start-up company, you have no historical figures to work from. You can budget in two directions (often it is helpful to do both and compare the results).

"Revenue down" budgeting starts by working out how many units you expect to sell and at what price. This gives you total revenue. Then estimate what percentage of revenue is accounted for by the various costs – Cost of sales (50% perhaps), Salaries (25%), Overheads (20%), leaving a net profit margin of 5%. Be careful with this method, since it's all too easy to scale up your budget beyond the point where you have exceeded your capacity to produce.

"Cost up" budgeting starts from the cost of making the product. To this, you add a profit margin big enough to cover marketing expenses, salaries, overheads and a profit. Multiply the total of product cost and the margin by the number of units you expect to sell to get total revenue. The difficulty with this method is that your selling price is unrelated to the market. In fact, inefficiencies in production are disguised by this method – until your product reaches the market-place.

Target costing is a relatively new method of costing, introduced from Japan. Here you identify the maximum price customers will pay for the product and manufacture within this. Usually, this means that you have to look very hard at quantity, suppliers, materials used, the use of technology and alternative sources.

In the Operating Budget, you forecast:

- **Turnover** – total sales
- **Gross profit** – the difference between the turnover and its purchase cost
- **Overheads** – all the expenses incurred in order to keep the business going
- **Net profit** – the gross profit less the overheads.

In developing your Operating Budget, take into account the expenses you will incur to keep the business running and to provide you, as the entrepreneur, with an income (your personal expenses from the last section), as well as the cost of meeting repayments if you have borrowed money.

If you have a good idea of the overheads involved, you can calculate what the turnover figure will need to be, using the formula:

Turnover – Purchases = Gross Profit
Gross profit – Overheads = Net profit.

Work out what you expect to sell (turnover) and how you are going to achieve this target.

Bear in mind that, because you will have busy times and not so busy times, your turn-over will not remain constant throughout the year. Budget for peaks and troughs.

At the same time, look at the forecast in light of overheads. Test these again against the turnover forecast. For example: Does the number of visits planned to customers agree with the mileage that you have included in the Transport and travel category?

Gross profit is the difference between the total amount for sales (turnover excluding VAT) and the purchase cost of the goods you have sold.

This gross profit can also be expressed as a percentage of the turnover (excluding VAT). A gross profit percentage of 45% signifies that for every €100 of turnover, €55 is purchases and €45 is regarded as the gross profit of the business.

Overheads

This section looks at the expenses that you will have in running your business, including:
- Staff

OBJECTIVES
o Understand the budgeting process
o Be able to prepare an Operating Budget

*Know when to spend,
And when to spare,
And you need not be busy,
And you'll never be bare.*
JAMES KELLY

Spare no expense to make everything as economical as possible.
SAM GOLDWYN

- Production
- Premises
- Transport
- Selling and promotion
- General expenses
- Finance
- Depreciation.

Staff

These expenses are only incurred if you actually have employees working for you (full or part-time). In addition to wages/salaries, you may (depending on the contract of employment) have to include travelling expenses, work clothes or uniforms, study expenses for employees, and so on. Bonuses, employers' PRSI and other staff-related costs should be included here.

Production overheads

If your business has a production unit, you will have costs that cannot be directly associated with items of production – heat, light and power, maintenance, etc - that can be treated as overheads.

Premises

This covers all expenses that are directly connected with your premises:
- Rent of premises (bear in mind the need to have the rental agreement checked by your solicitor)
- Mortgage interest, if you own the property under a mortgage
- A percentage of your personal accommodation expenses, if you begin your business from your own house (rent or mortgage split between the part used for business and the total, in m^2)
- Repairs and maintenance, depending on the condition of the premises and, if rented, the contract under which it is used
- Gas, water and electricity expenses (enquire about these at your local authority energy department)
- Business charges and taxes, including service charges (if levied by your local authority)
- Insurance – fire insurance is essential
- Cleaning expenses – cleaning consumables or the cost of hiring a cleaner
- Miscellaneous small items (for example, hand tools, kitchen equipment, etc.) that are not depreciated.

Transport and travel expenses

First, you should estimate all the journeys by public transport that you are likely to make for your business. For car expenses, estimate the distance that you will travel on behalf of the business. The mileage should be multiplied by the cost per km – which should include insurance, road tax, maintenance, depreciation, etc. Use Civil Service rates to avoid tax issues.

Selling and promotion

The costs you estimate for promotion should be based on "Marketing – Promotion", earlier.

General expenses

This category looks very simple but, in fact, it is frequently underestimated. General expenses include:
- **Telephone and postage** – Note that if you work from your own house and make use of your private telephone, only the business-related calls can be regarded as expenses for the business and not the line rental
- **Subscriptions and contributions** – For example, to employers' or small business representative organisations, professional and trade journals, Chambers Ireland, etc.
- **Insurance premiums** – Excluding the premiums for private insurance
- **Administration and office expenses** – Everything that you need in order to be able to perform your bookkeeping and carry on your correspondence (business stationery, envelopes, computer supplies, filing system, etc.)
- **Accountancy expenses** – Even though you may not have an in-house accountant, a bookkeeper can easily charge you several hundred euro annually for compiling VAT and PAYE/PRSI returns and preparing the year end accounts
- **Entertainment** – Business-related entertainment of customers or potential customers should be included here. Note that entertainment costs are not tax-deductible.

Finance costs

These cover not only the interest on the loans you have entered into but also the expenses that are associated with the loan, such as credit advice, assessment, solicitor's fees, costs of arranging credit, etc. Remember that the repayment of loans is not a business cost but must be made from net profit.

Depreciation

Depreciation expresses the annual reduction in value of your fixed assets. There are various methods of depreciation. Though your accountant will choose the best method for your accounts, you can use the "straight line" method for your operating budget. Under this method, all fixed assets are reduced each year by a fixed percentage.

For example, a machine costs €10,000, and will

OPERATING BUDGET – ANALYSIS OF OVERHEADS

	Year 1	Year 2	Year 3
Staff costs			
Gross staff salaries	€ _____	€ _____	€ _____
Employer's PRSI	€ _____	€ _____	€ _____
Bonuses, etc.	€ _____	€ _____	€ _____
Staff training costs	€ _____	€ _____	€ _____
Other staff costs	€ _____	€ _____	€ _____
Total staff costs	**€ _____**	**€ _____**	**€ _____**
Production overheads			
Use of auxiliary materials	€ _____	€ _____	€ _____
Maintenance	€ _____	€ _____	€ _____
Heat, light & power	€ _____	€ _____	€ _____
Rent/lease equipment	€ _____	€ _____	€ _____
Insurance equipment	€ _____	€ _____	€ _____
Other costs	€ _____	€ _____	€ _____
Total production costs	**€ _____**	**€ _____**	**€ _____**
Premises costs			
Rent	€ _____	€ _____	€ _____
Heat, light & power	€ _____	€ _____	€ _____
Insurance	€ _____	€ _____	€ _____
Cleaning	€ _____	€ _____	€ _____
Maintenance	€ _____	€ _____	€ _____
Other costs	€ _____	€ _____	€ _____
Deduct: Rent received	€ <__>	€ <__>	€ <__>
Total premises costs	**€ _____**	**€ _____**	**€ _____**
Transport costs			
Maintenance and repairs	€ _____	€ _____	€ _____
Lease costs	€ _____	€ _____	€ _____
Fuel	€ _____	€ _____	€ _____
Insurance	€ _____	€ _____	€ _____
Road Tax	€ _____	€ _____	€ _____
Public transport	€ _____	€ _____	€ _____
Air fares	€ _____	€ _____	€ _____
Deduct: Private use	€ <__>	€ <__>	€ <__>
Total transport costs	**€ _____**	**€ _____**	**€ _____**

	Year 1	Year 2	Year 3
Selling and promotion costs			
Advertising	€ _____	€ _____	€ _____
Packaging	€ _____	€ _____	€ _____
Promotion	€ _____	€ _____	€ _____
Trade fairs	€ _____	€ _____	€ _____
Commissions	€ _____	€ _____	€ _____
Other costs	€ _____	€ _____	€ _____
Total sales and promotion costs	**€ _____**	**€ _____**	**€ _____**
General expenses			
Telephone	€ _____	€ _____	€ _____
Postage	€ _____	€ _____	€ _____
Subscriptions	€ _____	€ _____	€ _____
Insurance	€ _____	€ _____	€ _____
Stationery	€ _____	€ _____	€ _____
Office expenses	€ _____	€ _____	€ _____
Accountancy fees	€ _____	€ _____	€ _____
Legal & other fees	€ _____	€ _____	€ _____
Other costs	€ _____	€ _____	€ _____
Total general expenses	**€ _____**	**€ _____**	**€ _____**
Finance costs			
Interest on loans/overdraft	€ _____	€ _____	€ _____
Mortgage interest	€ _____	€ _____	€ _____
Charges/fees	€ _____	€ _____	€ _____
Other	€ _____	€ _____	€ _____
Total finance costs	**€ _____**	**€ _____**	**€ _____**
Depreciation			
Property	€ _____	€ _____	€ _____
Fixtures & fittings	€ _____	€ _____	€ _____

Copy to Business Plan, page 130-131, and summarise on page 90.

last for five years, when its scrap value will be €500. The annual depreciation is calculated as: €10,000 – €500 = 9,500 / 5 = €1,900 per year. The depreciation term is not usually changed during the depreciation period. Commonly-used depreciation terms include: Buildings – 40 years; Extensions/renovations – 10 years; Machines – 5 or 7 years; Cars – 3 or 5 years.

Downloads for this section are available @
www.startingabusinessinireland.com

OPERATING BUDGET – ESTIMATE OF SALES AND GROSS PROFIT

Revenue by product

	Year 1	Year 2	Year 3
Cash sales			
A _____	€ ____	€ ____	€ ____
B _____	€ ____	€ ____	€ ____
C _____	€ ____	€ ____	€ ____
D _____	€ ____	€ ____	€ ____
	€ ____	€ ____	€ ____
Credit sales			
A _____	€ ____	€ ____	€ ____
B _____	€ ____	€ ____	€ ____
C _____	€ ____	€ ____	€ ____
D _____	€ ____	€ ____	€ ____
	€ ____	€ ____	€ ____
Total sales	€ ____	€ ____	€ ____
Deduct			
Opening stock	€ ____	€ ____	€ ____
Purchases	€ ____	€ ____	€ ____
	€ ____	€ ____	€ ____
Less Closing stock	€ ____	€ ____	€ ____
Cost of goods sold	€ ____	€ ____	€ ____
Gross profit	€ ____	€ ____	€ ____
Gross profit percentage	____ %	____ %	____ %

Copy to Business Plan, page 125, and summarise in the panel to the right.

Copy these Assumptions into your business plan, page 129.

OPERATING BUDGET – ASSUMPTIONS

What assumptions did you make in estimating these key figures for your operating budget?

Sales

Purchases

Stocks

Staff salaries

Production overheads

Premises costs

Transport costs

Selling and promotion costs

General expenses

Finance costs

Depreciation

OPERATING BUDGET – PROFIT AND LOSS ACCOUNT

	Year 1	Year 2	Year 3
Sales	€ ____	€ ____	€ ____
Cost of Sales	€ ____	€ ____	€ ____
Gross Profit	€ ____	€ ____	€ ____
Gross Profit %	____ %	____ %	____ %
Overheads:			
Staff	€ ____	€ ____	€ ____
Production	€ ____	€ ____	€ ____
Premises	€ ____	€ ____	€ ____
Transport	€ ____	€ ____	€ ____
Selling & promotion	€ ____	€ ____	€ ____
General expenses	€ ____	€ ____	€ ____
Finance	€ ____	€ ____	€ ____
Depreciation	€ ____	€ ____	€ ____
Total overheads	€ ____	€ ____	€ ____
Net Profit/(Loss)	€ ____	€ ____	€ ____
Tax on profit/(loss)	€ ____	€ ____	€ ____
	€ ____	€ ____	€ ____
Drawings	€ ____	€ ____	€ ____
Profit retained in business	€ ____	€ ____	€ ____

MINIMUM TURNOVER

To calculate the minimum turnover to meet all your business and personal expenses, the formula is:

Total expenses x 100/Gross profit percentage = Minimum turnover.

Calculate your own minimum turnover.

CASH-FLOW PLANNING

On paper you could be the richest person in the world and still not be able to pay the mortgage (or go for a pint!). That is because there is a clear distinction between cash flow and profits and between costs and expenditure.

You need to know when money is coming in, and when it is going out. The cash is the lifeblood of the business and should be monitored rigorously. More businesses fail because they run out of cash than from almost any other cause. Even profitable businesses can fail because of lack of cash! So always think CASH.

The main pitfalls in financing are:

- Underestimating the investment needed (the golden rule is to double your original estimate)
- Not including room to manoeuvre in your start-up budget
- Forgetting your own personal financial requirement (how much do you need to take out of the business for living expenses?)
- Not putting aside money to pay your taxes when they are due
- Underestimating the difficulties of getting paid (the average credit period in Ireland is around three months).

When you calculated your initial investment (see "Finance", page 84/85), you analysed your initial investment on a time basis – some items were needed now, others could be postponed for a month or two, or even more. Cashflow planning is the same exercise applied across your entire business. It means looking at every item of income and expenditure in your budgets and estimating when it will impact the business in cash terms. Timing of cash in or out can be critical – as you will find when your first big cheque comes in late!

Initial investment

You know when your initial investment needs to be acquired; now calculate when it needs to be paid for. Pencil in the amounts under the heading "Outgoing/Initial investment" in the appropriate months in the Cash flow projection (following pages).

Be careful of VAT. You must pay it when you buy things but, even if you are entitled to recover it, you will not get it back for some time (See "Taxation"). Your cash flow needs to be able to pay the full amount up-front. Next, look at sources of finance that you have agreed (see "Finance, page 85). When will these come in? Pencil the amounts into your cash flow projection in the appropriate months under "Incoming/Sources of finance").

Operating Budget

Look again at your Operating Budget:

- Which items of expenditure will occur every month? (Don't forget your own personal drawings)
- Are there any once-off payments such as legal fees, security deposit for rent, new phone lines, insurance, etc.?
- Any advance payments for suppliers, rent, etc.?

Check your diary. Does activity in a particular month mean extra expenditure for that month? (advertising, direct mail, networking, meeting with your mentor, holiday, travel, etc.). Fill in those extra expenses. If clients have paid you (or will pay you) in advance, put that in the appropriate month. Do you have any forward orders? When will the product or service be delivered and when will the customer pay? Fill in the amounts in the appropriate months.

Go back to your market research and marketing plan. Are there seasonal patterns? Will some of your promotional actions increase sales in particular months? What are your expectations of how sales will develop in the first few months? Try to estimate sales for each month. Write down how you came to that estimate and on which sources and assumptions you have based it. Fill in your sales estimates in the appropriate months.

Check your cost pricing and, more importantly, the costs directly related to the sales (variable costs). Most obvious ones are purchase of materials and travel. Fill in the variable costs, and keep the VAT separate again. Things to check include:

- Do you have to pay VAT (calculate incoming VAT minus outgoing VAT)?
- Can you claim VAT back?
- When must you pay taxes and how much?

OBJECTIVES
o Understand the difference between profit and cash-flow
o Be able to prepare cash-flow projections

Happiness is a positive cash-flow.
FRED ADLER, US venture capitalist

Take the cash and let the credit go.
EDWARD FITZGERALD

CASHFLOW PROJECTIONS – YEAR 1

Copy this to page 133.

	M1 €	M2 €	M3 €	M4 €	M5 €	M6 €	M7 €	M8 €	M9 €	M10 €	M11 €	M12 €	Year 1 €
Opening bal.	—	—	—	—	—	—	—	—	—	—	—	—	—
Incoming													
Sources of finance	—	—	—	—	—	—	—	—	—	—	—	—	—
Cash sales	—	—	—	—	—	—	—	—	—	—	—	—	—
Debtors	—	—	—	—	—	—	—	—	—	—	—	—	—
VAT refunds	—	—	—	—	—	—	—	—	—	—	—	—	—
Other income	—	—	—	—	—	—	—	—	—	—	—	—	—
Total income	—	—	—	—	—	—	—	—	—	—	—	—	—
Outgoing													
Initial investment	—	—	—	—	—	—	—	—	—	—	—	—	—
Cash purchases	—	—	—	—	—	—	—	—	—	—	—	—	—
Creditors	—	—	—	—	—	—	—	—	—	—	—	—	—
Overheads:													
Staff	—	—	—	—	—	—	—	—	—	—	—	—	—
Production	—	—	—	—	—	—	—	—	—	—	—	—	—
Premises	—	—	—	—	—	—	—	—	—	—	—	—	—
Transport	—	—	—	—	—	—	—	—	—	—	—	—	—
Selling/promo	—	—	—	—	—	—	—	—	—	—	—	—	—
Gen. expenses	—	—	—	—	—	—	—	—	—	—	—	—	—
Finance costs	—	—	—	—	—	—	—	—	—	—	—	—	—
Loan repayments	—	—	—	—	—	—	—	—	—	—	—	—	—
Private drawings	—	—	—	—	—	—	—	—	—	—	—	—	—
Fixed assets	—	—	—	—	—	—	—	—	—	—	—	—	—
VAT payable	—	—	—	—	—	—	—	—	—	—	—	—	—
Other taxes	—	—	—	—	—	—	—	—	—	—	—	—	—
Other expenses	—	—	—	—	—	—	—	—	—	—	—	—	—
Total expenses	—	—	—	—	—	—	—	—	—	—	—	—	—
Net cash flow	—	—	—	—	—	—	—	—	—	—	—	—	—
Final balance	—	—	—	—	—	—	—	—	—	—	—	—	—

SCRIBBLE BOX

CASHFLOW PROJECTIONS – YEAR 2

Copy this to page 134.

	M1 €	M2 €	M3 €	M4 €	M5 €	M6 €	M7 €	M8 €	M9 €	M10 €	M11 €	M12 €	Year 2 €
Opening bal.													
Incoming													
Sources of finance													
Cash sales													
Debtors													
VAT refunds													
Other income													
Total income													
Outgoing													
Initial investment													
Cash purchases													
Creditors													
Overheads:													
Staff													
Production													
Premises													
Transport													
Selling/promo													
Gen. expenses													
Finance costs													
Loan repayments													
Private drawings													
Fixed assets													
VAT payable													
Other taxes													
Other expenses													
Total expenses													
Net cash flow													
Final balance													

SCRIBBLE BOX

CASHFLOW PROJECTIONS – YEAR 3

Copy this to page 135.

	M1 €	M2 €	M3 €	M4 €	M5 €	M6 €	M7 €	M8 €	M9 €	M10 €	M11 €	M12 €	Year 3 €
Opening bal.													
Incoming													
Sources of finance													
Cash sales													
Debtors													
VAT refunds													
Other income													
Total income													
Outgoing													
Initial investment													
Cash purchases													
Creditors													
Overheads:													
Staff													
Production													
Premises													
Transport													
Selling/promo													
Gen. expenses													
Finance costs													
Loan repayments													
Private drawings													
Fixed assets													
VAT payable													
Other taxes													
Other expenses													
Total expenses													
Net cash flow													
Final balance													

SCRIBBLE BOX

CASHFLOW – 3-YEAR PROJECTIONS

	Year 1	Year 2	Year 3
Opening balance	€ _____	€ _____	€ _____
Incoming			
Sources of finance	€ _____	€ _____	€ _____
Cash sales	€ _____	€ _____	€ _____
Debtors	€ _____	€ _____	€ _____
VAT refunds	€ _____	€ _____	€ _____
Other income	€ _____	€ _____	€ _____
Total income	€ _____	€ _____	€ _____
Outgoing			
Initial investment	€ _____	€ _____	€ _____
Cash purchases	€ _____	€ _____	€ _____
Creditors	€ _____	€ _____	€ _____
Overheads:			
Staff	€ _____	€ _____	€ _____
Production	€ _____	€ _____	€ _____
Premises	€ _____	€ _____	€ _____
Transport	€ _____	€ _____	€ _____
Selling/promotion	€ _____	€ _____	€ _____
General expenses	€ _____	€ _____	€ _____
Finance costs	€ _____	€ _____	€ _____
Loan repayments	€ _____	€ _____	€ _____
Private drawings	€ _____	€ _____	€ _____
Fixed assets	€ _____	€ _____	€ _____
VAT payable	€ _____	€ _____	€ _____
Other taxes	€ _____	€ _____	€ _____
Other expenditure	€ _____	€ _____	€ _____
Total expenditure	€ _____	€ _____	€ _____
Net cash flow	€ _____	€ _____	€ _____
Final balance	€ _____	€ _____	€ _____

SCRIBBLE BOX

OBJECTIVES

o Understand the place of grants in financing your business

o Identify main sources of grant-aid and other assistance

o Understand grant-givers' criteria

There is a wide range of State bodies charged with assisting entrepreneurs and potential entrepreneurs to develop their businesses. The assistance they provide may be in the form of cash grants but increasingly includes advice, subsidies, training, workspace, etc.

Whatever form it takes, this assistance may be vital in providing the final piece of the jigsaw to get your business up and running, or it may provide just the push you need to get going. Sometimes, it may even be just the fact that someone else has confidence in you that makes it all come together.

Grant-aid, or other assistance, is a good thing. It can help your business to grow. Going through the application process, whether or not you are successful, will focus your planning. But don't let the need to meet grant-givers' criteria push your business where you don't want to go.

Too often, entrepreneurs start by asking "Where will I get a grant?". Grants are not the aim of the business – your work on developing a strategy and a mission statement should tell you that. Grants are an extra, which may help you do something that you couldn't otherwise have afforded. They come at the end of the financing process – not at the start of the planning process! However, if grants – or better still, relevant training courses – are available, take advantage.

This section outlines the main sources of assistance from State bodies. Other sources, including private sector organisations, appear on page 104.

Structure of State assistance

Overall responsibility for enterprise lies with the Department of Enterprise, Trade and Employment, which is responsible for promoting competitiveness in the economy and for creating a favourable climate for the creation of self-sustaining employment. It works to monitor and improve the environment for business by ensuring that the framework of law, regulation and Government policy promotes effective company performance and both public and business confidence.

It achieves this indirectly by creating an environment for enterprise and directly through the agencies it has established, which operate to stimulate industrial development at different levels:

• **Nationally** – Enterprise Ireland
• **Regionally** – Shannon Development and Údarás na Gaeltachta
• **Locally** – County/City Enterprise Boards and Area Partnerships.

Policy is determined by Forfás, which is the national Policy and Advisory Board for Enterprise, Trade, Science, Technology & Innovation. It reports to the Department of Enterprise, Trade & Employment.

IDA Ireland and Enterprise Ireland both report to Forfás and implement policy set by it. IDA Ireland focuses on inwards investment — bringing foreign multinationals into Ireland — while Enterprise Ireland is tasked with supporting indigenous (local) businesses.

There are also other State agencies whose role includes that of stimulating development, albeit often in specified sectors.

Where do I start?

Although there has been a huge shift away from a jobs focus among the enterprise support agencies, ironically the first question that you must answer to decide where you should look for help still relates to the employment potential of your new business.

If, within three years or so of start-up, you are likely still to employ under 10 people, you should make your way to the County/City Enterprise Boards and/or the other local support agencies.

Once you can show that you are likely to employ more than 10 people within three years or so of start-up (and meet some other criteria, including demonstrating significant turnover with strong export potential), Enterprise Ireland (or Shannon Development /Údarás na Gaeltachta, as appropriate) classifies your business as a "high potential start-up" and takes you under its wing.

County/City Enterprise Boards

County/City Enterprise Boards are probably the most important source of assistance for the start-up business. The 35 CEBs aim to encourage local initiative. Each is a company limited by guarantee, and has an executive staff, headed by a Chief Executive Officer. The 12-14 Board members are drawn from elected members of the local authority, the social partners, State agencies, ICTU, IBEC, the farming organisations, the county manager and community and other representatives.

The CEBs have responsibility for enterprise development in areas not already covered by the State industrial development agencies – specifically, enterprises employing (or likely to employ) fewer than 10 persons and service businesses. Where they receive applications for funding and advice that are more appropriate to the remit of existing agencies (say, Enterprise Ireland), such applications are directed to the appropriate agency.

Each Board has access to an Enterprise Fund which has been established to assist small projects. However, County/City Enterprise Boards do not normally consider proposals involving grant support in excess of €75,000 - and at this level, a proportion of the funding is likely to be repayable. Project promoters must demonstrate:

- There is a market for the proposed product/service
- Adequate overall finance will be available to fund the project
- They possess the management and technical capacity to implement the proposed project
- Projects to be assisted will add value so as to generate income or supplement income for those involved, and will have the capacity to create new direct employment whether full-time, part-time or seasonal, or will, as a minimum, contribute directly to maintaining employment in existing small businesses
- They will comply with existing policies on tax clearance, the certification of subcontractors, and related matters.

The Boards do not fund projects that are contrary to public policy, nor do they duplicate support for projects which would be eligible for assistance from any existing sectoral or grant structure, or which involve primary agricultural production.

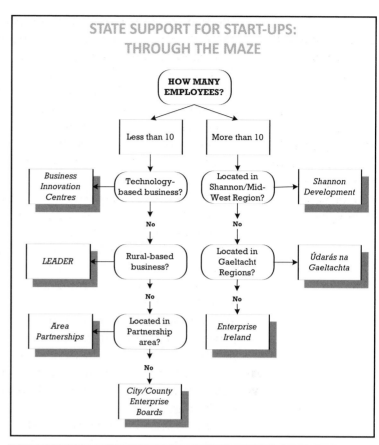

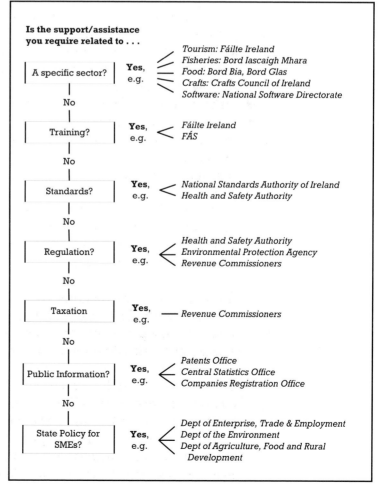

The following grants are available:

- Up to 50% of the capital cost to a maximum of €75,000
- Up to €7,500 per job, up to 10 jobs
- Up to of 60% (BMW region; 50% South & East) of the cost of preparing a feasibility study/business plan, subject to a limit of €6,350 (BMW region; €5,100 in South & East).

Assistance is not confined to grants, since the CEBs have authority to provide loans and loan guarantees and to take equity stakes in businesses. In addition, the CEBs act as a source of advice and information. Many provide training and mentoring services.

Increasingly, the focus of the CEBs has moved towards a broader range of "soft" supports — training (in particular, management development), mentoring and other forms of assistance — designed to increase the survival rates of start-ups and small businesses.

Since the activities of the CEBs are tailored to the needs of their local community, you should check with your local CEB for the full range of assistance available.

You should contact your local CEB before taking your project much beyond an initial stage. An initial informal discussion will quickly determine whether:

- The CEB can support your project

- A feasibility study grant may be available
- You should make changes to your project to make it acceptable to the CEB for assistance.

Your application should be on an official application form, obtainable from your local CEB. Read the notes with the application form carefully before completing. Almost always, except in cases where very small amounts of money are involved, CEBs will require a business plan with your application. A Feasibility Study Grant may help you prepare one (see the first chapter, **READY**).

Enterprise Ireland

Enterprise Ireland is the government organisation charged with assisting the development of Irish enterprise. Its mission is: "to work in partnership with client companies to develop a sustainable competitive advantage, leading to a significant increase in profitable sales, exports and employment". Its clients are mainly manufacturing and internationally-traded services companies employing more than 10 people.

Enterprise Ireland services are best described on its website (**www.enterprise-ireland.com**). but include:

- Funding for development and growth
- Assistance with intellectual property and technology transfer
- Linkages with EU technology support programmes
- Market information and supports
- Mentoring.

It also hosts an annual Student Enterprise Awards competition.

Enterprise Ireland assists "high potential" start-ups:

- In manufacturing or internationally traded services
- Based on technological innovation or exploitable market niche opportunity
- Likely to achieve projected sales of at least €1m and 10 jobs by Year 3
- Export-oriented

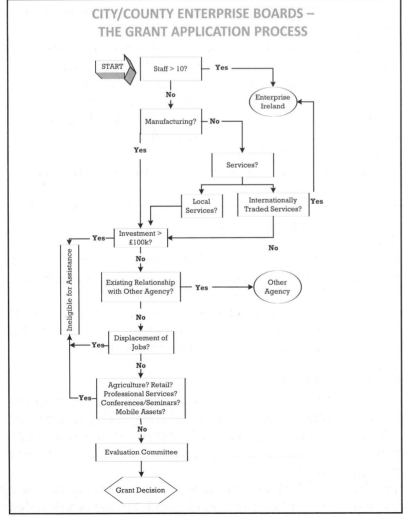

CITY/COUNTY ENTERPRISE BOARDS – THE GRANT APPLICATION PROCESS

- Capable in the longer term of significantly exceeding these levels
- Being established by experienced managers, academics or technical graduates.

Assistance provided by Enterprise Ireland nationally is provided in certain regions by Shannon Development or Údarás na Gaeltachta, as appropriate. Enterprise Ireland's approach involves:
- Detailed analysis of a company's requirements
- Determination of the level of need for State support
- Targeting of funds to meet the real needs of the business
- Provision of funds to companies that are forecast to deliver strong growth in both sales and exports.

In addition to financial support from its own resources, Enterprise Ireland can provide access to:
- Its Research, Technology and Innovation (RTI) scheme — grants to develop innovative products, awarded on a competitive basis
- Venture capital funds, often in conjunction with other organisations.

Shannon Development

Shannon Development is the Regional Development Agency responsible for development in the Shannon Region, comprising Counties Limerick, Clare, North Tipperary and South-west Offaly and North Kerry. It offers grants and other assistance to businesses in the Shannon region, broadly in line with the assistance available nationally from Enterprise Ireland.

Shannon Development operates the National Technological Park, which includes its Innovation Centre. It also launched the Kerry Technology Park, in association with the Institute of Technology Tralee, IDA Ireland, Tralee Urban District Council and Kerry County Council. It has developed its own range of venture capital funds and other facilities that make the Mid-West a prime technological base.

Údarás na Gaeltachta

Údarás na Gaeltachta combines an economic development role (that of creating sustainable jobs and attracting investment to the Gaeltacht regions) with community, cultural and language-development activities, working in partnership with local communities and organisations. Projects in manufacturing, internationally-traded services (such as software development and telemarketing/servicing) and natural resources such as mariculture are the priority for assistance. It offers grant schemes and

incentives to help small and medium-sized enterprises in the Gaeltacht areas, which are broadly in line with those available nationally from Enterprise Ireland. It also provides non-financial incentives, such as advice and consultation on legal documentation.

Údarás aims to establish and develop job-creating industries and services in the Gaeltacht regions of Donegal, Mayo, Galway, Kerry, Cork, Waterford and Meath.

Area Partnerships

The 38 Area Partnerships originally were set up under the Programme for Economic and Social Progress (PESP) in 1993. Their activities are co-ordinated by Pobal (formerly Area Development Management Ltd). One of the Partnerships' aims is to work at local level to generate more jobs through sustainable enterprises and through the promotion of local economic projects and initiatives.

Each Partnership is autonomous and agrees different work practices. Each works on an Area Action Plan for its own region. Practical measures are taken to discriminate in favour of the long-term unemployed and those who are socially excluded.

Partnerships provide support for unemployed people setting up their own business, through:
- Support for the development of business plans and business ideas
- Financial support, including non-repayable grants, interest subsidies, loan guarantees, small-scale investment and joint ventures
- Mentoring, including sources of advice
- Provision of workspace, including help in obtaining enterprise incubation units
- Rent subsidies
- Marketing, including identifying gaps in the market
- Training and education in enterprise, with the support of FÁS.

There is variety in what each Partnership offers, and would-be entrepreneurs should contact the Partnership in their area for further details.

Note that some of the Partnerships also operate LEADER programme in their areas, or provide support for other enterprise activities.

LEADER

LEADER is an EU initiative for rural development (part-funded by the Irish Government) that enables groups in rural areas to implement their own multi-sectoral integrated plans for the development of their areas.

LEADER is aimed at encouraging and supporting high quality and ambitious integrated strategies for local rural development, putting a strong emphasis on co-operation and networking between rural areas. All rural areas of the EU are, in principle, eligible under LEADER.

Typical LEADER activities include:
- Technical support to rural development including group administration
- Training and recruitment assistance
- Rural tourism
- Small firms, craft enterprises and local services
- Local exploitation and marketing of agricultural, horticultural, forest and fishery products
- Preservation and improvement of the environment and living conditions.

As each LEADER Group identifies and responds to needs within its own communities, its activities are unique to its own situation. Because of this, would-be entrepreneurs seeking assistance should make contact with their local LEADER Group to see whether and what help is available.

Border, Midland & Western Regional Assembly
The Border, Midland & Western Regional Assembly was established in 1999 and consists of 29 elected members from the constituent local authorities. The BMW Region consists of counties Cavan, Donegal, Galway, Laois, Leitrim, Longford, Louth, Mayo, Monaghan, Offaly, Roscommon, Sligo, Westmeath. Its role is to:
- Manage the BMW Regional Operational Programmes 2000-2006 and 2007-13
- Monitor the general impact of all EU and Irish exchequer-funded programmes in the Border, Midland and West region
- Promote the co-ordination of the provision of public services in the region; and
- Ensure that national policies take regional issues into account.

The BMW Assembly does not provide direct funding to individuals or organisations but funds through "Implementing Bodies".

Business Innovation Centres
The Business Innovation Centres are primarily targeted at technology-based businesses. They encourage and foster innovation in new or existing businesses, through services directed at the development of new ideas and their conversion into real business projects.

As BIC support services may vary between centres, would-be entrepreneurs seeking assistance should make contact with their local BIC to see whether and what help is available. There are BICs in Cork, Dublin, Galway, Waterford and Derry.

STATE AND SEMI-STATE AGENCIES
As mentioned earlier, there are a wide range of these agencies, covering a variety of roles and responsibilities and reporting to appropriate Government Departments. Useful websites for access are:
- **www.ask-ireland.com**
- **www.irlgov.ie** – the Government web-site
- **www.basis.ie** – Business Access to State Information Services, a single information point for all Government information and services.

Arts Council
The Arts Council is the development agency for the arts in Ireland and the primary source of support for the individual creative and interpretative artist. It provides support and financial assistance for artistic purposes to individuals and organisations. It annually funds over 350 arts and non-arts organisations and makes awards to over 450 individuals across all art forms, from €750 to €10,000.

Bord Bia - The Irish Food Board
Bord Bia (The Irish Food Board) is the Irish government agency charged with the promotion, trade development and marketing of the Irish food, drink and horticulture industry. Its mission is to deliver effective and innovative market development, promotion and information services to assist companies grow and win new business. Bord Bia works in partnership with this industry to increase the sales and exports of Irish food, drink and horticulture by developing long-term relationships between Irish companies and trade buyers. Bord Bia operates programmes to develop and foster contact between buyers and Irish companies, including participation under the 'Ireland' umbrella brand at international trade exhibitions, and co-coordinating inward buying visits. Bord Bia has its Head Office in Dublin and nine strategically located offices in key export markets.

Bord Iascaigh Mhara - Irish Sea Fisheries Board
Bord Iascaigh Mhara (BIM) is the Irish State Agency with responsibility for providing commercially relevant and innovative services to the Irish seafood industry that drive growth opportunities, add value, enhance competitiveness and create jobs in a sustainable, natural resource-based industry for the benefit of coastal communities. It provides a wide

range of financial, technical, educational, business innovation and trade development services for fishermen, processors, fish-farmers, retailers and exporters, organised through five divisions: Aquaculture, Business Development and Innovation, Fisheries Development, Marine Services and Secretariat.

Central Statistics Office
Since its establishment as a specialist national statistical agency in 1949 the CSO has pursued the same mandate, as set out in the Statistics Act 1993: 'The collection, compilation, extraction and dissemination for statistical purposes of information relating to economic, social and general activities and conditions in the State'. It is also responsible for co-ordinating official statistics of other public authorities and for developing the statistical potential of administrative records.

The CSO exists primarily to meet the needs of Government for quality statistical information which is a vital input to the formation, implementation and monitoring of policy and programmes at national, regional and local levels in a rapidly changing economic and social environment. It also serves the needs of the wider national and international community (business, EU, international organisations, media, researchers, and the public generally) for impartial and relevant information on social and economic conditions. Particular attention is paid to the specialist needs of business and the research/academic community for more detailed and focused data.

Companies Registration Office
The CRO is the authority for the incorporation of new companies and the registration of business names in the Republic of Ireland. It is also responsible for the receipt and registration of post-incorporation documents, for enforcement of the filing requirements of companies and for the provision of information to the public. Almost all of the information filed with the CRO is available for public inspection, usually for a small fee. Regsitration forms are available for download on the CRO's website (**www.cro.ie**).

Crafts Council of Ireland
The CCOI is the national design and economic development agency for the craft industry in the Republic of Ireland, funded by Enterprise Ireland and the EU. CCOI's services include:
* Showcase Ireland, a national trade fair
* Information services to wholesale and retail buyers on the availability of craft products, plus up-to-date, computerised information on retail outlets, courses, craftspeople and their craft products, development agencies, grant-aid bodies etc
* Business advisory service for craftspeople setting up their own craft business or craft-shop and for those already established, including grant applications and liaising with grant-aiding agencies, market research, business plans, company structure, finance and packaging
* Training and help for design enterprise through short courses, offered via local City/County Enterprise Boards, to enhance product and marketing development in craft businesses
* Training programmes in jewellery production and design skills, pottery skills and craft & design business development.

Department of Social & Family Affairs
The Department operates a "Back to Work" Allowance (Self-Employment) scheme to encourage people to become self-employed. To qualify, you must be:
* Setting up a self-employment business approved by a Partnership Company or Job Facilitator
* "Signing-on" for at least 12 months and getting Unemployment Benefit or Assistance
* Getting One-Parent Family Payment, Disability Allowance or Blind Person's Pension for 12 months.

You will receive support for up to two years. You will also retain and "secondary" benefits.

A new Short-Term Enterprise Allowance requires no qualifying period, provided you have an entitlement to Jobseeker's Benefit and two years' contributions or qualify for statutory redundancy. Under STEA, you keep your full benefits for up to one year.

ENFO – Environmental Information Service
ENFO is an environmental information service that promotes knowledge and care of the environment, through:
* A query-answering service
* Clear, authoritative content, constantly updated, on the www.enfo.ie website
* Access to downloadable information leaflets and posters
* A portal to Irish environmental sites providing newsfeeds and events' listings, and a search across environmental websites
* Online access to free environmental databases within public libraries

- Electronic environmental exhibitions
- An online Kid's ENFO section providing interactive learning resources for children and teachers supporting the children's play areas and reading material available in the 350 public libraries nationwide
- Environmental exhibitions and workshops in libraries throughout the country
- Access to environmental books and DVDs countrywide through www.borrowbooks.ie.

Environmental Protection Agency
The EPA's responsibilities include:
- Licensing and control of large scale waste and industrial activities to ensure that they do not endanger human health or harm the environment.
- National environmental policing
- Monitoring, analysing and reporting on the environment
- Regulating Ireland's greenhouse gas emissions
- Environmental research and development
- Strategic environmental assessment
- Environmental planning, education and guidance and
- Proactive waste management.

Fáilte Ireland - The National Tourism Development Authority
Fáilte Ireland provides an extensive range of training and support services and business solutions to tourism enterprises, large and small, designed to develop and sustain Ireland as a high-quality competitive tourist destination.

FÁS — The Training and Employment Authority
Through a regional network of Employment Services offices and Training Centres, FÁS operates training and employment programmes, provides a recruitment service to job-seekers and employers, an advisory service for industry and supports community-based enterprises.

FÁS encourages employers and employees to improve their work skills ('up-skilling') through its Services to Business division. With on-line training available 24/7 through FÁS eCollege and a range of business start-up advisory training programmes, FÁS also offers traineeships (formal training with workplace coaching) tailored to Irish industry and local businesses needs. For those experiencing major barriers in progressing to the workforce, there is a support grant (Technical Employment Support Grant) available for non-FÁS training programmes. In addition, employers can find staff or list vacancies on FÁS Jobs Ireland (freephone 1800 611 116) or meet with EURES advisers to discuss and access a database of European job-seekers.

Ireland's national standard for human resource management is awarded by FÁS' 'Excellence Through People', a successful business improvement tool designed to further an organisation's performance through its people.

Food Safety Authority of Ireland
The Food Safety Authority of Ireland's mission is to protect consumers' health and consumers' interests by ensuring that food consumed, distributed, marketed or produced in Ireland meets the highest standards of food safety and hygiene. The Authority offers advice and information on all aspects of food safety, including starting up a food business, food labelling, food safety training requirements, food safety legislation and HACCP. The Authority operates an Advice Line on 1890 33 66 77.

Government Publications
All Government publications are available from the sales office, including Central Statistics Office reports.

Health & Safety Authority
The Health and Safety Authority (HSA) is the national body in Ireland with responsibility for securing health and safety at work. It is a state-sponsored body, established under the Safety, Health & Welfare at Work Act and it reports to the Minister for Enterprise, Trade & Employment. Its responsibilities cover every type of workplace and every kind of work in the public and private sectors, ranging from workplaces where just one or two people are employed to corporations with multiple locations and thousands of employees.

Marine Institute
The Marine Institute is the national agency responsible for undertaking, co-ordinating, promoting and assisting in marine research and development, and providing such services related to marine research and development that, in the opinion of the Institute, will promote economic development, create employment and protect the environment.

National Standards Authority of Ireland
Among NSAI's objectives are:
- To formulate, publish and sell Irish Standards, which form part of the harmonised European and worldwide system of standards in which NSAI is a designated "National Standards Body"

- To assist all sectors of industry to understand and meet the technical, quality and safety requirements of harmonised European and international standards in the domestic and overseas markets
- To provide a comprehensive quality auditing and product certification service for industry and commerce in accordance with current European and international practice
- To improve the quality of products and services through the promotion and application of the IS EN ISO 9000 series of Quality Systems Management standards
- To provide training and information on standards and their application to the certification service provided by the NSAI.

Patents Office

The principal statutory functions of the Office are:
- The granting of patents
- The registration of industrial designs and trade marks
- Providing information in relation to patents, designs, copyright and trade marks.
- The regulation of copyright licensing bodies and dispute resolution involving same.

Registry of Business Names

By law, entrepreneurs are obliged by law to register their business with the Registry of Business Names, or the relevant body in the case of co-operatives, if it carries on a business under a name other than its own.

Registry of Friendly Societies

A co-operative society can be formed by any group of seven or more people over the age of 18, and can be registered with the Registry of Friendly Societies. The advantage of registration is limited liability. The Co-operative Development Society Ltd, Irish Co-operative Society Ltd, and National Association of Building Co-operatives Ltd have Model Rules for co-operatives that have been approved by the Registry of Friendly Societies for use by those wishing to form a co-operative.

Revenue Commissioners

Visit the Revenue website (www.revenue.ie) for a wide range of leaflets, forms and other information relating to the tax implications of starting your own business. Alternatively, contact your local tax office for advice - contact details are on the website.

Southern & Eastern Regional Assembly

The Southern & Eastern Regional Assembly was established in 1999 following the designation of Ireland into two regions for the purposes of EU Funding. The Assembly is made up of 41 councillors who are nominated by their respective Local & Regional Authorities. Their functions are:
- Managing and monitoring the Regional Operational Programme 2007-2013
- Promoting the co-ordination of public services in the region
- Monitoring & making proposals in relation to the general impact in the region of EU funding
- Making public bodies aware of the regional implications of their policies & plans.

Teagasc

Teagasc offers a Certificate in Rural Business for farmers exploring opportunities for starting new businesses, or expanding existing businesses, linked to the rural environment. The course covers technical and management skills as well as hands-on practical skills.

Teagasc also offers a comprehensive range of training courses at its National Food Centre and Dairy Products Research Centre, aimed at strengthening in-company capabilities in quality systems, food safety and hygiene, food technology and product development/marketing.

Through its Rural Enterprise Service, Teagasc provides foundation and advanced training courses for food entrepreneurs in rural areas. Teagasc research centres provide a range of technical services on a cost-recovery basis in support of the farming and food processing industries, government departments, local authorities and other clients.

Universities and Institutes of Technology

A final source of State support for enterprise are the Universities and Institutes of Technology. All have Industrial Liaison Officers or Heads of External Services or Development whose task it is to build links between the college and the business world. In many cases, this results in the college carrying out technical research for a local business or commercialising through a local business the fruits of their own research. In addition, all the ITs and most of the universities have incubator units and support enterprise through a variety of programmes.

OBJECTIVES

o Understand the role of the various organisations assisting enterprise development

o Be aware of the assistance available

Small and medium-sized enterprises are defined as independent businesses (fewer than 25% of the shares held by one or more large companies), that have no more than 250 employees, and have either turnover less than €50 million or total assets net of depreciation less than €43 million.

EU definition of small and medium-sized enterprises (SMEs)

Other organisations, some State-supported, some entirely financed by the private sector, assist the potential entrepreneur in starting up and/or developing their business. This section lists some of these organisations. For further details on each organisation and their services, contact them directly (see **Appendix 1** for addresses).

Accountants and consultants

Many accounting firms and consultants provide advice on obtaining grant-aid and on taking a business concept from viability assessment through to the production stage.

The initial meeting between a potential entrepreneur and the consultant is usually free and is used to gather information about the promoter and the business proposal. Based on the information available, the accountant/consultant will recommend appropriate action to progress the project.

Where further information is required, a structured feasibility study will be carried out, embracing key aspects such as products, markets, competitors, technology, funding etc. The consultant will prepare applications for feasibility study grant aid from a County or City Enterprise Board, Enterprise Ireland or other appropriate bodies, and provide hands-on assistance in planning and carrying out the study. A fee should be agreed before work starts.

If the proposal is viable, the consultant will assist in the preparation of a comprehensive business plan, at a further agreed cost. The consultant will make application for grants appropriate to the project and assist in raising finance from banks or private investors. The consultant will also help to obtain commercial partners.

Professional advice on taxation, accounting and financial matters can be obtained also from a firm of accountants and auditors.

Amárach Consulting

Amárach (Irish for "tomorrow") specialises in predictive market research and business forecasting. It focuses on understanding the changes taking place in Irish markets and on linking these insights to effective business strategies designed to profit from anticipated change, using a multi-disciplinary approach that draws on economics, demographics, social psychology and technological forecasting. Many of its reports are published on its website.

Bolton Trust

The Bolton Trust encourages and promotes new business enterprise in Ireland. We are an independent voluntary trust actively committed to assisting people create sustainable business. The Bolton Trust was established in 1986 by staff of the Dublin Institute of Technology, and currently has over 200 members. This membership is largely drawn from the various disciplines of DIT, Ireland's largest third-level technological Institute, and also from Ireland's entrepreneurial community. The expertise of the Trust can be mobilised to help budding entrepreneurs to create new business enterprise.

bPlans.ie

A website from Palo Alto Software., developers of Business Plan Pro, that that offers business planning advice and resources in an Irish context.

Chambers Ireland

Chambers Ireland is Ireland's largest business network with 13,000 member companies drawn from all sectors of the Irish economy. There are 59 chambers in Ireland, affiliated to Chambers Ireland. Each Chamber strives for local economic development, representation of its members' interests, and the provision of market-led services to the local business community.

creativeireland.com

Creative Ireland is the online home for the Irish creative design community. It provides news, a directory of designers, a jobsdesk, for those looking for work or designers, and a gateway to essential design resources on the Internet.

DIT Hothouse

Hothouse is the award-winning Innovation and Technology Transfer Centre at Dublin Institute of Technology. Hothouse draws in entrepreneurial and academic talent, ignites creativity and provides a dynamic environment to fast-track businesses and technologies to commercial success. Hothouse assists:

- Entrepreneurs to start and grow businesses
- Business leaders to find technologies, research partners, and funding
- Investors to find high potential opportunities
- DIT staff and students to commercialise their intellectual property (IP).

EIQA

EIQA (Excellence Ireland Quality Association is the Irish national quality association known specifically for hygiene and quality programmes (for example, Q mark). EIQA offers solutions to cutomers who are committed to improving their hygiene and quality standards and view a nationally-recognised accredited programme as key to their company's future.

European Commission

The European Commission provides support to European small and medium-sized enterprises. This is available in different forms such as grants, loans and, in some cases, guarantees. Support is available either directly or through programmes managed at national or regional level, such as the European Union's Structural Funds. SMEs can also benefit from a series of non-financial assistance measures in the form of programmes and business support services.

To help small and medium-sized businesses the European Commission has funded various programmes, details of which are available from:

- **Enterprise Europe Network**
  (http://www.enterprise-europe-network.ec.europa.eu/index_en.htm)
- **Europe Direct Centres**
  (http://ec.europa.eu/europedirect/)
- **DG Enterprise and Industry**
  (http://ec.europa.eu/enterprise/sme/fund_tools/fund_tools_theme_en.htm).

First Tuesday Network

Now online, First Tuesday provides a forum for entrepreneurs, start-ups, investors and service providers. Bi-monthly networking events provide opportunities for companies to pitch and raise their profile.

Food Product Development Centre

The Food Product Development Centre at the Dublin Institute of Technology develops innovative food concepts through investigating value-added opportunities in Irish and European markets. It provides a confidential service to clients. Its development work includes idea generation, concept and prototype development, ingredient sourcing and testing, shelf life studies, sensory assessment and market research, nutritional declaration and labelling.

Guaranteed Irish Ltd

Guaranteed Irish Limited aims to increase awareness of and demand for Irish products and services, thereby maximising employment and prosperity in Ireland through a definitive mark of excellence. For members, Guaranteed Irish provides an ongoing series of seminars, talks and buyers days. By creating consumer interest, awareness and passion for the Guaranteed Irish ethos and symbol, it helps members to increase their market share.

Innovator

Innovator is a consultancy that provides integrated innovation management, R&D management, intellectual property management, training and mentoring services to SMEs, entrepreneurs and large companies. Innovator helps companies achieve growth and success through innovation by transforming typically unstructured development activities into planned, managed and predictable processes.

Institute of Management Consultants & Advisers

IMCA is the professional body for management consultants and business advisers. It operates a Client Enquiry Service to help organisations locate and select management consulting firms to undertake a possible assignment or explore possible solutions to a specific problem.

International Fund for Ireland

The International Fund for Ireland was established as an independent international organisation by the British and Irish Governments in 1986. With contributions from the United States of America, the European Union, Canada, Australia and New Zealand, the total resources committed to the Fund to date amount to £628m/€753m, funding over 5,800 projects across the island of Ireland. The Fund's mission is to underpin efforts towards peace by promoting social and economic advance and encouraging contact, dialogue and reconciliation between nationalists and unionists throughout Ireland. Established by the International Fund for

Ireland, Enterprise Equity Fund Management (NI), based in Belfast, and Enterprise Equity (IRL) Limited, based in Dublin, provide venture capital and private equity to new and expanding businesses in Northern Ireland and the southern border counties.

IRD Duhallow Ltd

IRD Duhallow is a Community-Based Rural Development Company that operates in East Kerry and North West Cork. It operates a sustainable rural development model, which includes development of the human, cultural, economic and environmental resources of the Duhallow region.

IRD Duhallow implements a wide range of supports and programmes including LEADER, Local Development Social Inclusion, Rural Social Scheme, Rural Transport, Meals for the Elderly, Attic & Cavity Wall Insulation, Millennium Fund, Carers Support, DSFA-Mental Health, Bereavement Support, Afterschools Support, Summer Camps, Job Centre, Integration Programme for Migrants, and Support for Low Income Farmers. IRD Duhallow carries out Community Development work with 33 geographically-based groups.

The company provides support and assistance to small businesses, including technical support, training, mentoring and capital Grants.

IRD Kiltimagh

IRD Kiltimagh Ltd. operates two Enterprise Centres, with incubation workspace, and has undertaken the successful implementation of a re-development programme for the Kiltimagh area in conjunction with the State and private sectors. This has included work with the private sector business and tourism actors in the Kiltimagh area, including those with a business idea or looking to develop a project, in order to enhance economic activity and create jobs in the area. It has recently completed a new 35,000 sq. ft office based workspace development (Cairn International Trade Centre), which is available for private sector projects having requirements for office spaces in excess of 1,000 sq. ft.

Irish Business & Employers Confederation

IBEC (Irish Business & Employers Confederation) is the national umbrella organisation for business and employers in Ireland. Its policies and procedures, set by the national council and the board, are implemented by an executive management group.

IBEC provides its membership base of over 7,500 organisations with knowledge, influence and connections. IBEC staff offer practical employer services as well as the opportunity to network and lobby at an industry level through a web of over 60 business sector associations. It works to shape policies and influence decision-making in a way that develops and protects members' interests and contributes to the development and maintenance of an economy that promotes enterprise and productive employment.

Irish Exporters Association

The Irish Exporters Association is the national export support organisation that helps exporters to find new markets, to comply with all the export/import documentation requirements for each market, and to find the most cost-efficient route to foreign markets, and assists with exchange and credit insurance once the deal is done.

The IEA is run by exporters for exporters, with a modest membership fee, which supports exporters and international services providers with a range of services such as:

- Channel clinics: to assist members in managing their export channels and expand into new markets
- Brand audits: to help members improve sales and brand recognition
- Events to highlight the opportunities in new markets to members
- Expert advice from country directors to help members export into new countries in an efficient way
- Query service: to assist members when exporting into new markets
- Visa and legalisation service
- Regular export-related information
- Promoting members' products and services
- Representing members at Government, EU, UN and WTO/WCO
- First query legal advice service
- Boardroom facility
- Wide range of short courses industry focus
- Diplomas in International Trade and e-Business.

Irish Internet Association

The IIA is the professional body for those conducting business via the Internet in Ireland. IIA provides information to members on e-business, education & training, security, employer/employee rights, raising capital, marketing, design & development and languages/ platforms. The IIA website offers "iia internet resources", with catalogued links and articles within each topic.

IPC Consulting

IPC Consulting provides consulting and training support to growing SMEs - raising finance, planning growth, minimising unit cost, online strategy and expansion through acquisition.

Irish Small & Medium Enterprises Association

ISME's membership is composed exclusively of entrepreneurs who own and manage competitive businesses. It offers a range of services to members, including free advice on a 24 hour helpline on employment law, taxation and other areas affecting business. It issues publications on health & safety, employers' obligations, Government-sponsored grant schemes and a member-to-member sourcing directory.

Irish Venture Capital Association

The IVCA represents the venture capital industry in Ireland. Its website has a list of members and associates.

Libraries/Information Centres

Good libraries are a treasure trove for the entrepreneur conducting market research.

Check out the libraries/information centres in (phone first to check access, opening times, etc.):
* Central Business Library, ILAC Centre, Dublin
* Enterprise Ireland
* ENFO.

Limerick Enterprise Development Partnership

Limerick Enterprise Development Partnership (LEDP) was established in 1999 following the closure of the Krups factory in Limerick. LEDP is a partnership between the following organisations: Limerick City Council, Shannon Development, Paul Partnership, The RC Diocese Of Limerick, The Community Foundation for Ireland, and Limerick Enterprise Network. LEDP has a proven track record in assisting in the development of communities. LEDP is actively engaged in supporting innovation in community and education development. Over 700 people participate daily in LEDP in
employment, training & education activities.

MAC (National Microelectronics Application Centre)

MAC provides consultancy and complete innovative electronic, software and e-Service/Web technological products and services for Irish entrepreneurs and industry.

MAC can help an entrepreneur by:
* Discussing the market opportunity, concept, product or eService idea
* Help to identify similar products/services, potential competitors, and competing technologies
* Designing and building a working prototype, in a feasibility study
* Designing for commercial operation, manufacture, sourcing appropriate state-of-the-art components, adhering to standards and regulations

MAC normally works on fixed-price contracts to agreed schedules, so the entrepreneur's exposure is defined and can be budgeted to a grant application.

National Software Centre

The Centre, in Mahon, Cork, has been funded on a public-private partnership basis, with backing from Cork Corporation, Enterprise Ireland, the National Software Directorate and private investors. Managed in association with the Cork Business Innovation Centre, the campus provides cutting-edge voice, data and conferencing communications and houses the main carrier telecommunications hub and internet co-location centre for Southwest Ireland. The NSC Campus provides a multi-tenanted, purpose-built environment with community, flexibility and scalability in mind.

Network

Network is a national organisation for women in business, management, the professions and the arts. It facilitates women in the promotion and development of their careers through regular meetings and educational seminars. It provides a forum where members can exchange ideas and increase their business contacts and markets the skills and expertise of Network members, promoting women as worthy contributors to the Irish economy and decision-making bodies and, through the joint effort of members, promoting the welfare of the community.

Partas

The aim of Partas is to build an inclusive and thriving community by being a leading source of excellence in development of local enterprise and of social economy. It promotes and develops self-employment opportunities for people living in Tallaght. It also offers affordable office and workshop space in four centres in Tallaght, including the Brookfield Enterprise Centre. Partas also provides consulting and training for community and enterprise groups.

PLATO Ireland

PLATO Ireland is a business and management development network for owner/managers of SMEs.

107

There are PLATO regional groups in Belfast, Cork, Dun Laoire, Louth, Newry & Mourne, Monaghan, North Dublin, South Dublin/Kildare and the South East, involving over 1,000 SMEs and 100 of Ireland's largest companies. An owner/manager can join the network for an initial two-year cycle and can continue to use it as a resource to meet their own needs.

Regional Development Centre

The Regional Development Centre was established by Dundalk Institute of Technology to contribute, in partnership with State, European and international developmental organisations, to the industrial and commercial development of the East Border Region and to enhance the region's science and technology infrastructure. The Centre acts as a commercially-oriented interface between the Institute and the industrial, commercial and business life of the region, making available the Institute's expertise, facilities and resources for the wider benefit of the regional economy. It offers:

- Entrepreneurial development programmes
- Incubation facilities for knowledge and technology-based enterprises
- Industrial applied research, consultancy and information services.

Small Firms Association

The Small Firms Association is the "Voice of Small Business in Ireland", representing and providing economic, commercial, employee relations and social affairs advice and assistance to over 8,000 member companies. As a full social partner, it directly meets government at the table and interacts with key decision-makers at all levels to ensure that the economic environment is conducive to small business establishment and development.

The SFA secures the best deal for small firms by providing dedicated professional support and by offering a range of services to members, including economic, commercial, employee relations and social affairs advice and assistance. It also provides training in the management of people and related topics for managers at all levels.

SPADE Enterprise Centre

The SPADE Enterprise Centre opened in 1990 in the former St Paul's Church, offering incubator workspace for start-up businesses. The incubator units cater for food production and office space. SPADE currently accommodates over 40 businesses. The facilities in the Centre are kept to a high standard. Tenants have access to in-house secretarial services, central reception facility, use of the conference room, and off-street car parking. Space is available on a monthly licence.

Terenure Enterprise Centre

Terenure Enterprise Centre is a long established centre for new enterprise and entrepreneurs. Services include business incubator units, business advice, coaching and mentoring as well as practical assistance with business plans and funding applications, etc.

Tipperary Institute

Tipperary Institute provides a range of education, training, mentoring and support services to rural businesses and communities, including courses in accounting and finance, business, management and marketing.

Updates for this section are available @
www.startingabusinessinireland.com

REDUCING RISK

This workbook sets out what is probably the best way of reducing the risk involved in your start-up – producing a well-thought-out business plan. Next, you need to quantify the risks. The panel opposite helps you to do that. It shows you what is at risk (your personal investment and any borrowings), how long for, and other factors that help you assess the risk.

Sensitivity analysis

This technique looks at how sensitive your business plan projections are to changes – in sales, in costs, in the environment generally. Ask yourself these questions:

- What happens if sales do not take off until month 8, even though the business plan projects month 3? How likely is this?
- What happens if sales are half the level projected? How likely is this?
- What happens if ... ? How likely is this?

Break-even analysis

Another useful analysis tool is "break-even", the sales volume at which your business begins to make profit. This happens when Sales less Variable Costs (those that vary directly with output) covers Fixed Costs (costs that remain fixed over a wide range of activity).

Use the panel to calculate the break-even point for your business. If your sales expectations fall below this level, you have some work to do!

Other risks

The other risk is that things can just go wrong. You can be unlucky. Answer the questions in the 'At Risk' panel to see how at risk your business may be.

Protection

When you have identified the risks to which you are (or may be) exposed:

- Reconsider your Business Plan and look at alternatives
- Review your insurance situation (personal and business)
- Review your dependency (if any) on specific suppliers
- Review your dependency (if any) on specific customers.

QUANTIFYING THE RISKS

Personal investment	€ _____
Total borrowing	€ _____
Annual cash flow	€ _____
Period personal investment is at risk	€ _____
Period borrowing is at risk	€ _____
Security given	€ _____
Time commitment over risk period	€ _____
Expected profit over risk period	€ _____
Salary required over risk period	€ _____

BREAK-EVEN

Sales price per unit	€ _____
Variable Costs per unit	€ _____
Fixed Costs (total)	€ _____

Break-even volume:

Fixed Costs (total) divided by	€ _____
Sales – Variable Costs per unit	€ _____
equals Number of Units	_____

Number of Units x Sales Price equals Break-even Sales value	€ _____

AT RISK?

What happens if:
You get sick for a long period?
Your spouse/partner gets sick?
Your computer breaks down?
Your machinery breaks down?
Your transport breaks down?
How dependent are you on specific suppliers?
How dependent are you on specific customers?

Consider both the probability of the situation happening AND its likely impact.

First ask yourself: What is the worst that can happen? Then prepare to accept it. Then proceed to improve on the worst.
DALE CARNEGIE

If your project doesn't work, look for the part you didn't think was important.
ARTHUR BLOCH

MENTORS

OBJECTIVES

o Understand the role of a mentor
o Understand how to select a mentor
o Understand how to work with a mentor

Discover someone to help shoulder your misfortunes. Then you will never be alone ... neither fate, nor the crowd, so readily attacks two.

BALTASAR GRACIAN

Loneliness and a sense of isolation are the two most common complaints among entrepreneurs (after the difficulty in getting anyone to finance their business!). That's why it is so important to have the support of your family when you run your own business. But sometimes you need more than support – you need someone who has been there, done that, someone who has experienced what you are going through. This is where a mentor can be helpful.

A mentor is an experienced businessperson who makes available their experience and expertise to small businesses, usually for very modest reward. Most mentors are "putting something back into the system". There are several mentor schemes available – including Enterprise Ireland and the County & City Enterprise Boards. Sometimes your bank may be able to suggest a suitable mentor.

Why a mentor? Then, who?

The first question to ask yourself is why you want a mentor. Use the questions in the panel below to help you answer the question. Next, you need to build a profile. Use the second panel for this. Then, when you apply to the relevant agency, you will have a head-start.

When selecting a mentor, act as if you were interviewing for a vacancy with your business (you are – for a trusted adviser to yourself). Aim to meet about three potential mentors and prepare carefully (re-read "Recruiting Staff" again). Go through the skills/experience match carefully. You may not be able to judge how good the mentor is at his/her specialist area but you can judge the chemistry between the two of you. This will be important, especially if you are looking for a confidante rather than an expert to solve a specific problem.

Working with a mentor

Your mentor must keep totally confidential everything you say to him/her. If you don't trust them to keep your secrets, get rid of them. By the same token, you must be totally honest with your mentor. You are wasting your time (and theirs) if you are not telling them the full picture - deliberately or otherwise - and you may get wrong advice as a result.

Structure the mentor/business relationship as follows:

1. Express your expectations from the mentoring process. (Write them down.)
2. Allow the mentor to express their expectations. (If you have selected carefully, there will be no surprises.)
3. Agree on what the mentor will do and what they will not do. Confirm confidentiality.
4. Decide on what information the mentor needs to be able to help you.

WHAT DO YOU WANT IN A MENTOR?	
A sounding-board for ideas?	☐ YES ☐ NO
Advice based on previous experience?	☐ YES ☐ NO
Hands-on assistance, perhaps in implementing something new in your business?	☐ YES ☐ NO
Contacts, to open doors that might otherwise be closed?	☐ YES ☐ NO
Expertise/experience in specific areas: Marketing, sales, finance, production, legal?	☐ YES ☐ NO
Market knowledge?	☐ YES ☐ NO

WHO DO YOU WANT AS A MENTOR?	
Someone:	
Older than yourself?	☐ YES ☐ NO
Younger than yourself?	☐ YES ☐ NO
With entrepreneurial experience?	☐ YES ☐ NO
With managerial experience?	☐ YES ☐ NO
With specific expertise?	☐ YES ☐ NO
With specific industry background?	☐ YES ☐ NO
From your own personal or business network?	☐ YES ☐ NO
A complete stranger?	☐ YES ☐ NO
Who will become more than a mentor (friendship as part of the mentoring)?	☐ YES ☐ NO

An entrepreneur has to be a master of all trades. But, as your business expands, you may need to hire a consultant or specialist to assist in implementing a project or dealing with a problem that you are unable to solve on your own.

Choose carefully – a good consultant can add immeasurably to your business, while a bad one could cost you a lot of money with nothing to show for it. Ignore qualifications – they are necessary but not the basis for choosing a consultant. Look instead for experience. A good consultant will refer you to his/her previous clients. Ask other entrepreneurs whose opinions you value for recommendations.

Areas in which you should seriously consider employing a consultant (depending on your own skills, of course) include computers, accounting, taxation and law.

Reasons for hiring an outside consultant might be:
- To save time
- You need information, knowledge and expertise in a specific area
- You want an independent view
- You want a second opinion.

Selecting the right adviser is difficult. Just as with a mentor, before deciding on taking on an adviser, you should formulate some selection criteria.

Things to consider are:
- The consultant's knowledge of your business area and your specific project/problem
- His/her experience as a consultant and entrepreneur
- His/her way of working (dedicated to you until the project is done/available as necessary?)
- Ethics/confidentiality (can you trust him/her?)

- Costs (how/when will you be billed?)
- Time-frame (can the work be done when you want?).

Develop a clear briefing of what you expect from the adviser and ask for several quotes before you decide which one you are going to deal with.

Accountants

For information or advice on accounting or taxation matters, you are advised to consult your accountant.

If you do not know an accountant, check the Golden Pages or contact one of the following accounting bodies:
- Association of Chartered Certified Accountants
- Institute of Certified Public Accountants in Ireland
- Chartered Accountants Ireland.

Any of these bodies will be happy to put you in touch with one of their members close to where you live/work. Ask other entrepreneurs whose opinions you value for recommendations to their accountants.

Most accountants will not charge you for a first meeting. Use this to help you decide whether you want to engage the accountant or look further.

Solicitors

You need a solicitor to:
- Check out any lease, loan agreement or contract you may be asked to sign
- Advise you on relevant legislation
- Act as the final step in your credit control process
- Act for you if you are sued.

If you do not know a solicitor, check the Golden Pages or contact the Law Society for a recommendation.

OBJECTIVES
o Understand how to work with, and what to expect from, professional advisers

I don't want a lawyer who tells me what I can't do. I hire a lawyer to tell me how I can do what I want.
JP MORGAN

To spot the expert, pick the one who predicts the job will take the longest and cost the most.
MURPHY'S LAW, BOOK TWO

OBJECTIVES

o Understand the process of business planning

o Combine work done on earlier sections of the guide into a Business Plan

The discipline you impose on yourself by writing things down is the first step towards getting them done.
LEE IACOCCA

A three sentence course on business management:
You read a book from the beginning to the end.
You run a business the opposite way.
You start with the end, and then you do everything you must to achieve it.
HAROLD GENEEN

It is always wise to look ahead, but difficult to look further than you can see.
SIR WINSTON CHURCHILL

A good business plan is nine parts implementation for every one part strategy.
TIM BERRY

All the research into success and failure factors of small businesses show that one of the most important success factors is business planning – over 70% of failures are due to bad planning.

Planning becomes even more important as the business develops. Business planning should be an ongoing process. All major companies have a business plan which is updated regularly. The same should apply for a small company.

A business plan has many functions, which change as the business develops:

o It makes an idea measurable
o It gives a complete picture of a business
o It gives insight into all the aspects of the business
o It is an exercise to assess the viability of an idea
o It helps people to familiarise themselves with all kinds of possible problems
o It is a communication tool for use with suppliers, clients, advisers, banks, funds, etc.
o It can be used as a reference point in history
o It is a planning tool for the future
o It is a teaching tool for the entrepreneur
o It provides a step-by-step approach towards reaching a decision
o It is a way of assessing an existing business
o It is a working manual for the entrepreneur
o It is a checklist for the entrepreneur, bank, funding agency, etc.

Which functions apply to your Business Plan? Tick them above.

As a business goes through various stages in its life, it has different needs (see panel). In each, the Business Plan plays a vital role.

Writing a Business Plan before starting a business reduces the trial and error factor (which is a very costly process) and will prevent obvious mistakes. The more you put into the Business Plan, the more you will get out of the plan.

Writing a Business Plan

The type of Business Plan you are going to write depends on the audience you are

---

BUSINESS PLANNING IN THE DIFFERENT STAGES OF A BUSINESS' LIFE CYCLE

1. **Existence and survival**
   - Thinking it through
   - Ensure solid base
   - Check viability
   - Convince yourself, your spouse/partner and investors

2. **Consolidation and control**
   - Decide further direction
   - Ensure progress
   - Confidence
   - Financing growth/survival

3. **Control and planning**
   - Secure finance
   - Communication tool to employees, partners and investors

4. **Expansion**
   - Maximise potential
   - Secure finance of growth

5. **Stagnation**
   - Revitalise company
   - Assess viability
   - Convince investors

6. **Selling off the company**
   - Sales document
   - Maximise selling price
   - Set terms of agreement

---

writing the plan for. It might be for:

o Yourself
o Your partner/spouse
o Potential business partner
o Private investors
o Suppliers
o Banks
o City/County Enterprise Boards
o Others.

A good Business Plan is:
- Practical
- Honest
- Consistent

BUSINESS PLAN – STRUCTURE

I   **Executive Summary**

II   **Introduction and Background**
- Background to the company

III   **Project Outline**
- Overview of what the business is proposing to do over the period of the business plan – sales increase, employment increase, turnover increase, profit level increase

IV   **Ownership, Management and Employment**
- Founders/Management
- Employee levels

V   **Market and Marketing Strategy**
- Overview of the market
- Projected share of the market
- Target markets
- Main competitors
- Key competitive advantages
- Marketing strategy
- Distribution

VI   **Production**
- Products
- Increased capacity required
- New capital expenditure required
- Efficiency levels
- Skills and numbers of staff required
- Training requirements
- Quality
- Raw material sources

VII   **Financial**
- Summary of projected performance

VIII   **Funding Proposal**
- Funding requirements
- Proposed sources of funding

IX   **Detailed Projections**
- Assumptions
- Profit and Loss account
- Balance Sheet
- Cash-flow

He hath made good progress in a business that hath thought well of it before-hand.
THOMAS FULLER (1654-1734)

Growth is the goal, profit is the measure, security is the result.
SIR OWEN GREEN, BTR

Think of these things: whence you came, where you are going, and to whom you must account.
BENJAMIN FRANKLIN

Sit down to write what you have thought and not to think about what you shall write.
WILLIAM COBBETT

Always keep in mind that your Business Plan tells your story to those reading it when you are not present.
ANON.

- Based on research and facts
- Complete
- Realistic
- Gives a clear picture of the personality and the quality of the entrepreneur
- Turn-key.

Structuring your Business Plan

Your Business Plan must have a structure that is easily followed and understood by the person reading it. Use the structure set out in the panel on the previous page and work through the example layout on the following pages.

Executive Summary

This is the first part of a Business Plan to read – and the last to be written. Here, in less than a page, you summarise the key points of your plan. It's easiest if you can put them in bullet point, like this:

This Business Plan:
- *Explains how XYZ Company came to be*
- *Describes the products we intend to make*
- *Describes the market*
- *Shows how we will reach that market*
- *Costs the products*
- *Includes Operating Budgets and cash-flow projections*
- *Requests grant aid of €xxk, based on equity already committed of €xxk and loans agreed of €xxk.*

See page 116.

Introduction and Background

This is the start of your Business Plan. Here you set out the basic information that a reader will want to know about your business:
- The purpose of the Plan
- Business name and contact details
- Whether it is in operation or has yet to start
- The business objective
- The product/service range.

See page 116.

Project outline

Here you can go into more detail about the business:
- A description of the business
- Your Mission Statement
- Trends in the industry
- Targets that you have set.

This gives the reader a sense of what you are setting out to achieve.
   See page 117.

Ownership, Management and Employment

You, the entrepreneur, are one of the critical success factors of the business. For this reason, the reader of your Business Plan will want to know about you. This is not a place for boasting – simply explain why you believe you are a good bet to make a success of the business, based on:
- Your education
- Your work experience
- Your other experience.

If you have business partners, they should also complete this section. If your start-up is big enough to have managers employed (or key staff whose presence or absence will be critical to the business), you should consider getting them to complete this section too.

   If several people are included in this section, it may be best to summarise each person's details here and include the full information in an Appendix.

   Since most of the State agencies, the City/County Enterprise Boards, etc. are focused on job creation, it makes sense to tell them about the extent to which your business will contribute to job creation. Even though the agencies cannot grant aid part-time jobs, include them in your calculations anyway. And, where you are sub-contracting manufacturing or other aspects of your business, (even though again these are not grant-aided) include them also as "downstream" employment.

   See page 118.

Marketing and marketing strategy

A critical section that will be read carefully by any investor. Because readers are unlikely to be familiar with your market, you need to set the scene for them:
- An overview
- Key indicators
- Target groups/customers
- Competitors
- Your key competitive advantages
- Your marketing strategy
- Your distribution.

See page 119.

Production

Again, because your readers may have no experience of your market, you need to explain:
- Your product/service
- How it is made/delivered
- The experience you have with the process
- What equipment you need (this ties in with your financial projections later)

- How you will assure quality
- Where you will source supplies.

If there is too much detail, put it in an Appendix.
See page 123.

Financial

Most readers of business plans not only have a financial background, they are preparing to invest in your business. Therefore they pay special attention to your financial section.

Here, you set out your financial projections – profit and loss account and cash-flow. Whatever your own background, you need to be sufficiently sure of your financial projections to be able to withstand severe questioning. No one will invest or lend you money if you appear to be incapable of controlling it.
See page 125.

Funding proposal

This is the important bit – from your point of view. Here you lay out your stall. You have already explained what the business does, the market, the product, the financial projections. Now you are saying "I need €xxk, made up as follows. I have €xxk of my own. I have tied down €xxk more from these sources. I need €xxk, please".

Again, you need to be very sure of your calculations here. If some figures are loose – you think you need €10k but it could be as high as €12k for some item – say so. Don't get found out when you run out of money!
See page 127.

Detailed projections

Almost an Appendix, this is where the real number-crunching is put – out-of-the-way at the back. The critical part here are your assumptions. Expect to be quizzed on these when you make a presentation of your Business Plan to a City/County Enterprise Board or bank.
See page 129.

Almost finished

Your Business Plan is now almost finished – except that, just like your market research and testing of your product – you must test your Business Plan.

Perform the Reality Check in the panel. Then give it to a few trusted friends to read through. Ask them to pick holes in it. Don't be defensive. Use their comments to improve the plan.

A REALITY CHECK

You have finished your Business Plan. You are ready to submit it to your local City/County Enterprise Board or bank. Before you do, run these final checks:

Is the Executive Summary:
- Short? ☐
- Relevant? ☐
- To the point? ☐
- Interesting? ☐
- Packed with "Ooomph"? ☐

Check the entire Business Plan
(get help if you need it) for:
- **Spelling mistakes** – Use a spelling checker ☐
- **Grammatical mistakes** – Use a grammar checker (but be careful) ☐
- **Page numbering** – Are the pages all in order, with no gaps or duplication? ☐
- **Chapter/section numbering** – Are the chapters/sections all in order, with no gaps or duplication? ☐
- **Cross-references between sections/pages** – Are these correct? ☐
- **Logical structure** – Does the plan flow in a sensible order? ☐
- **Jargon/use of language** – Do you introduce concepts, explain jargon, demystify complicated things for the reader? ☐
- **Length** – Is it too long? Could you cut parts out, without damaging it? Could sections be moved into an Appendix? ☐
- **Type size/style** – Is it easy to read? Are headings clearly identifiable? ☐
- **Colour** – If you are using coloured type, does it help or does it distract? Keep it simple. ☐

I EXECUTIVE SUMMARY

Use this section to write a brief summary (no more than 1 page) of the whole Business Plan.

II INTRODUCTION AND BACKGROUND

Introduction
This Business plan is written to:
- ☐ Document strategy
- ☐ Act as a management tool in monitoring performance
- ☐ Raise € _____ k equity funding from _____
- ☐ Raise € _____ k grant aid from _____
- ☐ Other (specify):

Explain here the purpose of the Business Plan. Put it in your own words.

Background
Business name:

Address:

Telephone/Facsimile/E-mail:

Status:	☐ Sole trader	☐ Partnership	☐ Limited company
Registered for:	☐VAT	☐ PAYE/PRSI	☐ Corporation tax ☐ Income tax
Formed as:	☐ Purchase of existing business	☐ Purchase of franchise	
	☐Start-up	☐ Other (specify)	

Business in operation? Yes, started on _____

No, planned to start on _____

Product/service range

Product/service	*Description*	*Price*
A _____	_____	€ _____
B _____	_____	€ _____
C _____	_____	€ _____
D _____	_____	€ _____
E _____	_____	€ _____
F _____	_____	€ _____

Copy this from "Products and Production", page 53.

III   PROJECT OUTLINE

General description of proposed business

Mission statement

Copy this from "Developing a Mission Statement", page 28.

Trends in industry

Copy this from "Developing a Strategy", page 30.

Targets

Copy this from "Developing a Strategy", page 30.

IV   OWNERSHIP, MANAGEMENT AND EMPLOYMENT

Founders/Management
Name:
Address:

The first four sections must be completed for EACH founder or key manager. Use additional pages, if necessary.

Telephone/Facsimile/E-mail:
Date of birth:
Nationality:
Marital status:
Percentage shareholding:

Education

	Year(s)		School/course	Degree/certificate
From	_____	to _____	_____	☐ YES ☐ NO
From	_____	to _____	_____	☐ YES ☐ NO
From	_____	to _____	_____	☐ YES ☐ NO
From	_____	to _____	_____	☐ YES ☐ NO

Work Experience

	Year(s)		Organisation	Position
From	_____	to _____	_____	_____
From	_____	to _____	_____	_____
From	_____	to _____	_____	_____
From	_____	to _____	_____	_____
From	_____	to _____	_____	_____

Other Experience
Describe other significant experience that could be useful for your business

Employer and employees
Initially, how will your staffing be organised?

You alone, while holding another wage-earning position ☐
You alone, full-time ☐
You and your partner: Full-time ☐
You and your partner: Part-time ☐
You and your business partner(s) ☐
You and your business partner(s) with employees at a wage ☐

Copy this from section "Staff", page 55.

How many employees full-time? _____
How many employees part-time? _____

Have you drawn up clear job descriptions for your employees? ☐ YES ☐ NO
If yes, enclose job description(s) as an Appendix
Do you plan to expand your employee numbers quickly? ☐ YES ☐ NO
If yes, do you think you can attract enough qualified people? ☐ YES ☐ NO
Who will replace you during any required absences? _____

V MARKET AND MARKETING STRATEGY

Overview of the market

Describe the market in which you operate and the level of competition you face. Copy information from "Marketing", pages 36-48.

What are the leading indicators in your market sector?
- Average annual turnover per employee   _____
- Average annual turnover per m² of selling space   _____
- Average annual purchases per head of population   _____
- Extent of the service area per outlet   _____ m²
- Other

What's your estimate of the Irish market for your product/service? _____
What part of this market do you intend to service?   _____%
Have you contacted future customers?   ☐ YES ☐ NO
What was their reaction?

Have you obtained any forward orders?   ☐ YES ☐ NO
What comments did you receive with the forward orders?

If Yes, enclose copies as an Appendix.

The forward orders total approximately € _____ k

Market
Who are your target groups?

What do you have to offer them?

Competitors

Competitor	Description of product/service	Turnover	Employees
A _____	_____	€ _____	_____
B _____	_____	€ _____	_____
C _____	_____	€ _____	_____
D _____	_____	€ _____	_____
E _____	_____	€ _____	_____
F _____	_____	€ _____	_____

Competitors' strengths compared to your own.
(Use + where you think your business is better, = where they are the same, and – where you think your competitors have an advantage.)

Competitor	A	B	C	D	E	F
Broad Range	—	—	—	—	—	—
Guarantee	—	—	—	—	—	—
Quality	—	—	—	—	—	—
Price	—	—	—	—	—	—
Service	—	—	—	—	—	—
Delivery	—	—	—	—	—	—
Proximity	—	—	—	—	—	—
Other	—	—	—	—	—	—
	—	—	—	—	—	—

In what ways do your products/services differ from your competitors'?
(If you can, describe differences for each competitor)

A _____

B _____

C _____

D _____

E _____

F _____

Key competitive advantages

What extras do you offer compared to the competition?

A _____

_____

B _____

_____

C _____

_____

D _____

_____

E _____

_____

F _____

_____

Marketing strategy

How are you going to present your business?

o Layout
o Colours
o Music
o Atmosphere
o Correspondence
o Brochures
o Business cards
o Van signs
o Website

Rate those areas your customers are most interested in, and your relative strengths in those areas.

Buying Motive	Customer Importance			Your Relative Strength		
Broad Range	☐ High	☐ Medium	☐ Low	☐ Strong	☐ OK	☐ Weak
Guarantee	☐ High	☐ Medium	☐ Low	☐ Strong	☐ OK	☐ Weak
Quality	☐ High	☐ Medium	☐ Low	☐ Strong	☐ OK	☐ Weak
Price	☐ High	☐ Medium	☐ Low	☐ Strong	☐ OK	☐ Weak
Delivery	☐ High	☐ Medium	☐ Low	☐ Strong	☐ OK	☐ Weak
Service	☐ High	☐ Medium	☐ Low	☐ Strong	☐ OK	☐ Weak
Proximity	☐ High	☐ Medium	☐ Low	☐ Strong	☐ OK	☐ Weak
Other	☐ High	☐ Medium	☐ Low	☐ Strong	☐ OK	☐ Weak
	☐ High	☐ Medium	☐ Low	☐ Strong	☐ OK	☐ Weak

How are you going to approach your customers and what buying motives are you going to emphasise?

What marketing and promotion resources will you emphasise?

Resource	Emphasis				Cost
Brochures	☐ A lot	☐ A little	☐ Not at all	☐ Not yet	€ _____
Mailings	☐ A lot	☐ A little	☐ Not at all	☐ Not yet	€ _____
Advertisements	☐ A lot	☐ A little	☐ Not at all	☐ Not yet	€ _____
Sponsorship	☐ A lot	☐ A little	☐ Not at all	☐ Not yet	€ _____
Word-of-mouth	☐ A lot	☐ A little	☐ Not at all	☐ Not yet	€ _____
Personal selling	☐ A lot	☐ A little	☐ Not at all	☐ Not yet	€ _____
Notice boards	☐ A lot	☐ A little	☐ Not at all	☐ Not yet	€ _____
Public relations	☐ A lot	☐ A little	☐ Not at all	☐ Not yet	€ _____
Website	☐ A lot	☐ A little	☐ Not at all	☐ Not yet	€ _____
Other	☐ A lot	☐ A little	☐ Not at all	☐ Not yet	€ _____

Explain your promotion methods (how, where, frequency, why, etc.)

Distribution

How will your products/services be distributed?

Are product deliveries insured?   ☐ YES ☐ NO
If yes, for how much?   € _____ k

If your goods or services are supplied under standard terms of trade, summarise them here.

Enclose a copy of your full terms of trade with this plan, as an Appendix.

VI PRODUCTION

Copy this from page 53.

Products

Product/service	Description	Price
A _____	_____	€ _____
B _____	_____	€ _____
C _____	_____	€ _____
D _____	_____	€ _____
E _____	_____	€ _____
F _____	_____	€ _____

Describe your production process.

What experience do you have with this process?

Are you involved with (or will you be using) new techniques or new
products in your production processes?   ☐ YES ☐ NO
If yes, are you receiving assistance from experts?   ☐ YES ☐ NO
If yes, who are they and how are they engaged?

New capital expenditure required
What equipment are you using in the production process?

List the equipment you intend to lease, buy new, or buy used.

Description	New/Used?	If used, Age	Buy/Lease?	Cost
_____	☐ N ☐ U	___ years	☐ B ☐ L	€ _____
_____	☐ N ☐ U	___ years	☐ B ☐ L	€ _____
_____	☐ N ☐ U	___ years	☐ B ☐ L	€ _____
_____	☐ N ☐ U	___ years	☐ B ☐ L	€ _____
_____	☐ N ☐ U	___ years	☐ B ☐ L	€ _____
_____	☐ N ☐ U	___ years	☐ B ☐ L	€ _____
_____	☐ N ☐ U	___ years	☐ B ☐ L	€ _____
_____	☐ N ☐ U	___ years	☐ B ☐ L	€ _____
_____	☐ N ☐ U	___ years	☐ B ☐ L	€ _____
_____	☐ N ☐ U	___ years	☐ B ☐ L	€ _____
_____	☐ N ☐ U	___ years	☐ B ☐ L	€ _____

What guarantees do you have for this equipment in case of malfunction
(re-purchase, service contract, insurance)?

Does the available production equipment provide enough capacity
to achieve the revenue you have budgeted?   ☐ YES ☐ NO

Quality

Will your production process be accredited to a Quality Standard?

If yes, which?   ☐ Quality Mark   ☐ Hygiene Mark
                          ☐ ISO 9000/2000 ☐ ISO 14000
                          ☐ Other

Have you checked your products and production processes for environmental
considerations? (pollution, noise, undesirable waste products)   ☐ YES ☐ NO
If yes, are there any environmental objections?   ☐ YES ☐ NO
If yes, what are you planning to do about it?

Raw material sources

Have you contacted your future suppliers?   ☐ YES ☐ NO
If yes, what are their terms of trade? (Payment conditions, delivery times, etc.)

Are there alternative suppliers?   ☐ YES ☐ NO
If yes, list them

What advantages do these alternative suppliers offer you?

VII   FINANCIAL

Copy this from page 90.

Summary of projected performance
Profit and loss account

Revenue by product	Year 1	Year 2	Year 3
Cash sales			
A			
B			
C			
D			
E			
Credit sales			
A			
B			
C			
D			
E			
Total sales			
Deduct			
Opening stock			
Purchases			
Less Closing stock			
Cost of goods sold			
Gross profit			
Gross profit percentage	___ %	___ %	___ %

Overheads

	Year 1	Year 2	Year 3
Staff costs			
Production overheads			
Premises costs			
Transport costs			
Sales and promotion costs			
General expenses			
Finance costs			
Depreciation costs			
Total costs			
Net profit			
Less tax on profits			
Drawings			
Profit retained			

Copy this from page 130-131.

What effect will any shortfall in turnover have on your business and how do you plan to handle it?

What is your minimum required turnover?   € _____ k

Cash flow

	Year 1	Year 2	Year 3	
Opening bank balance	_____	_____	_____	Copy this from page 132.
Cash in				
Cash sales	_____	_____	_____	
Debtors	_____	_____	_____	
VAT refunds	_____	_____	_____	
Other income	_____	_____	_____	
Total income	_____	_____	_____	
Cash out				
Cash purchases	_____	_____	_____	
Creditors	_____	_____	_____	
Overheads:				
Staff	_____	_____	_____	
Production	_____	_____	_____	
Premises	_____	_____	_____	
Transport	_____	_____	_____	
Selling and promotion	_____	_____	_____	
General expenses	_____	_____	_____	
Finance costs	_____	_____	_____	
Loan repayments	_____	_____	_____	
Private drawings	_____	_____	_____	
Fixed assets	_____	_____	_____	
VAT payable/(due)	_____	_____	_____	
Other taxes	_____	_____	_____	
Other expenditure	_____	_____	_____	
Total expenditure	_____	_____	_____	
Net cash flow	_____	_____	_____	
Final bank balance	_____	_____	_____	

VIII FUNDING PROPOSAL

Funding requirements   Copy this from page 85.

                          Year 1

1. Fixed assets
Property   _____
Renovations   _____
Fixtures and fittings   _____
Transport   _____
Machines and equipment   _____
Goodwill, security deposits _____
Other   _____
Total fixed assets   _____

2. Current assets
Stock of raw material   _____
Stock of finished goods   _____
Work in progress   _____
Debtors   _____
Other   _____
Total current assets _____

3. Liquid assets
Cash   _____
Bank   _____
Other   _____
Total liquid assets   _____

4. Start-up costs
Prepaid expenses   _____
Promotion, opening   _____
Other   _____
Total start-up costs _____

*5. Margin for unforeseen
    costs*   _____

Total investment   _____

Proposed sources of funding

Personal assets available: €

Fixed assets _____ Copy this from page 85.

Car _____

Additional private mortgage _____

Savings _____

Deferred loans (family) _____

Other _____

Total personal assets _____

Introduced as:

Equity _____

Loans _____

External equity:

Source _____

Agreed?

☐ YES ☐ NO

External debt:

Long/medium-term finance

	Term	Amount	Agreed?
Mortgage on company building	_____ years	€ _____	☐ YES ☐ NO
Loans	_____ years	€ _____	☐ YES ☐ NO
Leasing (cars, machines, etc.)	_____ years	€ _____	☐ YES ☐ NO
Other	_____ years	€ _____	☐ YES ☐ NO
	_____ years	€ _____	☐ YES ☐ NO
Total long/medium term finance	_____		

Short-term finance

	Amount	Agreed?
Overdraft	€ _____	☐ YES ☐ NO
Suppliers' credit	€ _____	☐ YES ☐ NO
Payments received in advance	€ _____	☐ YES ☐ NO
Other	€ _____	☐ YES ☐ NO
	€ _____	☐ YES ☐ NO
Total short term/other finance	€ _____	

Subsidies/grants

	Amount	Agreed?
Agency	€ _____	☐ YES ☐ NO
Enterprise Board	€ _____	☐ YES ☐ NO
Other	€ _____	☐ YES ☐ NO
	€ _____	☐ YES ☐ NO
Total subsidies/grants	€ _____	

Total available finance € _____

Can you support the required investment in fixed assets with quotations from suppliers?   ☐ YES ☐ NO

In your estimates, did you take seasonal business influences into account, and calculate based on your maximum requirements?   ☐ YES ☐ NO

If Yes, enclose quotations as an Appendix.

How did you estimate your stock levels?

How did you estimate the value of your work-in-progress?

How did you estimate the value of your debtors?

Do you have sufficient liquid assets to cope with disappointments, delays and unexpected expenses?   ☐ YES ☐ NO

IX DETAILED PROJECTIONS

Assumptions

Copy this from page 90.

SCRIBBLE BOX

Analysis of Overheads

Copy this from page 89.

	Year 1	Year 2	Year 3
Staff costs			
Gross staff salaries	_____	_____	_____
Employer's PRSI	_____	_____	_____
Bonuses, etc	_____	_____	_____
Staff training costs	_____	_____	_____
Other staff costs	_____	_____	_____
Total staff costs	_____	_____	_____
Production overheads			
Use of auxiliary materials	_____	_____	_____
Maintenance	_____	_____	_____
Heat, light and power	_____	_____	_____
Rent/lease equipment	_____	_____	_____
Insurance equipment	_____	_____	_____
Other costs	_____	_____	_____
Total production costs	_____	_____	_____
Premises costs			
Rent	_____	_____	_____
Heat, light & power	_____	_____	_____
Insurance	_____	_____	_____
Cleaning	_____	_____	_____
Maintenance	_____	_____	_____
Equipment rent/lease	_____	_____	_____
Other costs	_____	_____	_____
Deduct: Rent received	€<___>	€<___>	€<___>
Total premises costs	_____	_____	_____
Transport costs			
Maintenance and repairs	_____	_____	_____
Lease costs	_____	_____	_____
Fuel	_____	_____	_____
Insurance	_____	_____	_____
Road Tax	_____	_____	_____
Public transport	_____	_____	_____
Air fares	_____	_____	_____
Deduct: Private use	€<___>	€<___>	€<___>
Total transport costs	_____	_____	_____

Analysis of Overheads

	Year 1	Year 2	Year 3
Sales and promotion costs			
Advertising			
Packaging			
Promotion			
Trade fairs			
Commissions			
Other costs			
Total sales & promotion			
General expenses			
Telephone			
Postage			
Subscriptions			
Insurance			
Stationery			
Computer supplies			
Office expenses			
Accountancy fees			
Legal & other fees			
Bad debts			
Profit/loss on sale of assets			
Other costs			
Total general expenses			
Finance costs			
Interest on loans/overdraft			
Mortgage interest			
Charges/fees			
Other			
Total finance costs			
Depreciation			
Property			
Fixtures and fittings			
Transport			
Machines and equipment			
Other			
Total depreciation			

SCRIBBLE BOX

SCRIBBLE BOX

Bring forward from pages 133-135.

Cash-flow

	Year 1	Year 2	Year 3
Opening bank balance			
Income			
Cash sales			
Debtors			
VAT refunds			
Other income			
Total income			
Expenditure			
Cash purchases			
Creditors			
Overheads:			
Staff			
Production			
Premises			
Transport			
Selling and promotion			
General expenses			
Finance costs			
Loan repayments			
Private drawings			
Fixed assets			
VAT payable/(due)			
Other taxes			
Other expenditure			
Total expenditure			
Net cash flow			
Final bank balance			

SCRIBBLE BOX

Cash-flow: Year 1

	M1 €	M2 €	M3 €	M4 €	M5 €	M6 €	M7 €	M8 €	M9 €	M10 €	M11 €	M12 €	Year 1 €	
Opening balance	—	—	—	—	—	—	—	—	—	—	—	—	—	
Income														
Cash sales	—	—	—	—	—	—	—	—	—	—	—	—	—	Copy
Debtors	—	—	—	—	—	—	—	—	—	—	—	—	—	this
VAT refunds	—	—	—	—	—	—	—	—	—	—	—	—	—	from
Other income	—	—	—	—	—	—	—	—	—	—	—	—	—	page
Total income	—	—	—	—	—	—	—	—	—	—	—	—	—	92.
Expenditure														
Cash purchases	—	—	—	—	—	—	—	—	—	—	—	—	—	
Creditors	—	—	—	—	—	—	—	—	—	—	—	—	—	
Overheads:														
Staff	—	—	—	—	—	—	—	—	—	—	—	—	—	
Production	—	—	—	—	—	—	—	—	—	—	—	—	—	
Premises	—	—	—	—	—	—	—	—	—	—	—	—	—	
Transport	—	—	—	—	—	—	—	—	—	—	—	—	—	
Selling/promotion	—	—	—	—	—	—	—	—	—	—	—	—	—	
General expenses	—	—	—	—	—	—	—	—	—	—	—	—	—	
Finance costs	—	—	—	—	—	—	—	—	—	—	—	—	—	
Loan repayments	—	—	—	—	—	—	—	—	—	—	—	—	—	
Private drawings	—	—	—	—	—	—	—	—	—	—	—	—	—	
Fixed assets	—	—	—	—	—	—	—	—	—	—	—	—	—	
VAT payable	—	—	—	—	—	—	—	—	—	—	—	—	—	
Other taxes	—	—	—	—	—	—	—	—	—	—	—	—	—	
Other expenses	—	—	—	—	—	—	—	—	—	—	—	—	—	
Total outgoings	—	—	—	—	—	—	—	—	—	—	—	—	—	Take
Net cash flow	—	—	—	—	—	—	—	—	—	—	—	—	—	Year 1 total to
Final balance	—	—	—	—	—	—	—	—	—	—	—	—	—	page 132.

SCRIBBLE BOX

Cash-flow: Year 2

	M1 €	M2 €	M3 €	M4 €	M5 €	M6 €	M7 €	M8 €	M9 €	M10 €	M11 €	M12 €	Year 2 €
Opening balance													
Income													
Cash sales													
Debtors													
VAT refunds													
Other income													
Total income													
Expenditure													
Cash purchases													
Creditors													
Overheads:													
Staff													
Production													
Premises													
Transport													
Selling/promotion													
General expenses													
Finance costs													
Loan repayments													
Private drawings													
Fixed assets													
VAT payable													
Other taxes													
Other expenses													
Total outgoings													
Net cash flow													
Final balance													

Copy this from page 93.

Take Year 2 total to page 132.

SCRIBBLE BOX

Cash-flow: Year 3

	M1 €	M2 €	M3 €	M4 €	M5 €	M6 €	M7 €	M8 €	M9 €	M10 €	M11 €	M12 €	Year 3 €
Opening balance													
Income													
Cash sales													
Debtors													
VAT refunds													
Other income													
Total income													
Expenditure													
Cash purchases													
Creditors													
Overheads:													
Staff													
Production													
Premises													
Transport													
Selling/promotion													
General expenses													
Finance costs													
Loan repayments													
Private drawings													
Fixed assets													
VAT payable													
Other taxes													
Other expenses													
Total outgoings													
Net cash flow													
Final balance													

Copy this from page 94.

Take Year 3 total to page 132.

SCRIBBLE BOX

OBJECTIVES

o Understand the importance of presentation

o Prepare to present your Business Plan

The minute you start talking about what you're going to do if you lose, you have lost.

GEORGE SCHULTZ

The Business Plan is your ticket to financing your business. It should communicate your ability to make your business a success. Therefore, when you are asked to make a presentation of your Business Plan, there are two critical aspects:

• The Business Plan itself
• You.

Of these, at this stage, the Business Plan is the least important. If you have worked through this guide to this point and put into practice its suggestions, your Business Plan should be an effective communication tool.

If you have been asked to make a presentation on it, you know that it has worked. It's now up to you!

You must show:
• Credibility
• Willingness to work and prepare
• Ability to sell
• A positive attitude
• Professionalism.

Remember, the people you are presenting to are asking themselves, "Should we be lending/investing our money with this person?"

Start with the Executive Summary from your Business Plan. Put a bullet-point for each paragraph on a PowerPoint slide. If it won't fit, it's arguably too long. If you can't make it shorter, break it up and put it on two slides.

Make your business idea real. Bring it to life. Show your product or a prototype. Demonstrate it. Show its features, particularly the ones that your market research has shown are important to customers. Explain why these are important. "Sell" the product to your listeners.

When you come to discuss the financial aspects of your Business Plan, make sure that you know every single figure, its origin, its calculation, the reason it is in the plan, the impact it has on other figures – all of this off by heart.

You must **BE** the business plan. If you cannot explain and defend its contents, it reflects badly on you as a potential business partner.

Preparing your presentation

Prepare your presentation carefully. This is no time for a few notes scribbled out on a scrap of paper. Write out what you want to say.

Anticipate questions that you might be asked. Try and build the answers into your presentation, so that you have answered them before they can be asked.

Rehearse your presentation in front of family and friends. Ask them to be critical and to shoot as many holes in the plan as they can. Build their reactions into your presentation. And practise, practise, practise.

On the day, make sure you are at the appointed venue in plenty of time – not too early and definitely not late.

Try to find out in advance who you will be meeting. Ask around to find out what their preferences are – use this information in your presentation.

If you can, see the room a day or so before the presentation and check (and double-check) that any equipment you need, like overhead projectors, etc., will be available. If you are using your own technology, check, double and triple-check that it works – and bring a back-up with you anyway.

And then relax. It's your business. You know more about it than any investor, Enterprise Board officer or banker will ever learn. You are a self-confident, capable, well-organised entrepreneur with a good Business Plan. Go for it!

PITCHING YOUR PLAN TO INVESTORS

Pitching to investors should now be part of the skillset of every ambitious entrepreneur, since at this level of financing it has almost superseded the business plan as a tool used to communicate the business proposition. Pitching to investors is about understanding what investors need to know about you and your venture and shaping that into a compelling story.

Follow the 30-1-10-20 rule:

• **30 seconds (think "YouTube"):** Start by developing a very short story (30 seconds or so - longer, if you can keep it interesting) about your business.

What (big) problem do you solve? What solution are you offering and what is the magic behind that solution? Record your pitch.

- **One sentence (think "Twitter"):** Now explain the magic of your business in one tweet.
- **10-slide presentation (think "Dragons' Den"):** 1. Title; 2. Problem; 3. Solution; 4. Competitive position (real analysis); 5. Team (industry knowledge, track record, expertise); 6. Business strategy (your plan to grow beyond launch); 7. Financial projections; 8. Funding sought (amount, use); 9. Milestones (product launch, next funding, breakeven, etc); 10. Exit strategy (IPO, acquisition, who?/when?).
- **20 minutes:** Make sure your presentation is less than 20 minutes in duration.

The presentation itself:

- **'Tell them what you are going to tell them' opening:** On the 1.Title slide, show them where you are going to take them - the agenda. Number the key elements so subsequent slides reinforce the elements in turn.
- **Put forward a clear, simple case:** On the 2. Problem slide, show the simple ABC situation/gap analysis: A = Today (the current market situation); B = Tomorrow (the place where the market should be/the big opportunity); C = Gap (what's missing to get there/the special play you have to fill the gap)
- **Tell them why your play is better than everyone else's:** On the 3. Solution slide, set out your clear market positioning - 'We have the only X product that solves Y customers' problem in Z unique way and we can back this up with ... (team's track record, customer traction, real competitive analysis, etc)', where X = Product category (the specific product type market for your business), Y = Target buyer (the person who actually writes the cheque) and Z = Differentiation (advantage or positive distinction over the competition). And remember, proofs are better than 'claims'
- **Go with the best foot first:** Adapt your pitch and how you tell it to the stage of your company's development. Always put the strongest case elements first.

For example, at seed financing, relatively small amounts of capital are made available to support the entrepreneur's exploration of an idea or product concept.

Pitch first about initial market validation (quotes from prospects in target industry), then about the product specification, the team (such as it is) and then the other slides. If you are at start-up financing stage, you should have a clear competitive advantage and a prototype. Pitch first about initial customer traction (some demonstration of willingness to try and pay for the product), then the best real numbers you have, the product specification, the team and then the other slides. At first-stage financing, your venture normally is not yet profitable, but there is an established organisation, a working product and preferably some revenues. Capital is required primarily for the company's first major marketing efforts, to hire sales and support personnel in anticipation of higher sales volumes. Pitch first about the momentum of the business (the progress made, milestones achieved), then show the sales numbers and the trends, then the product specifications, the team and then the other slides.

Some other guidelines for pitching:

- Wrap up, recap and go for the close. Tell them again in summation what your pitch story was and deliver your prepared, thought-out, aggressive enough 'ask'
- Handle questions competently
- Always show progress as a team, product and with customers.
- Understand the management, market, financial, technological and operational risks to your venture and the industry it will compete in - investors will ask.
- Know the 10 companies across the different verticals who will want to acquire your venture and why - investors will ask.
- Keep the business model specific, simple and non-aggressive. It shouldn't be a total innovation.
- Understand that the deal must make lots of money for the investor - multiples of 5 to 10 x initial capital to be earned in an exit 5 to 8 years down the line.

OBJECTIVES

o Appreciate balance in life

Don't hurry, don't worry.
You're only here for a short visit.
So be sure to stop and smell the flowers.

WALTER HAGEN

TWELVE THINGS TO REMEMBER

1. The value of time.
2. The success of perseverance.
3. The pleasure of working.
4. The dignity of simplicity.
5. The worth of character.
6. The power of kindness.
7. The influence of example.
8. The obligation of duty.
9. The wisdom of economy.
10. The virtue of patience.
11. The improvement of talent.
12. The joy of origination.

MARSHALL FIELD

Starting and running your own business is all-consuming. Everything falls back on you. And you are doing it for yourself – so there is a temptation to do too much.

Certainly, it is hard (and may even be damaging to your business) to turn down work but, at some point, you need to take time out to decide what is really important to you, what you are achieving at present and what you need to do about it. This is where time management comes in.

Time management

An average working week for an entrepreneur is between 70 and 80 hours. As well as handling all aspects of the business – book-keeping, selling, clients, networking, etc. – you also must know how to handle your time and how to maintain your entrepreneurial drive.

You, the entrepreneur, are the most important success factor in the business. It is vital that this success factor is maintained. An entrepreneur needs to know when to peak and when to rest and take it easy. It is impossible to go full throttle all the time.

Go back to the first chapter, **READY**, and ask yourself how much time you are willing to spend on the business. Discuss it with your partner/spouse.

Go back to your assessment of your strong and weak points. Then go back to your market research and your identification of the critical success factors for your business.

Next, decide whether you are a morning person or an evening person. When do you function best? Whenever it is, aim to do your best work then. Start late and keep your heavy thinking till late at night if that suits – or start at six in the morning and knock off at four in the afternoon.

As an entrepreneur, you can choose your hours. Choose them to make the most of yourself.

Now some tips for managing your time:

- Make a daily "To Do list"
- Learn to say "NO"
- Protect yourself, take time off regularly
- A healthy mind in a healthy body
- Never handle documents more than once (no paper shuffling, deal with it and get it off your desk)
- Keep things simple
- Do the things you hate first
- Manage your stress levels (meditate, exercise)
- Delegate
- To handle paperwork – **TRAF**: Toss, Refer, Act or File – only do one, and only once!

Make time for yourself

However pressured your business, you need to take some time out to unwind – to "smell the flowers". Without it, you will burn out. Add time to your diary – every day, every week, every month – for yourself. Cut yourself free from the business and the other demands on your life. Allow your batteries to recharge – and you will come back to the business better able to make it succeed.

In the earlier chapters in this guide, you:
- Assessed your own suitability (and that of your business partners) for business and decided to proceed to the next stage
- Considered all the many factors that impact on the success of a start-up – from a mission statement and strategy, through marketing, finance and budgeting – and took these into account in developing your business plan.

This chapter of the workbook takes you onwards from the business plan, into the detail of starting and running your new business.

It starts with sample documents, designed to save you time and difficulty, including:
- Sample accounts pages
- Sample Job Application - adapt this as necessary
- Sample Job Description - adapt this as necessary
- Sample Employment Contract - where necessary, take professional HR or legal advice on any changes needed to this sample contract to adapt it to the circumstances of your business
- Sample Safety Statement - again, where necessary, take professional advice on adapting this sample statement to the circumstances of your own business
- Sample Advertising Control Sheet - use this to measure and monitor the effectiveness of your advertising / promotion activities.

Download these documents at **www.startingabusinessinireland.com**.

The chapter then covers topics whose importance only becomes apparent once a business is up and running. They have been touched upon in the STEADY chapter, but here they are considered in a little more detail.

However, most could fill a book on their own and so further research and reading is recommended, depending on your own specific circumstances.

Unlike the other chapters, there are no Key Questions here – just a genuine wish to see you succeed. Keep going!

OBJECTIVES
o To assist in establishing a business by providing sample documents
o Understand core topics relevant to the continued success and development of a business

The accounts pages shown opposite are based on the discussion in "Accounting" in the previous chapter, **STEADY**. This section explains how to use them.

Purchases on credit

This page records all the goods and services that you buy on credit and will have to pay for later.

The core information you are recording is:
* The date – in the first column
* The type of transaction – on the top of the page (Purchases on credit)
* The other person involved – the supplier, in the second column
* The amount involved – in the third column, headed up "Total".

Next, if your business is registered for VAT, you need to analyse the Total amount for VAT purposes – between the VAT itself and the "net" amount. (If your business is not registered for VAT, ignore the fourth and fifth – VAT and Net – columns).

Last, you need to analyse your purchases across the overhead categories defined earlier. This analysis will help you manage your business better by showing how your money is being spent. Write the net amount of the transaction in one of the remaining columns – Staff, Production, Premises, Transport, Selling, General, Finance or Other – according to where it belongs.

At the end of each week, or month, depending on the number of transactions, total the page and start a new one.

Sales on credit

Sales on credit accounts for all sales which you invoice and have to wait to get paid for. You complete the page in much the same way as the Purchases on credit page.

Write the date in the first column, and the customer in the second. The total amount of the transaction goes in the third, with a breakdown between VAT and "net" in the next two columns.

Then analyse your sales on credit across product categories to suit your information needs. Any unusual sales can go in the "Other" column.

Total the page at the end of the month and start a new one.

Receipts

It is critically important that you account for all cash coming into the business. You do this by writing all incoming cash transactions in a Receipts page. For one, the taxman will want this information and you need it anyway to protect yourself from loss.

Again, similar information is required. The date and name of the other party involved, the total amount, split between VAT and "net" where it is a new transaction (not if it has been accounted for earlier, as happens when you receive payment for sales on credit).

It is useful to know the breakdown of where cash comes from:
* Are your debtors building up or paying on time?
* How much of your business is from cash sales?
* What other sources of cash have you? Record these in the appropriate columns.

Total the page at the end of the week or month and start a new one.

Payments

Just as it is important to record cash coming in, it's also important to record cash paid out. The Payments page helps here.

Again, date and the other party to the transaction, as well as the amount, are essential information. Again, also only account for VAT on new transactions. In some cases here, you will be paying for purchases made earlier on credit – record these in the "Suppliers" column. Other purchases made for cash should be analysed into the appropriate category.

Petty Cash

This is like the Payments page but on a smaller scale of spending. It should be totalled and checked every week, so that money does not go astray. You also should have receipts for all petty cash expenditure – set this as a habit from the very start.

Bank balance book

The operation of this page is explained in the previous chapter, **page 72**.

Summary

These are very simple "books", which give you the absolute basics of information that you need to control your business.

Talk to your own accountant about the specific needs of your business but always keep in mind that book-keeping is a means (to information for management purposes) not an end in itself.

Accounts pages: Purchases on Credit

Date	Supplier	Total	VAT	Net	Staff	Production	Premises	Transport	Selling	General	Financial	Other
TOTAL												

Accounts pages: Sales on Credit

Date	Customer	Total	VAT	Net	Staff	Product A	Product B	Product C	...	Service Y	Service Z	Other
TOTAL												

Accounts pages: Receipts

Date	Received from	Total	VAT	Net	Staff	Debtors	Cash Sales	Loans	Other
TOTAL									

Accounts pages: Payments

Date	Paid to	Total	VAT	Net	Suppliers	Staff	Production	Premises	Transport	Selling	General	Other
TOTAL												

Accounts pages: Petty Cash

Date	Paid to	Total	VAT	Net	Postage	Stationery	Office Expenses	Transport	Other
TOTAL									

Accounts pages: Bank Balance Book

Date	Transaction	IN	OUT	Balance
TOTAL				

JOB APPLICATION FORM

POSITION

_____

NAME (Mr/Mrs/Miss/Ms)   _____
ADDRESS   _____
                                   _____
                                   _____
TELEPHONE / EMAIL   _____
DATE OF BIRTH   _____
STATUS   [] Single   [] Married   [] Divorced   [] Separated   [] Widowed
CHILDREN (Number/Ages)   _____
HEALTH (Illnesses/Disabilities) _____
                                   _____

EDUCATION

Year(s)		School/course	Degree/certificate
From _____ to _____		_____	o Yes o No
From _____ to _____		_____	o Yes o No
From _____ to _____		_____	o Yes o No
From _____ to _____		_____	o Yes o No

WORK EXPERIENCE

Year(s)		Organisation	Position
From _____ to _____		_____	_____
From _____ to _____		_____	_____
From _____ to _____		_____	_____
From _____ to _____		_____	_____
From _____ to _____		_____	_____

OTHER EXPERIENCE
Describe other significant experience that could be useful in this position

_____
_____
_____

HOBBIES/INTERESTS

_____
_____
_____

OTHER INFORMATION

_____
_____
_____
_____

I wish to apply for the position of _____ .
I declare the information above to be correct to the best of my knowledge and belief.

Signed _____   Date _____

JOB DESCRIPTION

POSITION _____

NAME _____

DATE APPOINTED _____

REPORTING TO _____

SUBORDINATES _____

_____

_____

CORE RESPONSIBILITY

_____

_____

_____

KEY TASKS
Daily _____

_____

Weekly _____

_____

Monthly _____

_____

Yearly _____

_____

TARGETS

_____

_____

_____

EMPLOYMENT CONTRACT

(Name)   **Company Letterhead**
(Address)
(Date)

Dear

The following are the terms and conditions of your employment, which I am required to give you. Should you require clarification on any point, please feel free to ask me.

Position

You will be employed primarily as (POSITION), commencing on (DATE). A job specification for the position is attached. You will be required to be flexible in this position and to undertake such other work as may be assigned to you by the company from time to time, outside the area of your normal duties. This work may be for such subsidiary or associate companies of the company as the company may require.

Hours of work

Your normal working week will be _____ days, ___day to _____day. Your normal working hours will be ___ am to _____ pm on those days, with _____ hour for lunch. Your position may require you to work in excess of these hours from time to time, especially when deadlines have to be met.

Remuneration

You will be paid monthly in arrears by credit transfer. Your salary at commencement will be €_____ pa and will be reviewed on (DATE). There is no payment for overtime. If additional responsibilities or working hours in excess of normal working hours become part of your regular work, your salary may be reviewed before the review date above.

Annual leave

The company's holiday year runs from 1 January to 31 December. Your annual holiday entitlement will be 20 working days and shall be given in accordance with the Organisation of Working Time Act, 1997. Your entitlement in 20__ will be _____ days. Holiday dates must be agreed in advance with the Managing Director and are subject to management discretion. Public holidays shall also be given in accordance with the Organisation of Working Time Act, 1997.

Maternity Leave (female staff only)

You have a statutory entitlement to Maternity Leave and Maternity Benefit as provided for under the **Maternity Protection Acts** and the Social Welfare Acts. You are also entitled to have your existing job, or a suitable alternative, held open for you pending your return to work following maternity leave, which is calculated as **four weeks before the expected date of the birth of your child and 22 weeks** following that date. To ensure your entitlement, you must:

* Provide a letter from your doctor, certifying that you are pregnant and the expected date of birth of your child
* Write a letter to the Managing Director, stating that you are pregnant, advising the dates you intend to be absent on maternity leave and stating whether you intend to return to work following your maternity leave.

Maternity Benefit is paid by the Department of Social, Community and Family Affairs on a weekly basis throughout your maternity leave. The amount paid is not taxable, and is based on your earnings in the previous tax year. The maximum benefit payable is currently € _____ per week. In addition, you have a statutory entitlement to **an additional 16 weeks' unpaid leave immediately following the end of your statutory maternity leave.** No benefit is payable by the Department of Social & Family Affairs during these weeks which must be taken entirely at your own expense. You must advise the Managing Director of your intention to take this unpaid leave at least four weeks before the end of your statutory maternity leave.

Sick Pay

If you are sick and unable to attend at work, you must notify the Managing Director or another senior member of staff before 10 am on the first day of non-attendance, to advise of your absence and to state how long you expect to be absent. Medical certificates must be provided to the Managing Director for absences of more than two days.

The company will pay you your normal salary, less PAYE and PRSI, for up to ____ weeks' sick leave in any calendar year. You must claim Social Welfare benefits, where applicable, during such sick leave and must pay any such benefits received to the company immediately on receipt. The company reserves the right to reduce the period of paid sick leave or withdraw the scheme at any time.

Retirement

Normal retirement age is ___. A pension/No pension is payable at retirement.

Grievances

If you have a grievance in relation to any aspect of your employment, you have a right to a hearing by your immediate superior. If you are unhappy with the outcome of that hearing, you may appeal to the Managing Director. You may be accompanied by a fellow employee at this appeal meeting. Where the circumstances warrant it, you may refer your grievance directly to the Managing Director. If the matter cannot be resolved within the company, it shall be referred through procedures, which shall include, as appropriate, reference to a Rights Commissioner, the Labour Relations Commission, the Labour Court, the Employment Appeals Tribunal or the Equality Officer.

Notice of Termination

Except in circumstances justifying immediate termination of your employment by the company, you are entitled to receive ____ month's notice of termination of your employment. The company reserves the right to pay you ____ month's salary in lieu of notice. Your employment may be terminated without notice for serious misconduct or unreasonable failure to carry out such duties as may be assigned to you from time to time.

You must give the company ____ month's notice of your intention to terminate your employment. The company reserves the right to pay you ____ month's salary in lieu of this period of notice.

Dismissal

The company hopes that it will not be necessary to dismiss you. However, you may be dismissed for: Incompetence or poor work performance, serious or persistent misconduct, incapacity, failure to carry out reasonable instructions, redundancy, or some other substantial reason. The following procedures will be carried out before a decision to dismiss you from the company's employment is taken:

- A full investigation will be carried out by the company. You may be suspended, with or without pay at the company's discretion, during this investigation
- You will be informed of the reasons for the proposed dismissal
- You will have a right to state your case and may be accompanied by a fellow employee at any meeting that you are asked to attend concerning your proposed dismissal.

If you wish to challenge your dismissal, it shall be referred in accordance with normal procedures to a Rights Commissioner, the Labour Court, the Labour Relations Commission or the Employment Appeals Tribunal, as appropriate.

Health and safety

The company is committed to fulfilling its obligations under applicable health and safety legislation and has prepared a Safety Statement. It is a condition of your employment that you sign the Health and Safety Statement and abide by its requirements.

On behalf of (BUSINESS NAME), I wish you well in your employment. Please sign one copy of this letter to indicate your acceptance of the terms and conditions of your employment and return it to me as soon as possible.

Signed _____ Managing Director

I accept and agree to be bound by the above terms and conditions of employment.

Signed _____ (EMPLOYEE)

SAFETY STATEMENT

BUSINESS NAME: _____

ADDRESS: _____

_____

_____

_____

BUSINESS ACTIVITY:

_____

_____

_____

NAME/TEL NO of:

Doctor: ` _____

Hospital: _____

Ambulance: _____

Fire: _____

Garda: _____

Safety Rep: _____

First Aider: _____

HSA: _____

"This Safety Statement is aimed at protecting our employees from workplace accidents and ill-health at work. It is our programme in writing to manage health and safety. We provide protective equipment, guards, etc., as well as information, training and supervision necessary to protect our employees. The Safety Statement is available to our employees, outside contractors and inspectors of the Health and Safety Authority. We will update it as necessary and it will be reviewed at least once a year."

Signed: _____ **Date:** _____
(Proprietor/Manager)

Deputy: _____

CHECKLIST OF HAZARDS AND RELATED ISSUES

Is your workplace safe, clean and tidy?

Are your work systems safe?

Is your equipment and machinery safe (guarded if necessary and maintained regularly)?

Are machinery and equipment suppliers' instructions followed?

Is portable equipment (such as ladders, welders, electrical tools, etc) properly maintained?

Are boilers, air receivers, lifts and cranes examined and maintained?

Can manual lifting, pushing, pulling or dragging of heavy weights be avoided?

Is care taken with chemicals? Remember to read the labels and chemical safety sheets.

Are there health hazards – processes giving rise to dust or fumes?

Have you made arrangements for emergencies and fire-fighting? Are escape routes clear?

Is there safe means of access to heights?

Are goods safely stacked?

Is there training, consultation, information and supervision of employees in health and safety?

Are records kept of safety training?

Is ventilation adequate?

Is personal protective equipment provided and used?

Do your VDUs comply with safety standards?

Are First Aid provisions adequate?

Is there any history of accidents/ill-health in the business?

Are accidents reported to the Health and Safety Authority?

Are there any other hazards in the workplace?

Are employees adhering to all remedial steps to avoid injury?

Are the welfare facilities (toilets/washing/eating/drink) adequate?

Are employees and outside contractors aware of this Safety Statement?

Have you displayed your Health and Safety poster?

Reproduced by permission of the Health and Safety Authority

ADVERTISING CONTROL SHEET

ADVERTISING OBJECTIVE:

Media selected	Ad	Timing	Responsibility Whose?	Budget cost	Actual cost	Criteria	Evaluation

It goes without saying that your product is top quality.
HARRY CROSBIE, on developing a brand

Quality is no longer a competitive advantage.
It is a minimum entry requirement in any market.
BRIAN TRACY

Quality is in – big time! Quality has always been important as a means of differentiating products and delivering higher value-added but there is no escaping the current management focus on quality as a means of achieving higher profits through customer satisfaction.

What is quality?

Quality is an attitude of mind that results in everyone in a business working together towards:

- Eliminating (or minimising) errors and faults
- Meeting deadlines
- Mapping out clear lines of responsibility
- Continuous improvement.

Think about what quality means to you. What does it mean for your customer? What does it mean for your product/ service? Write your answers in the space below.

Quality systems

Quality systems help ensure that quality is delivered every time.

Quality certification provides independent assurance that the quality systems meet approved standards. Surveys show that quality assurance marks/logos give customers valued guidance when buying products and services and influence their decision to buy at point of sale. However, too few companies trading in Ireland have either the Q-Mark or ISO 9000 certification.

Quality standards

The key quality standards in Ireland are:

- **The Q-Mark** – Excellence Ireland Quality Association's most successful programme to date and one of the most coveted brands on the Irish market. The Q-Mark is regarded as the national symbol of quality and is essentially a framework through which a business can continually improve
- **Hygiene Mark Certification**
- **The Triple Hygiene Mark**
- **ISO 9000** – The Quality Standard, the most successful international standard ever produced and currently in use in over 70 countries world-wide
- **ISO 14000** – The Environmental Standard.

The Q-Mark

The Quality Systems Q-Mark is a systems and processes framework used to help continuously improve the practices that underpin the way an organisation operates. As well as giving internal confidence to organisations, enabling them to consistently deliver good product/s and/or services, the Q-Mark also enhances the organisation and its products as a brand, thus sustaining customer confidence.

The granting of the Q-mark is based on a two-fold asessment of an organisation's quality system. First, the

What does quality mean to you?

What does it mean for your customer?

What does it mean for your product/service?

business completes a questionnaire from Excellence Ireland Quality Association (EIQA), which evaluates the quality system. This is followed by an in-depth, interactive, on-site audit of the system. The business is audited annually to ensure that its operations and systems are being improved upon.

The Q-Mark is only given to organisations that demonstrate to EIQA's independent auditors that their standards of quality management are rigorous and consistent. Benefits include:
- Increased management control through service delivery system
- A constructive audit
- Public recognition through display of the Q-Mark logo
- Motivational impact on employees
- Deepened understanding of customer needs and requirements
- Independent feedback to assist the organisation's development.

The Hygiene Mark

The Hygiene Mark is awarded to those organisations that have successfully completed an audit against the requirements of the EIQA Hygiene and Food Safety Programme Technical Standard.

The EIQA Hygiene and Food Safety Programme provides a framework for ensuring that organisations are meeting and exceeding legal requirements for food safety management whilst also providing guidance on continuous improvement and best practice. The Hygiene and Food Safety Programme encompasses emerging standards, codes and legal requirements in hygiene and food safety, both in Ireland and internationally.

ISO 9000

ISO 9001: 2008 is a strategic management tool, facilitating effective control over design, manufacturing and service delivery processes. Applying an ISO 9001 system for Quality Management within an organisation can result in significant benefits, including:
- Management effectiveness: Through structured, organised and defined authorities, responsibilities and reporting structures
- Operating efficiency: Through clearly documented practices and procedures
- Cost reduction: Through the identification and elimination of potential system deficiencies and product failures
- Increased marketability: Through the identification of a registered company with a quality philosophy and international standard
- Customer satisfaction: Through the receipt of enhanced service or product quality levels.

As ISO 9001 is a harmonised European and international standard, certification to the standard opens up international markets to companies where previously technical trade barriers may have been a major impediment.

ISO 9001 requires an organisation to implement a documented quality management system addressing all organisational activities from the definition of its quality policy and objectives to the detailing of various methodologies and controls applicable to its service delivery or product manufacturing processes. This takes the form of a Quality Manual, supported by procedures manuals, work instructions, etc. defining:
- The processes in the organisation
- The inter-relationship between the process and the customer / stakeholder
- The criteria by which the effectiveness of each process can be judged
- The activities within each process (What, Who, When and How)
- The methodologies for process improvement processes and corrective action

The business' Quality Manual is assessed to ensure that it adequately and completely conforms to the requirements of the relevant standard. The assessment is conducted on the applicant's premises by an experienced team of assessors. On approval, the business is awarded 'Registered Firm' status and can use the mark on advertising material, letterheads and for other promotional purposes. Once registered, on-going inspections ensure that quality standards are maintained.

ISO 14000

ISO 14001:2004 is a standard for the management of the environment and a business' relationship with it. It is applicable to processes of any size and is ideal for managing more complex activities within a regulatory framework (such as IPPC licensing).

As explained in "Developing a Mission Statement" in the STEADY chapter, customers increasingly expect companies to be concerned about their impact on the environment, both socially and physically. At the same time, EU regulations on environmental issues are becoming stricter.

Businesses tend to react in three ways:

- **Do nothing** – Wait to be pushed into complying with emerging regulations
- **Act now** – Identify potential environmental hazards and take steps to eliminate them. Use this as a "competitive edge"
- **Identify new businesses** that will be created by these trends and get in first.

Areas to consider include:

- Materials used, both in manufacture and packaging (toxic, recyclable, replaceable)
- Machines used
- Odour
- Noise
- Risks (health, fire, etc.)
- Waste.

In the meantime, control over the impact of your activities on the environment is an important part of the management of your business. There are, of course, legal requirements in this area, but more than that, good environmental management can lead to cost savings, enhanced customer relations and a positive product image. If you are interested in exporting your product, you will find that compliance with an environmental management standard is invaluable, especially when dealing with other European businesses.

And, more generally, businesses should be looking at their carbon footprint - customers increasingly are doing so when selecting suppliers.

Environmental Protection Agency

The Environmental Protection Agency was established under the Environmental Protection Agency Act, 1992. The Agency has a wide range of statutory duties and powers. Its main responsibilities include:

- The licensing and regulation of large/complex industrial and other processes with significant polluting potential, on the basis of integrated pollution control (IPC) and the application of best available technologies for this purpose
- The monitoring of environmental quality, including the establishment of databases to which the public will have access, and the publication of periodic reports on the state of the environment
- Advising public authorities in respect of environmental functions and assisting local authorities in the performance of their environmental protection functions
- The promotion of environmentally sound practices through, for example, the encouragement of the use of environmental audits, the setting of environmental quality objectives and the issuing of codes of practice on matters affecting the environment
- The promotion and co-ordination of environmental research
- The licensing and regulation of all significant waste recovery activities, including landfills and the preparation and updating periodically of a national hazardous waste plan for implementation by other bodies
- Generally overseeing the performance by local authorities of their statutory environmental protection functions.

Environmental Management Systems

An environmental management system can take many forms:

- **IS EN ISO 14001** – Published by the NSAI
- **ISO 14000** – See "Quality Certification"
- **Self-audited systems** – Such as that outlined in *A guide to environmental self-auditing* published by the Chambers of Commerce in Ireland
- **EU Eco-Management & Audit Scheme.**

HEALTH AND SAFETY

Health and safety in the workplace has become a major issue in industry in recent years, driven largely by EU regulations and by an increasing awareness of employers' social responsibilities. Put simply, an employer is responsible in so far as is reasonably practicable for the safety, health and welfare of his/her employees. Employees also have a duty to ensure their own health and safety as well as that of other staff and others in the workplace.

Safety, Health & Welfare at Work Act, 2005

This updated Act applies to all places of work, regardless of size or activity, all employers and self-employed persons, manufacturers, suppliers and importers.

Under the Act, an employer must:

- Consult with employees on health and safety issues and allow employees to select a Safety Representative to represent them in these discussions
- Prepare a Safety Statement, which outlines the hazards identified in the place of work and details how they are controlled in order to safeguard the health and safety of employees
- Ensure that working practices and procedures, means of access and exit, and articles or substances used at the workplace or provided for use at work are safe and not dangerous to employees' health. This duty extends beyond the company's own employees to include employees of other businesses who happen to be in the workplace
- Test plant, equipment or materials he/she manufactures, designs, imports or supplies and give adequate information on associated hazards.

Other legislation

Where the 2005 Act forms the skeleton, the detail is provided by the Safety, Health and Welfare at Work (General Application) Regulations, 2006 and other industry-specific legislation.

Areas covered include:

- Risk assessment
- Design of the workplace
- Use of work equipment
- Manual handling methods
- Use of visual display units
- Electricity
- Protective equipment
- The availability of first aid
- Notification of accidents and dangerous occurrences.

Specific legislation covers hazards such as noise, chemicals and certain named substances, asbestos, lead, infection, and biological risks, safety signs and conditions for pregnant employees, etc.

The Health & Safety Authority has a range of publications that provide guidance on the Act and subsequent regulations, though industry-specific legislation is outside its remit.

The Health & Safety Authority

The Health and Safety Authority (HSA) is the national body in Ireland with responsibility for securing health and safety at work, in every type of workplace and every kind of work in the public and private sectors.

Its functions include:

- Providing advice and information
- Promoting safety
- Undertaking research
- Enforcing health and safety laws generally.

HSA inspectors may visit any workplace at any time to inspect documents, books, registers, and the physical environment. A range of enforcement mechanisms may be used, such as improvement directions, plans and notices and prohibition notices.

OBJECTIVES

o Understand the law relating to health & safety
o Understand the application of health & safety in the workplace

OBJECTIVES

o Understand the different types of intellectual property
o Be aware of application/ registration procedures

Inventors are warned that it is unwise to make any public disclosure of an invention or to put it into use publicly before an application for a patent has been made, as such action may prejudice the obtaining of a valid patent.
THE PATENTS OFFICE

Patents

A patent is an exclusive right given by the State and enforceable in the Courts. It gives the "patentee" a monopoly to make, use and sell the invention for a fixed period of time and the right to stop others manufacturing, using or selling the patented invention during that period unless they have obtained the patent owner's authorisation to do so. In return for this monopoly, the patentee pays fees to cover the costs of processing the patent application and granting the patent. Annual renewal fees are also paid in order to keep the patent in force. A patent can last for 10 years (short term) or 20 years. A patent granted in Ireland gives no rights in other countries.

To be eligible for the grant of a valid patent, an invention must be:
• New
• Involve an inventive step
• Capable of industrial application.

Not all inventions qualify for the grant of a patent. The Patents Act 1992 specifically excludes:
• A discovery, scientific theory or a mathematical method
• An aesthetic creation
• A scheme rule or method for performing a mental act, playing a game or doing business or a programme for a computer
• The presentation of information
• Methods of treatment of the human or animal body by surgery or therapy
• Plant and animal varieties or essentially biological processes for their production
• Inventions which are contrary to public order or morality.

An example of a well-known patented invention is the "widget" at the bottom of a Guinness can which promotes froth on canned beer similar to that of draught beer.

European Patents

The European Convention (EPC) came into force in 1977 and established the European Patent Office (EPO). A European patent application can be filed either with the Irish Patents Office or directly with the Hague Branch of the EPO and the applicant can choose to designate any of the 18 contracting states including Ireland. When granted, a European patent has the effect of a national patent in each of the countries designated. Therefore, an applicant may find it considerably cheaper to lodge a single patent application to the EPO, designating a number of contracting states, as opposed to lodging individual patent applications with each of the countries.

Patent Co-operation Treaty (PCT)

The Patent Co-operation Treaty (PCT) came into effect in 1978. Its main aim is to streamline patent application filing and novelty search procedures for applicants wishing to obtain patent protection in a wide number of countries around the world. The PCT provides a system whereby a single international application in one of the contracting states allows for the designation of up to 80 other countries in which one wishes to have patent protection. The applicant designates those in which a patent is desired and eventually the relevant national authority may grant a patent. The Patents Office acts as a receiving office for PCT applications.

Trade Marks

Once a business has a product to sell, it needs something which distinguishes its goods and services from those of competitors. A trade mark is a sign which is capable of being represented graphically (in words or pictures written down) and which is capable of distinguishing the goods or services of one business from those of other businesses. It may consist of words (including personal names), designs, letters, numerals, or the shape of the goods or of their packaging. An applicant is required to pay fees to register a trade mark and renewal fees to keep it in force.

The Trade Marks Act 1996 allows for the first time registration of a trade mark for a service.

A trade mark should be:

- Distinctive
- Not deceptive
- Not descriptive
- Not among certain excluded items listed in the Act (such as national emblems, immoral or offensive language).

When registered, a trade mark is valid for 10 years and may be renewed every 10 years. Validity is effective from the date of application.

Well-known Irish trade marks include Guinness, Kerrygold and Aer Lingus.

You apply for registration of a trademark to:
- (For Ireland) Patents Office, Government Buildings, Hebron Road, Kilkenny
- (For EU) Office for Harmonisation in the Internal Market, Avenida de Europa 4, Apartado de Correos 77, E-03080, Alicante, Spain.

Industrial Designs

A design is a new idea or a conception of the external "shape, configuration, pattern or ornament" intended to be assumed by any article. Designs may be registered in respect of such diverse items as toys, lamps, articles of furniture, containers, clothes, fabrics and wallpaper.

A design applied to an article should not be confused with what may be a patentable invention, or a "device" trademark (a trademark containing or consisting of a picture or drawing). A trademark is only used for the purpose of indicating the origin of the goods/service on which it is used.

To be eligible for registration, a design must be new or original and must not have been published previous to the application.

A design may be registered initially for five years and may be renewed for further periods of five years, subject to a maximum of 15 years.

The Industrial Designs Act, 2001 updated and enhanced Irish industrial design law, broadening the civil and criminal remedies available in respect of infringements of design rights, implementing the EU Directive on the legal protection of designs and enabling future access for Irish designs to an international system of design protection under the Geneva Act of the Hague Agreement.

Copyright Protection

Copyright is the creator's (or legal owner's) rights in creative works like paintings, writings, computer software, photographs, drawings, sound recordings, films and television broadcasts. No formality such as registration or deposit of the work or payment of fees is required in order that copyright may subsist in a work.

The author of a work is the first owner of copyright in the work, except in the case of a work made under a contract of service in the course of employment. Subject to any agreement with the author, copyright in Government publications belongs to the Government.

To avoid others copying your work, it is essential to be able to show proof of ownership. It is advisable for an author to sign, date and witness his/her work as proof of ownership and to display the international copyright symbol © prominently on his/her work.

The law relating to copyright was updated by the Copyright and Related Rights Act, 2000. This is a complex area, and it is advisable to seek legal advice on any matter of doubt or dispute.

Information and Advice

The Patent Office has a library at its Kilkenny offices, containing various legal and technical reference works which may be of interest to inventors. In addition to providing access to a wide range of patent and trademark information in paper form, the Library also offers some electronic patent information services through CD-ROM computer terminals and also provides a document delivery service to the public.

The laws relating to intellectual property are complex and it is advisable for intending applicants to consult a registered patent or trade mark agent in advance. Application forms, information leaflets and lists of registered patent/trademark agents are available free of charge from the Patents Office (**www.patentsoffice.ie**).

MONITORING PERFORMANCE

OBJECTIVES
o Understand the importance of monitoring performance
o Be aware of monitoring techniques

If it's working,
keep doing it.
If it's not
working,
stop doing it.
If you don't know
what to do,
don't do anything.
**MEDICAL
SCHOOL
ADVICE**

It is important that you monitor the progress of your business against your business plan forecasts on a quarterly, monthly, even weekly basis. If you do not, there is a danger that things will go wrong without you knowing about it. In particular, if you do not watch your cash-flow carefully, you could run into difficulties very quickly.

Most lenders are keen to have regular financial information on the performance of the businesses to which they lend money. How they get it depends on the local manager and the arrangements he makes, since few small businesses have the capacity or ability to supply monthly or quarterly accounts.

The panel below provides a simple system both for you to monitor the financial performance of your business and to communicate it to your bank manager.

The first column is taken from your business plan and represents your forecast performance. The second is your actual performance to date, which you will get from your accounts. Calculate the difference between budget and actual, both in money and in percentages.

WHAT STAGE IS YOUR BUSINESS AT?

1. **Existence and survival**
   - Owner is business
   - Problem is finding customers and cash flow
2. **Consolidation and control**
   - Developing systems
   - Problem is to generate repeat sales and financial control
3. **Control and planning**
   - Taking on staff
   - Focus on management
   - Problem is fighting competition, development of new markets and control of margins and costs
4. **Expansion**
   - Delegation and decentralisation
   - Market expansion (new products and/or markets)
   - Tight financial control

Month/Quarter/Year ended _____

	Budget	Actual	Difference		Comment
Revenue by product					
A _____	€ _____	€ _____	€ _____	____%	_____
B _____	€ _____	€ _____	€ _____	____%	_____
C _____	€ _____	€ _____	€ _____	____%	_____
D _____	€ _____	€ _____	€ _____	____%	_____
E _____	€ _____	€ _____	€ _____	____%	_____
Total revenue	€ _____	€ _____	€ _____	____%	_____
Gross profit	€ _____	€ _____	€ _____	____%	_____
Gross profit % of turnover	_____%	_____%	_____%	____%	_____
Staff costs	€ _____	€ _____	€ _____	____%	_____
Production costs	€ _____	€ _____	€ _____	____%	_____
Premises	€ _____	€ _____	€ _____	____%	_____
Transport costs	€ _____	€ _____	€ _____	____%	_____
Sales and promotion	€ _____	€ _____	€ _____	____%	_____
General expenses	€ _____	€ _____	€ _____	____%	_____
Finance costs	€ _____	€ _____	€ _____	____%	_____
Depreciation	€ _____	€ _____	€ _____	____%	_____
Total overheads	€ _____	€ _____	€ _____	____%	_____
Net profit	€ _____	€ _____	€ _____	____%	_____
Net cash flow	€ _____	€ _____	€ _____	____%	_____

Key: T: Telephone
      F: Facsimile
      E: E-mail
      W: Web
      C: Contact

ACT Venture Capital Ltd, Jefferson House, Eglinton Road, Dublin 4 T: (01) 260 0966 F: (01) 260 0538 E: info@actvc.ie W: www. actventure.com C: Niall Carroll

Action Tallaght, Brookfield Enterprise Centre, Brookfield, Tallaght, Dublin 24 T: (01) 462 3222 F: (01) 462 3433 C: Olive Whelan

AIB Seed Capital Fund, Dublin Business Innovation Centre, The Tower, TCD Enterprise Centre, Pearse Street, Dublin 2 T: (01) 671 3111 F: (01) 671 3330 E: bif@dbic.ie W: www.dbic.ie C: Alex Hobbs

Amárach Consulting, 37 Northumberland Road, Dublin 4 T: (01) 660 5506 F: (01) 660 5508 E: info@amarach.com W: www.amarach.com Contact: Gerard O'Neill

Arts Council, 70 Merrion Square, Dublin 2 T: (01) 618 0200 F: (01) 676 1302 E: paul@artscouncil.ie W: www.artscouncil.ie C: Paul Johnson

Ashdown Food Research Centre, Ashdown, Dublin 15 T: (01) 805 9500 F: (01) 805 9550 E: carmell.farrell@teagasc.ie W: www.teagasc.ie C: Carmel Farrell, Information Officer

Association of Chartered Certified Accountants, 9 Leeson Park, Dublin 6 T: (01) 498 8900 F: (01) 496 3615 E: kevin.kernan@ie.accaglobal.com W: www.accaglobal.com C: Kevin Kernan

Athlone Institute of Technology, Dublin Road, Athlone, Co Westmeath T: (0906) 424400 F: (0906) 424417 E: hfitzsimons@ait.ie W: www.ait.ie C: External Services Manager

Balbriggan Enterprise Development Group, The BEAT Centre, Stephenstown Industrial Estate, Balbriggan, Co Dublin T: (01) 802 0417 F: (01) 802 0455 E: info@ bedg.ie W: www.bedg.ie C: Ria Stubbs

Ballyfermot / Chapelizod Partnership, 4 Drumfinn Park, Ballyfermot, Dublin 10 T: (01) 623 5612 F: (01) 623 0922 E: info@ballyfermotpartnership.ie W: www.ballyfermotpartnership.ie C: Justin Purcell

Ballymun Partnership, North Mall, Ballymun Town Centre, Dublin 11 T: (01) 842 3612 F: (01) 857 7518 E: info@ballymun.org W: www.ballymun.org C: Terence Kavanagh, Economic Development Advisor

Bank of Ireland Business Banking, 40 Mespil Road, Dublin 4 T: (01) 665 3438 F: (01) 665 3480 E: damian.young@ boimail.com W: www.bankofireland.ie C: Damian Young, Head of Small Business

Bank of Ireland Kernel Capital Partners Private Equity Fund, Kernel Capital Partners, Rubicon Centre, Rossa Avenue, Bishopstown, Cork T: (021) 492 8974 F: (021) 492 8977 E: nolden@ kernelcapital.ie W: www.kernelcapital.ie C: Niall Olden

Bank of Scotland (Ireland) Ltd, Bank of Scotland House, 124-127 St Stephen's Green, Dublin 2 T: (01) 267 4000 F: (01) 267 4010 W: www. bankofscotland.ie

Blanchardstown Area Partnership, Unit 106, Coolmine Industrial Estate, Clonsilla, Dublin 15 T: (01) 820 9550 F: (01) 820 9551 E: ncomber@bap.ie W: www.bap.ie C: Niall Comber

Bolton Trust, 128-130 East Wall Road, Dublin 3 T: (01) 240 1300 F: (01) 240 1310 E: info@boltontrust.com W: www.boltontrust.com C: Michael Drennan

Borders Midlands & Western Regional Assembly, The Square, Ballaghaderreen, Co Roscommon T: (0907) 62970 F: (0907) 62973 E: info@bmwassembly.ie W: www.bmwassembly.ie

Bord Bia - The Irish Food Board, Clanwilliam Court, Lower Mount Street, Dublin 2 T: (01) 668 5155 F: (01) 668 7521 E: info@bordbia.ie W: www.bordbia.ie C: Eileen Bentley, Manager, Small Business

Bord Iascaigh Mhara - Irish Sea Fisheries Board, PO Box 12, Crofton Road, Dun Laoire, Co Dublin T: (01) 214 4100 F: (01) 284 1123 E: info@bim.ie W: www.bim.ie C: Imelda Bradley

Bplans.ie, W: www.bplans.ie

Bray Partnership, 4 Prince of Wales Terrace, Quinsboro Road, Bray, Co Wicklow T: (01) 286 8266 F: (01) 286 8700 E: info@braypartnership.org C: Peter Brennan

Breffni Integrated, Unit 6A Corlurgan Business Park, Ballinagh Road, Cavan T: (049) 433 1029 F: (049) 432 7280 E: reception@cavpart.ie C: Terry Hyland, Enterprise Officer; Brendan Reilly, CEO

Business Expansion Scheme, Office of the Revenue Commissioners, Stamping Building, Dublin Castle, Dublin 2 T: (01) 702 4107 F: (01) 671 0012 E: cillbyrn@ revenue.ie W: www.revenue.ie C: Cillian Byrnes

Business Information Centre, Dublin City Public Library, ILAC Centre, Henry Street, Dublin 1 T: (01) 873 4333 F: (01) 872 1451 E: businesslibrary@dublincity.ie W: www.dublincitypubliclibraries.ie C: Anne Collins

Campus Companies Venture Capital Fund, Molesworth House, Moleworth Street, Dublin 2 T: (01) 679 0818 F: (01) 679 9014 E: info@campuscapital.com W: www.campuscapital.com C: Pat Ryan

Canal Communities Partnership, 197 Tyrconnell Road, Inchicore, Dublin 8 T: (01) 473 2196 F: (01) 453 4857 E: enterprise@canalpartnership.com W: www.canalpartnership.com C: Liz Byrne, Enterprise Co-ordinator

Carlow County Enterprise Board, Enterprise House, O'Brien Street, Carlow T: (059) 913 0880 F: (059) 913 0717 E: enterprise@carlow-ceb.com W: www.carlow-ceb.com C: Michael P. Kelly, CEO

Cavan County Enterprise Board, Cavan Innovation & Technology Centre, Dublin Road, Cavan T: (049) 437 7200 F: (049) 437 7250 E: info@cceb.ie W: www.cavanenterprise.ie C: Vincent Reynolds, CEO

Central Statistics Office, Skehard Road, Mahon, Cork T: (021) 453 5000 F: (021) 453 5555 E: information@ cso.ie W: www.cso.ie C: Kevin Moriarty Also at: Ardee Road, Rathmines, Dublin 6 T: (01) 497 7144 F: (01) 497 2360

Centre for Co-operative Studies, O'Rahilly Building, University College Cork, Cork T: (021) 490 2570 F: (021) 490 3358 E: ccs@ucc.ie W: www.ucc.ie/en/ccs/ C: Michael Ward

Centre for Entrepreneurial Studies, University of Limerick, Limerick T: (061) 202 183 F: (061) 338 171 E: naomi.birdthistle@ul.ie W: www.ul.ie C: Dr Naomi Birdthistle

Chambers Ireland, 17 Merrion Square, Dublin 2 T: (01) 661 2888 F: (01) 661 2811 E: info@chambers.ie W: www. chambers.ie C: James Kiernan

Chartered Accountants Ireland, Chartered Acountants House, 47-49 Pearse Street, Dublin 2 T: (01) 637 7200 F: (01) 668 0842 E: ca@chartered accountants.ie W: www.charteredaccountants.ie C: Conal Kennedy, Practice Advisory Executive

City of Dublin Vocational Education Committee, Town Hall, Merrion Road, Ballsbridge, Dublin 4 T: (01) 668 0614 F: (01) 668 0710 E: jim.boland@cdvec.ie W: www.cdvec.ie C: Jim Boland, Management Services; Jacinta Stewart, CEO

Clare County Enterprise Board, Enterprise House, Mill Road, Ennis, Co Clare T: (065) 684 1922 F: (065) 684 1887 E: clareceb@clareceb.ie W: www.clareceb.ie C: Eamonn Kelly

Comhair Chathair Chorcaí - Cork City Partnership, Heron House, Blackpool Park, Cork T: (021) 430 2310 F: (021) 430 2081 E: info@partnershipcork.ie C: Ann O'Sullivan

Companies Registration Office, Parnell House, 14 Parnell Square, Dublin 1 T: (01) 804 5200 F: (01) 804 5222 E: info@cro.ie W: www.cro.ie Postal address: O'Brien Road, Carlow

Co-operation Ireland, 20 Herbert Place, Dublin 2 T: (01) 661 0588 / 676 3608 F: (01) 661 8456 E: info@ cooperationireland.org W: www.cooperationireland.org C: Peter Sheridan

Co-operative Development Society Ltd, Dominick Court, 41 Lower Dominick Street, Dublin 1 T: (01) 873 3199 F: (01) 873 3612 E: coopsoc@tinet.ie W: www. ablaze.ie/cds C: Dermot McKenna

Cork Business Innovation Centre, NSC Campus, Mahon, Cork T: (021) 230 7005 F: (021) 230 7020 E: postmaster@corkbic.com W: www.corkbic.com C: Michael O'Connor, Chief Executive

Cork City Enterprise Board, 1-2 Bruach na Laoi, Union Quay, Cork T: (021) 496 1828 F: (021) 496 1869 E: info@corkceb.ie W: www.corkceb.ie C: Dave Cody, CEO

Cork Institute of Technology, Rossa Avenue, Bishopstown, Cork T: (021) 432 6100 F: (021) 454 5343 E: jsomullane@cit.ie W: www.cit.ie C: Josette O'Mullane, Industrial Liaison Officer

Cork North County Enterprise Board, The Enterprise Office, 26 Davis Street, Mallow, Co Cork T: (022) 43235 F: (022) 43247 E: corknent@iol.ie W: www.theenterpriseoffice.com C: Rochie Holohan

County Wexford Partnership, Millpark Road, Enniscorthy, Co Wexford T: (054) 37033 F: (054) 37026 Also at: Gorey T: (055) 22477, New Ross T: (051) 425 028 E: info@wexfordpartnership.ie W: www.wexfordpartnership.ie C: John Nunn

CPLN Area Partnership, Unit D, Nangor Road Business Park, Nangor Road, Clondalkin, Dublin 22 T: (01) 450 8788 F: (01) 450 8748 E: reception@cpln.ie W: www.cpln.ie C: Aileen O'Donoghue, CEO

Crafts Council of Ireland, Castle Yard, Kilkenny T: (056) 776 1804 F: (056) 776 3754 E: info@ccoi.ie W: www.ccoi.ie C: Emer Ferran, Enterprise Development Manager

CreativeIreland.com, W: www.creativeireland.com

Cross Atlantic Capital Partners, Alexandra House, The Sweepstakes, Ballsbridge, Dublin 4 T: (01) 664 1721 F: (01) 664 1806 E: gmccrory@xacp.com W: www. xacp.com C: Gerry McCrory

Dairy Products Research Centre, Moorepark, Fermoy, Co Cork T: (025) 42222 F: (025) 42340 E: eileen.lehane@teagasc.ie W: www.teagasc.org/research/research_centres.htm C: Dr WJ Donnelly, Head of Centre

Delta Partners, South County Business Park, Leopardstown, Dublin 18 T: (01) 294 0870 F: (01) 294 0877 E: frank@delta.ie W: www.delta.ie C: Frank Kenny

Department of Agriculture, Fisheries & Food, Agriculture House, Kildare Street, Dublin 2 T: (01) 607 2000 F: (01) 678 5214 E: info@agriculture.gov.ie W: www.agriculture.gov.ie

Department of Enterprise, Trade & Employment, Head Office, Kildare Street, Dublin 2 T: (01) 631 2121 F: (01) 631 2827 E: info@entemp.ie W: www.entemp.ie C: Information Section

Department of Social & Family Affairs, Information Services, Social Welfare Services, College Road, Sligo T: (1890) 662244 F: (071) 919 3284 E: info@welfare.ie W: www.welfare.ie

Department of the Environment & Local Government, Custom House, Dublin 1 T: (01) 888 2000 F: (01) 888 2888 E: press-office@environ.irlgov.ie W: www.environ.ie

DIT Hothouse, Docklands Innovation Park, 128-130 East Wall Road, Dublin 3 T: (01) 240 1300 F: (01) 240 1310 E: hothouse@dit.ie W: www.dit.ie/hothouse C: Bernadette O'Reilly

Donegal County Enterprise Board, Enterprise Fund Business Centre, Ballyraine, Letterkenny, Co Donegal T: (074) 916 0735 F: (074) 916 0783 E: info@donegalenterprise.ie W: www.donegalenterprise.ie C: Michael Tunney, CEO

Donegal Local Development Company, 1 Millennium Court, Pearse Road, Letterkenny, Co Donegal T: (091) 27056 F: (091) 21527 E: info@dldc.org W: www. dldc.org C: Caoimhín Mac Aoidh, Manager

Drogheda Partnership Company, Workspace Centre, Mayoralty Street, Drogheda, Co Louth T: (041) 984 2088 F: (041) 984 3358 E: info@droghedapartnership.ie W: www.droghedapartnership.ie C: Mary-Ann McGlynn, Manager

Dublin Business Innovation Centre, The Tower, TCD Enterprise Centre, Pearse Street, Dublin 2 T: (01) 671 3111 F: (01) 671 3330 E: info@dbic.ie W: www.dbic.ie C: John McInerney

For an entrepreneur
nothing is written in stone.

Except for two little words.

Get the right people behind you

❊ Ulster Bank

As a business owner you don't see problems but opportunities waiting to be mined. You don't accept the status quo but revel in changing it. You don't sit and wait but get up and go, never accepting can't. You don't ask why but ask why not?

Running a business is continuously challenging yet rich with potential.

Our people support ideas and business vision every day. Whether it's funding for your idea through our Business Start-up package* or access to cashflow management solutions, athat can help your business grow, call into one of our Branches or Business Centres or visit www.ulsterbank.com

Terms and conditions apply. Please see Business Start up brochure in branch for details. Ulster Bank Ireland Limited. A private company limited by shares, trading as Ulster Bank, Ulster Bank Group and Banc Uladh. Registered in Republic of Ireland. Registered No 25766. Registered Office: Ulster Bank Group Centre, George's Quay, Dublin 2. Member of The Royal Bank of Scotland Group. Ulster Bank Ireland Limited is regulated by the Financial Regulator.

ENTERPRISE ACCELERATION CENTRE

THE IDEAL START-UP LOCATION WITH

- Leading edge business environment
- Award Winning Businesses
- Microsoft Bizspark Network Partner
- Conduit to supports provided by Enterprise Support Agencies
- 3rd Level Collaboration

FOR MORE INFORMATION

Contact: Donncha Hughes
Tel. 061 490151

Email. donncha.hughes@lit.ie
Web. www.lit.ie/eac

DEVELOP YOUR INVESTOR READY BUSINESS PLAN WITH:

- Management Training
- One to One Mentoring
- Business Plan Coaching
- Peer Networking
- End of Year Business Plan Competition

FOR MORE INFORMATION

Contact: Graham Royce
Tel. 061 490152

Email. graham.royce@lit.ie
Web. www.leap.ie

Investing in your Future

Dublin City Enterprise Board, 5th Floor, O'Connell Bridge House, D'Olier Street, Dublin 2 T: (01) 677 6068 F: (01) 677 6093 E: info@dceb.ie W: www.dceb.ie C: Greg Swift, CEO

Dublin City University, Invent, Glasnevin, Dublin 9 T: (01) 700 5175 F: (01) 836 0830 E: richard.stokes@dcu.ie W: www.dcu.ie C: Richard Stokes, CEO, Invent

Dublin Inner City Partnership, Equity House, 16-17 Upper Ormond Quay, Dublin 7 T: (01) 872 1321 F: (01) 872 1330 E: office@dicp.ie W: www.dcip.ie C: Peter Nolan, Employment & Enterprise Co-ordinator

Dublin Institute of Technology, Central Office: Fitzwilliam House, 30 Upper Pembroke Street, Dublin 2 T: (01) 402 3379 F: (01) 402 3393 E: rea.oneill@dit.ie W: www.dit.ie C: Rea O'Neill, Industrial Liaison Officer

Dundalk Employment Partnership Ltd, Partnership Court, Park Street, Dundalk T: (042) 933 0288 F: (042) 933 0552 E: partnership@dep.ie W: www.dep.ie C: John Butler, Chief Executive

Dundalk Institute of Technology, Dublin Road, Dundalk, Co Louth T: (042) 937 0200 F: (042) 933 3505 E: gerry.carroll@dkit.ie W: www.dkit.ie C: Gerard Carroll, Head of Development

Dún Laoghaire/Rathdown County Enterprise Board, Nutgrove Enterprise Centre, Nutgrove Way, Rathfarnham, Dublin 14 T: (01) 494 8400 F: (01) 494 8410 E: michael@dlrceb.ie W: www.dlrceb.ie C: Michael Johnson, CEO

ENFO - Environmental Information Service T: (01) 676 1167 F: (01) 676 6721 W: www.askaboutireland.ie C: Anne Marie O'Dwyer

Enterprise Equity, Dublin Road, Dundalk, Co Louth T: (042) 933 3167 F: (042) 933 4857 E: info@enterpriseequity.ie W: www.eeirl.com C: Conor O'Connor

Enterprise Europe Network, Enterprise Ireland, The Plaza, East Point Business Park, Dublin 3 T: (01) 727 2729 F: (01) 727 2069 E: jan.gerritsen@enterprise-ireland.com W: www.enterprise-ireland.com

Enterprise Europe Network Cork, Cork Chamber, Fitzgerald House, Summerhill North, Cork T: (021) 450 9044 F: (021) 450 8568 E: cosullivan@corkchamber.ie W: www.corkchamber.ie C: Cathy O'Sullivan

Enterprise Europe Network Dublin, Dublin Chamber of Commerce, 7 Clare Street, Dublin T: (01) 644 7200 F: (01) 676 6043 E: marion@dublinchamber.ie W: www.dublinchamber.ie C: Marion Jammet

Enterprise Europe Network Galway, Galway Chamber of Commerce & Industry, Commerce House, Merchants Road, Galway T: (091) 563536 F: (091) 561963 E: cbrady@galwaychamber.com W: www.galwaychamber.com C: Carol Brady

Enterprise Europe Network Sligo, Sligo Chamber of Commerce & Industry, 16 Quay Street, Sligo T: (071) 916 1274 F: (071) 916 0912 E: lorraine@sligochamber.ie W: www.sligochamber.ie C: Lorraine McDonnell

Enterprise Europe Network Waterford, Waterford Chamber of Commerce Ltd, 8 George's Street, Waterford T: (051) 311138 F: (051) 876002 E: michelle.mchugh@waterfordchamber.ie W: www.waterford-chamber.ie C: Michelle McHugh

Enterprise Ireland, The Plaza, East Point Business Park, Dublin 3 T: (01) 727 2000 E: client.service@enterprise-ireland.com W: www.enterprise-ireland.com Regional Offices in Athlone, Cork, Dublin, Dundalk, Galway, Letterkenny, Killarney, Shannon, Sligo, Waterford

Environmental Protection Agency, P.O. Box 3000, Johnstown Castle Estate, Co Wexford T: (053) 916 0600 F: (053) 916 0699 E: info@epa.ie W: www.epa.ie

Europa W: europa.eu

European Commission, European Union House, 18 Dawson Street, Dublin 2 T: (01) 634 1111 F: (01) 634 1112 E: eu-ie-info-request@ec.europa.eu W: ec.europa.eu/ireland/ C: Library

Europe Direct.ie Blanchardstown, Blanchardstown Library & Offices, Blanchardstown Centre, Fingal, Dublin 15 T: (01) 890 5563 F: (01) 890 5786 E: blanchlib@fingalcoco.ie W: www.fingalcoco.ie/livinginfingal/libraries/ C: Betty Boardman

Letterkenny
Institute of Technology

Institiúid Teicneolaíoch
Leitir Ceanainn

An Institiúid Teicneolaíochta, Sligeach

Innovative programme is a pipeline for successful NW entrepreneurs

A recent survey shows that participants of the CÉIM programme (Commercialising Entrepreneurial Ideas and Manageme Development) are more likely to succeed in business. This is an innovative programme for prospective entrepreneurs in t North West of Ireland. CÉIM is delivered in collaboration between the Institute of Technology Sligo (IT Sligo) and Letterken Institute of Technology (LYIT) to bring relevant, tangible support to people with innovative business ideas that have hi commercial and export potential.

What it provides to entrepreneurs:
• Training in all areas of business
• Mentoring from experienced business advisors and practitioners relevant to participant's projects
• Office and other business incubation facilities at the Innovation Centre IT Sligo or the Colab LYIT
• Networking with other entrepreneurs and business development agencies
• Introduction to seed and early stage capital investment organisations
• Grant aid from Enterprise Ireland or Údarás na Gaeltachta for eligible applicants

The programme, which is currently recruiting, is an innovative course for North West entrepreneurs which in 4 years ha produced 36 'knowledge' businesses that employ over 110 people in the North West. Over half the entrepreneurs on t intensive 12 month programme are exporting their products and services, some to markets as far away as Japan. Twer seven percent have grown their companies since they began and the remainder are set to expand in the next 2 years. It's impressive track record. This hands-on approach is proving to be a pipeline for high quality business ventures in the No West. **Anyone who has an idea for a new product or service and wants to find out more can contact:**

Patsy Donaghey, LYIT on 074 9186703, Janette Gillen, IT Sligo 071 9155315 or Ultan Faherty at 074 9186070.

www.ceim.ie

Current CEIM Innovators. Pic: Declan Doherty

Europe Direct.ie Carraroe & Ballinasloe, Carraroe Branch Library, An Scailp Chultúrtha, An Cheathrún Rua, Co na Gaillimhe T: (091) 595 733 F: (091) 565 039 E: carraroelibrary@eircom.net W: www.galwaylibrary.ie C: Peigi Vaughan; Ballinasloe Library, Fairgreen, Ballinasloe, Co Galway T: (090) 964 3464 F: (091) 565 039 E: ballinasloe@galwaylibrary.ie C: Mary Dillon

Europe Direct.ie Dundalk, Roden Place, Dundalk T: (042) 935 3190 F: (042) 933 7635 E: libraryhelpdesk@louthcoco.ie

Europe Direct.ie Killarney, Rock Road, Killarney T: (064) 663 2655 F: (064) 663 6065 E: killarney@kerrycolib.ie W: www.kerrylibrary.ie/killarneybranch.asp C: Mary Murray

Europe Direct.ie Letterkenny, Central Library, Oliver Plunkett Road, Letterkenny, Co Donegal T: (074) 912 4950 F: (074) 912 4950 E: library@donegallibrary.ie W: www.donegallibrary.ie C: Marianne Lynch

Europe Direct.ie Thurles, The Source, Cathedral Street, Thurles, Co Tipperary T: (0504) 29720 F: (0504) 21344 E: eudirect@tipperarylibraries.ie W: www.tipperarylibraries.ie C: Ann Marie Brophy

Europe Direct.ie Waterford City, Lady Lane, Waterford T: (051) 849 975 E: europedirect@waterfordcity.ie W: www.waterfordcity.ie C: Sinead O'Higgins

Excellence Ireland Quality Association, 9 Appian Way, Ranelagh, Dublin 6 T: (01) 660 4100 F: (01) 660 4280 E: info@eiqa.com W: www.eiqa.com C: Petrina Duggan

Fáilte Ireland - The National Tourism Development Authority, Baggot Street Bridge, Dublin 2 T: 1890 525525 E: info@failteireland.ie W: www.failteireland.ie

FÁS - The Training & Employment Authority, Services to Business, 27-33 Upper Baggot Street, Dublin 4 T: (01) 607 0500 F: (01) 607 0608 E: info@fas.ie W: www.fas.ie C: John McGrath, Services to Industry

Fingal County Enterprise Board, Mainscourt, 23 Main Street, Swords, Co Dublin T: (01) 890 0800 F: (01) 813 9991 E: info@fingalceb.ie W: www.fingalceb.ie C: Oisin Geoghegan, CEO

Fingal Employees Youth Business Fund, Fingal County Enterprise Board, Mainscourt, 23 Main Street, Swords, Co Dublin T: (01) 890 0800 F: (01) 813 9991 E: info@fingalceb.ie W: www.fingalceb.ie C: Oisin Geoghegan, CEO

Finglas Business Initiative, Rosehill House, Finglas Road, Dublin 11 T: (01) 836 1666 F: (01) 864 0211 E: info@ fcp.ie W: www.fcp.ie C: David Orford

First Step, Jefferson House, Eglinton Road, Donnybrook, Dublin 4 T: (01) 260 0988 F: (01) 260 0989 E: info@first-step.ie W: www.first-step.ie

Food Product Development Centre, Dublin Institute of Technology, Cathal Brugha Street, Dublin 1 T: (01) 814 6080 F: (01) 874 857 E: fpdc@dit.ie W: www.fpdc.dit.ie C: Mary Dineen

Food Safety Authority of Ireland, Abbey Court, Lower Abbey Street, Dublin 1 T: (01) 817 1300 F: (01) 817 1301 E: info@fsai.ie W: www.fsai.ie

Forfás, Wilton Park House, Wilton Place, Dublin 2 T: (01) 607 3000 F: (01) 607 3030 E: aideen.fitzgerald@forfas.ie W: www.forfas.ie C: Aideen Fitzgerald, Communications Manager

Fountain Healthcare Partners Fund, Delta Partners, Guild House, 4th Floor, Guild Street, IFSC, Dublin 1 T: (01) 522 5100 F: (01) 636 6230 E: manus@fh-partners.com W: www.fh-partners.com C: Manus Rogan

Galway Business Innovation Centre, *see* WestBIC

Galway City Partnership, 3 The Plaza, Headford Road, Galway T: (091) 773466 F: (091) 773468 E: info@gcp.ie W: www.gcp.ie C: Declan Brassil

Galway County & City Enterprise Board, Woodquay Court, Woodquay, Galway T: (091) 565269 F: (091) 565384 E: lynchc@iol.ie W: www.galwayenterprise.ie C: Charles Lynch, CEO

Galway-Mayo Institute of Technology, Dublin Road, Galway T: (091) 753161 F: (091) 751107 E: andrew.darcy@gmit.ie W: www.gmit.ie C: Andrew D'Arcy, Head of Development

Galway Rural Development Company, Mellows Campus, Athenry, Co Galway T: (091) 844335 F: (091) 845465 E: grdc@grd.ie W: www.grd.ie C: Delia Colahan, CEO

Government Publications, 51 St. Stephen's Green, Dublin 2 T: (01) 647 6000 F: (01) 661 0747 E: pubsales@opw.ie Also at: Sales Office: Sun Alliance House, Molesworth Street, Dublin 2

Growcorp Innovation Centre, 3015 Lake Drive, Citywest Business Campus Park, Dublin 24 T: (01) 466 1000 F: (01) 466 1002 E: grow@growcorp.net W: www.growcorp.net

Guaranteed Irish Ltd, 1 Fitzwilliam Place, Dublin 2 T: (01) 661 2607 F: (01) 661 2633 E: info@guaranteedirish.ie W: www.guaranteedirish.ie

Guinness Enterprise Centre, Taylor's Lane, Dublin 8 T: (01) 410 0600 F: (01) 410 0602 E: info@guinness-enterprisectr.com W: www.guinness-enterprisectr.com C: Dolores Dempsey, Administration Manager

Guinness Ulster Bank Equity Fund, NCB Ventures Ltd, 3 George's Dock, IFSC, Dublin 1 T: (01) 611 5611 F: (01) 611 5987 W: www.ncb.ie C: Michael Murphy, michael.murphy@ncb.ie; Mark Mulqueen, mark.mulqueen@ncb.ie

Guinness Workers' Employment Fund Ltd, St James's Gate, Dublin 8 T: (01) 453 6700 F: (01) 454 6520 C: Rowena Thornburgh, Andy Shirran (part-time)

Health & Safety Authority, The Metropolitan Building, James Joyce Street, Dublin 1 T: (01) 614 7000 F: (01) 614 7020 E: wcu@hsa.ie W: www.hsa.ie

IBEC, Confederation House, 84-86 Lower Baggot Street, Dublin 2 T: (01) 605 1500 F: (01) 638 1500 E: info@ibec.ie W: www.ibec.ie

IDA Ireland, Wilton Park House, Wilton Place, Dublin 2 T: (01) 603 4000 F: (01) 603 4040 E: idaireland@ida.ie W: www. idaireland.com

IE Domain Registry Ltd, Windsor House, 14 Windsor Terrace, Sandycove, Co Dublin T: (01) 236 5400 F: (01) 230 0365 E: customerrelations@iedr.ie W: www.iedr.ie

Inishowen Partnership Board, St Mary's Road, Buncrana, Co Donegal T: (074) 936 2218 F: (074) 936 2990 E: inishpar@indigo.ie W: www.inishpar.ie C: Shauna McClenaghan, Manager

InnovationWorks, National Technological Park, Limerick T: (061) 338177 F: (061) 338065 E: prendergaste@ shannondevelopment.ie W: www.shannondevelopment.ie C: Eoghan Prendergast

Innovator, 174 Ivy Exchange, Granby Place, Parnell Square, Dublin 1 T: (01) 879 4010 F: (01) 879 4001 E: info@innovator.ie W: www.innovator.ie C: James Bourke, Sean McNulty

Institute of Certified Public Accountants in Ireland, 17 Harcourt Street, Dublin 2 T: (01) 425 1000 F: (01) 425 1001 E: nbornschein@cpaireland.ie W: www.cpaireland.ie C: Nicole Bornschein

Institute of Directors in Ireland, Heritage House, Dundrum Office Park, Dublin 14 T: (01) 296 4093 F: (01) 296 4127 E: skirwan@iodireland.ie W: www.iodireland.ie C: Maura Quinn, Chief Executive

Institute of Management Consultants & Advisers, 19 Elgin Road, Dublin 2 T: (01) 634 9636 F: (01) 281 5330 E: info@imca.ie W: www.imca.ie C: Tom Moriarty, Development Executive

Institute of Technology Blanchardstown, Blanchardstown Road North, Blanchardstown, Dublin 15 T: (01) 885 1000 F: (01) 885 1001 E : info@itb.ie W: www.itb.ie C: Tom Doyle, Head of Development

Institute of Technology Carlow, Kilkenny Road, Carlow T: (059) 917 0400 F: (059) 917 0500 E: info@itcarlow.ie W: www.itcarlow.ie C: Jim McEntee, Head of External Services

THE INNOVATION SPACE

synergy centre
at ITT Dublin

If you have
  - a creative idea
  - for an innovative business
then ...
> Test your ability to become an entrepreneur in the **Enterprise Launch Programme**
> Take your business from concept to a knowledge-based, high technology business that is investor-ready on the Synergy Enterprise Programme.

Synergy Centre

will put you at the heart of a vibrant entrepreneurial community, with:

- Mentoring
- Advice
- Training
- Networking
- Office Space
- Café
- Research links
- Funding links.

www.synergycentre.ie

The Synergy System

Business Idea		Viable Concept		Trading Business
Enterprise Launch Programme		**Synergy Enterprise Programme**		**Synergy Business Incubation**

Institute of Technology Sligo, Ballinode, Sligo T : (071) 55222 F: (071) 44096 E: info@itsligo.ie W: www. itsligo.ie C: Padraig Ryan, Head of Learning Environment

Institute of Technology Tralee, Clash, Tralee, Co Kerry T: (066) 714 5600, 714 5611 (Development) F: (066) 714 5636 E: brenda.clifford@ittralee.ie W: www.ittralee.ie C: Brenda Clifford, Development Dept

International Fund for Ireland, PO Box 2000, Dublin 2 T: (01) 478 0655 F: (01) 475 1351 W: www.internationalfundforireland.com

IPC Consulting, Alexandra House, The Sweepstakes, Ballsbridge, Dublin 4 T: (01) 631 9320 F: (01) 631 9001 E: ipc@ipc.ie W: www.ipc.ie C: Declan Duke

IRD Duhallow Ltd, James O'Keeffe Institute, Newmarket, Co Cork T: (029) 60633 F: (029) 60694 E: duhallow@eircom.net C: Maura Walsh, Manager

IRD Kiltimagh, Enterprise House, Aiden Street, Kiltimagh, Co Mayo T: (094) 938 1494 F: (094) 938 1884 E: info@ ird-kiltimagh.ie, ird@iol.ie W: www.ird-kiltimagh.ie C: Joe Kelly

Irish BICs Seed Capital Fund, Dublin BIC, The Tower, TCD Enterprise Centre, Pearse Street, Dublin 2 T: (01) 671 3111 F: (01) 671 3330 E: dscf@indigo.ie W: www.indigo.ie/dbic C: Alex Hobbs

Irish Co-operative Society Ltd, Plunkett House, 84 Merrion Square, Dublin 2 T: (01) 676 4783 F: (01) 662 4502 E: info@icos.ie W: www.icos.ie

Irish Energy Centre, Enterprise Ireland, Glasnevin, Dublin 9 T: (01) 808 2070, 836 9080 F: (01) 837 2848 E: info@irish-energy.ie W: www.irish-energy.ie C: Tom Halpin, Manager

Irish Exporters Association, 28 Merrion Square, Dublin 2 T: (01) 661 2182 F: (01) 661 2315 E: iea@irishexporters.ie W: www.irishexporters.ie C: John Whelan, Chief Executive

Irish Internet Association, The Digital Hub, 101 James Street, Dublin 8 T: (01) 542 E: info@iia.ie W: www.iia.ie C: Roseanne Smith (Membership), Irene Dehaene (Events)

Irish LEADER Network, Clare Local Development Co., Westgate Business Park, Kilrush Road, Ennis, Co Clare T: (065) 686 6800 E: info@ irishleadernetwork.org W: www.irishleadernetwork.org C: Doirin Graham, CEO

Irish League of Credit Unions, 33-41 Lower Mount Street, Dublin 2 T: (01) 614 6700 F: (01) 614 6701 E: info@creditunion.ie W:www.creditunion.ie

Irish Small & Medium Enterprises Association, 17 Kildare Street, Dublin 2 T: (01) 662 2755 F: (01) 661 2157 E: info@isme.ie W: www.isme.ie C: Mark Fielding

ITT Dublin, Tallaght, Dublin 24 T: (01) 404 2000 F: (01) 404 2700 E: eamon.tuffy@ it-tallaght.ie W: www.it-tallaght.ie C: Eamon Tuffy, Head of Development and External Services

Kernel Capital Partners, Rubicon Centre, Rossa Avenue, Bishopstown, Cork T: (021) 492 8974 F: (021) 492 8977 E: nolden@kernelcapital.ie W: www.kernelcapital.ie C: Niall Olden

Kerry County Enterprise Board, Manor West Complex, Ratass, Tralee, Co Kerry T: (066) 718 3522 F: (066) 712 6712 E: kerryceb@kerrycoco.ie W: www.kerryenterprise.ie C: Tomas Hayes, CEO

Kerry Technology Park, Dromtacker, Tralee, Co Kerry T: (066) 719 0000 F: (066) 719 0070 E: lynchm@shannon-dev.ie W: www.shannondevelopment.ie C: Marie Lynch, Projects Executive

Kildare County Enterprise Board, The Woods, Clane, Co Kildare T: (045) 861707 F: (045) 861712 E: info@ kildareceb.ie W: www.kildareceb.ie C: Donal Dalton, CEO

Kilkenny County Enterprise Board, 42 Parliament Street, Kilkenny T: (056) 775 2662 F: (056) 775 1649 E: enquiries@kceb.ie W: www.kceb.ie C: Sean McKeown, CEO

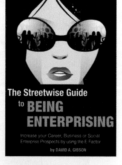
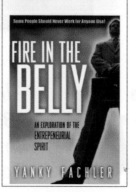

Laois County Enterprise Board, Portlaoise Enterprise Centre, Clonminam Business Park, Portlaoise, Co Laois T: (057) 866 1800 F: (057) 866 6989 E: admin@ laoisenterprise.com W: www.laoisenterprise.com C: Maria Callinan, CEO

Law Society of Ireland, Blackhall Place, Dublin 7 T: (01) 672 4800 F: (01) 672 4801 E: general@lawsociety.ie W: www.lawsociety.ie C: Ken Murphy, Director General

Leitrim Development Company, Church Street, Drumshambo, Co Leitrim T: (071) 964 1770 F: (071) 964 1741 E: info@ ldco.ie W: www.ldco.ie C: Tom Lavin, CEO

Leitrim Enterprise Board, Carrick-on-Shannon Business Park, Dublin Road, Carrick-on-Shannon, Co Leitrim T: (071) 962 0450 F: (071) 962 1491 E: info@ leitrimenterprise.ie W: www.leitrimenterprise.ie C: Joe Lowe, CEO

Letterkenny Institute of Technology, Port Road, Letterkenny, Co Donegal T: (074) 918 6000 F: (074) 918 6005 E: john.bonnar@lyit.ie W: www.lyit.ie C: John Andy Bonnar, Head of Development

Limerick City Enterprise Board, The Granary, Michael Street, Limerick T: (061) 312611 F: (061) 311889 E: info@limceb.ie W: www.limceb.ie C: Eamon Ryan, CEO

Limerick County Enterprise Board, Lissanalta House, Dooradoyle, Co. Limerick T: (061) 496 520 F: (061) 582 954 E: info@lcoeb.iol.ie W: www.lcoeb.ie C: Ned Toomey, CEO

Limerick Enterprise Development Partnership, Limerick Enterprise Development Park, Roxboro Road, Limerick T: (061) 469060 F: (061) 313 786 E: lmcelligott@ledp.ie W: www.ledp.ie C: Liam McElligott

Limerick Food Centre, Raheen Industrial Park, Limerick T: (061) 302033 F: (061) 301172 E: kehellyo@ shannon-dev.ie W: www.shannon-dev.ie/foodcentre C: Oliver Kehelly

Limerick Institute of Technology, Moylish Park, Limerick T: (061) 208803 F: (061) 208209 E: information@lit.ie W: www.lit.ie C: Colin McLean, Head of External Services / Fergal Barry, Head of Development

Longford Community Resources Ltd, Longford Community Enterprise Centre, Templemichael, Ballinalee Road, Longford T: (043) 334 5555 F: (043) 334 4093 E: enquiries@ lcrl.ie W: www.lcrl.ie C: Adrian Greene, Manager

Longford County Enterprise Board, Longford Enterprise Centre, Templemichael, Ballinalee Road, Longford T: (043) 334 2757 F: (043) 334 0968 E: info@longofordceb.ie W: www.longfordceb.ie C: Michael Nevin, CEO

Louth County Enterprise Board, Enterprise House, Quayside Business Park, Mill Street, Co Louth T: (042) 932 7099 F: (042) 932 7101 E: info@lceb.ie W: www.lceb.ie C: Ronan Dennedy, CEO

M50 Enterprise Platform Programme, LINC Centre, Institute of Technology Blanchardstown, Blanchardstown Road North, Blanchardstown, Dublin 15 T: (01) 885 1000 F: (01) 885 1001 E : info@itb.ie W: www.itb.ie C: Claire Quigley, Programme Manager

MAC (National Microelectronics Application Centre), Suparule House, Lonsdale Road, Plassey Technology Park, Limerick T: (061) 334699 F: (061) 338500 E: info@mac.ie W: www.mac.ie C: Dr John J. O'Flaherty, MD

Marine Institute, 80 Harcourt Street, Dublin 2 T: (01) 476 6500 F: (01) 478 4988 W: www.marine.ie

Mayo County Enterprise Board, Top Floor, The Cedar Building, Moneen, Castlebar, Co Mayo T: (094) 902 2887 E: info@ mayoceb.com W: www.mayoceb.com C: Frank Fullard, CEO

Meath County Enterprise Board, Navan Enterprise Centre, Trim Road, Navan, Co Meath T: (046) 907 8400 F: (046) 902 7356 E: mhceb@meath.com W: www.meath.com C: Pauline Baker

Meitheal Forbartha na Gaeltachta Teo, An Mhainistir, An Daingean, Co Chiarraí T: (066) 915 2280 F: (066) 915 1790 E: eolas@mfg.ie W: www.mfg.ie C: Antaine M Ó Sé

Meitheal Mhaigh Eo, Lower Main Street, Foxford, Co Mayo T: (094) 56745 F: (094) 56749 E: meithealm@ eircom.net C: Justin Sammon, Manager

MFG Teo, Ionad Fiontair, Ros Muc, Co. na Gaillimhe T: (091) 574 353 Fax: (091) 574 047 E: eolas@cumas.ie C: Trevor/Joe

Monaghan County Enterprise Board, Unit 9, M: TEK Building, Knockaconny, Monaghan T: (047) 71818 F: (047) 84786 E: info@mceb.ie W: www.mceb.ie C: John McEntegart, CEO

Monaghan Integrated Development, Monaghan Road, Castleblaney, Co Monaghan T: (042) 974 9500 F: (042) 974 9504 E: info@monaghanpartnership.ie W: www.planet.ie C: Gabriel O'Connell

National Association of Building Co-operatives Ltd, 33 Lower Baggot Street, Dublin 2 T: (01) 661 2877 F: (01) 661 4462 E: admin@nabco.ie W: www.nabco.ie

National Irish Bank Ltd, National House, Airton Road, Dublin 24 T: (01) 638 5000 F: (01) 638 5198 W: www.nib.ie C: Brian Leydon

National Microelectronics Application Centre, see MAC

National Software Centre, NSC Campus, Mahon, Cork T: (021) 230 7000 F: (021) 230 7020 E: info@nsc-campus.com W: www.nsc-campus.com C: Sue O'Brien, Facilities Manager

National Standards Authority of Ireland, 1 Swift Square, Northwood, Santry, Dublin 9 T: (01) 807 3800 F: (01) 807 3838 Also at: Plassey Park, Limerick T: (061) 411872 E: delaneyv@nsai.ie W: www.nsai.ie C: Vincent Delaney, Business Development Manager

National Technology Park, Limerick T: (061) 336555 F: (061) 338065 E: corcoranj@shannondevelopment.ie W: www.shannon-dev.ie C: Joan Corcoran, Marketing Executive

National University of Ireland Galway, Galway T: (091) 524411 F: (091) 525700 E: joe.watson@mis.nuigalway.ie W: www.nuigalway.ie C: Dr Joe Watson, Industrial Liaison Officer

NCB Ventures, 3 George's Dock, IFSC, Dublin 1 T: (01) 611 5611 F: (01) 611 5766 E: will.prendergast@ncb.ie W: www.ncb-ventures.com C: Will Prendergast

Northside Partnership, Coolock Development Centre, Bunratty Drive, Coolock, Dublin 17 T: (01) 848 5630 F: (01) 848 5661 E: cepta.dowling@ northsidepartnership.ie W: www.northsidepartnership.ie C: Cepta Dowling, Employment & Enterprise Programme Manager

Oak Tree Press, 19 Rutland Street, Cork T: (021) 431 3855 F: (021) 431 3496 E: brian.okane@oaktreepress.com W: www.oaktreepress.com C: Brian O'Kane, Managing Director

Offaly County Enterprise Board, Enterprise House, Cormac Street, Tullamore, Co Offaly T: (057) 935 2971 F: (057) 935 2972 E: info@offalyceb.ie W: www.offalyceb.ie C: Seán Ryan, CEO

Offaly Local Development Company, Millennium House, Main Street, Tullamore, Co Offaly T: (057) 935 2467/932 2850 F: (057) 935 2574 E: info@offalyldc.ie W: www.offalyldc.ie C: Carmel Ormond

Páirtíocht Chonamara & Árann, Ionad Fiontar, Rosmuc, Co na Gaillimhe T: (091) 574353 F: (091) 574047 E: cumas@eircom.net C: Máire Uí Ghiobúin, Manager

Páirtíocht Gaeltacht Thír Chonaill, MFG Teo, An Screabán, Na Doirí Beaga, Thir Chonaill, Co Dún na nGall T: (074) 953 2017 F: (074) 953 2428 E: eolasmfg@ eircom.net C: Seamus Sweeney, Acting Manager

Partas, Bolbrook Enterprise Centre, Avonmore Road, Tallaght, Dublin 24 T: (01) 414 5700 F: (01) 414 5799 E: ltwamley@partas.ie W: www.partas.ie C: Linda Twamley, Enterprise Officer

Partnership Trá Lí, 7 Ashe Street, Tralee, Co Kerry T: (066) 718 0190 F: (066) 712 9562 E: mail@partnershiptrali.com W: www.partnershiptrali.com C: Seamus O'Hara, Manager

Office Units for Start Up Companies in the heart of International Financial Services Centre

National College of Ireland – Business Incubation Centre (Finance, Education and Learning Technologies)

Individual offices ranging from 2 to 10 person offices. The Centre is recommended by successful Enterprises for its flexibility and its facilities for Start up companies.

Register your interest for space or to attend free information seminars by contacting Bertie Kelly at **014498704** or **bkelly@ncirl.ie**

National College of Ireland,
Mayor Street, IFSC, Dublin 1

Patents Office, Government Buildings, Hebron Road, Kilkenny T: (056) 772 0111 F: (056) 772 0100 E: patlib@ entemp.irlgov.ie W: www.patentsoffice.ie C: Yvonne Cassidy

PAUL Partnership Limerick, Unit 25a, The Tait Centre, Dominic Street, Limerick T: (061) 419388 F: (061) 418098 E: info@paulpartnership.ie W: www.paulpartnership.ie C: Ann Kavanagh, Manager

permanent tsb, 56-59 St Stephen's Green, Dublin 2 T: (01) 669 5000 E: info@ permanenttsb.ie W: www.permanenttsb.ie Contact: Local branch manager

PLATO Ireland, 58 Fitzwilliam Square North, Dublin 2 T: (01) 676 3973 F: (01) 676 3985 E: marion.walshe@plato.ie W: www.plato.ie C: Marion Walshe, Regional Manager

Pobal, Holbrook House, Holles Street, Dublin 2 T: (01) 240 0700 F: (01) 661 0411 E: enquiries@pobal.ie W: www.pobal.ie

Rabobank, Business Banking Unit, Charlemont Place, Dublin 2 T: (01) 418 4052 F: (01) 418 4809 E: padraig. kiernan@accbank.ie W: www.accbank.ie C: P. Kiernan

Rathmines Information Centre, *see* Terenure Enterprise Centre

Regional Development Centre, Dundalk Institute of Technology, Dublin Road, Dundalk, Co Louth T: (042) 933 1161 F: (042) 933 1163 E: gerry.carroll@dkit.ie W: www.rdc.ie C: Gerard Carroll, Head of Development

Registry of Business Names, Companies Registration Office, Parnell House, 14 Parnell Square, Dublin 1 T: (01) 804 5200 F: (01) 804 5222 W: www.cro.ie

Registry of Friendly Societies, Parnell House, 14 Parnell Square, Dublin 1 T: (01) 804 5499 F: (01) 804 5498

Revenue Commissioners, Dublin Castle, Dublin 2 T: (01) 679 2777 F: (01) 679 2035 W: www.revenue.ie Personal Callers: Central Revenue Information Office, Cathedral Street, off O'Connell Street, Dublin 1; Central Telephone Information Office: (01) 414 9700; Forms and leaflets: (01) 1890 30 67 06 (24 hours a day, 7 days a week)

Richmond Business Campus, North Brunswick Street, Dublin 7 T: (01) 809 0400 F: (01) 872 6252 E: richmond@iol.ie W: www. richmondbusinesscampus.com C: Rory O'Meara

Roscommon County Enterprise Board Ltd, Library Buildings, Abbey Street, Roscommon T: (090) 662 6263 F: (090) 662 5474 E: ceb@roscommon.ie W: www. roscommon.ie C: Peter Wrafter, Acting CEO

Roscommon Partnership Company, The Square, Castlerea, Co Roscommon T: (0907) 21337/8/9 F: (0907) 21340 E: roscommonptnship@eircom.net W: www.planet.ie/partners/roscommon.html C: Patricia Murphy-Byrne, Manager

Seed Capital Scheme, Office of the Revenue Commissioners, Dublin Castle, Dublin 2 T: (01) 702 4107 F: (01) 679 9287 E: cillbyrn@revenue.ie W: www.revenue.ie C: Cillian Byrnes

Shannon Development, Town Centre, Shannon, Co Clare T: (061) 361 555 F: (061) 361 903 E: info@shannon-dev.ie W: www.shannon-dev.ie Also offices in Birr, Ennis, Limerick, Nenagh and Tralee

Sligo County Enterprise Board, Sligo Development Centre, Cleveragh Road, Sligo T: (071) 914 4779 F: (071) 914 6793 E: info@sligoenterprise.ie W: www.sligoenterprise.ie C: John Reilly, CEO

Sligo LEADER Partnership Company Ltd, Sligo Development Centre, Cleveragh Road, Sligo T: (071) 914 1138 F: (071) 914 1162 E: info@sligoleader.com W: www.sligoleader.com C: Michael Quigley

Small Firms Association, Confederation House, 84-86 Lower Baggot Street, Dublin 2 T: (01) 660 1011 F: (01) 638 1668 E: info@sfa.ie W: www.sfa.ie C: Patricia Callan, Director

South Cork Enterprise Board, Unit 6A, South Ring Business Park, Kinsale Road, Cork T: (021) 497 5281 F: (021) 497 5287 E: enterprise@sceb.ie W: www.sceb.ie C: Sean O'Sullivan, CEO

South Dublin County Enterprise Board, 3a Village Square, Old Bawn Road, Tallaght, Dublin 24 T: (01) 405 7073 F: (01) 403 1234 E: info@sdenterprise.com W: www.sdenterprise.com C: Loman O'Byrne, CEO

South East Business Innovation Centre, Unit 1B, Industrial Park, Cork Road, Waterford T: (051) 356300 F: (051) 354415 E: info@sebic.ie www.sebic.ie C: Denise Stoneman, Administrator

Southern & Eastern Regional Assembly, Assembly House, O'Connell Street, Waterford T: (051) 860700 F: (051) 879887 E: info@seregassembly.ie W: www.seregassembly.ie

South Kerry Development Partnership, An Tobar, West Main Street, Caherciveen, Co Kerry T: (066) 947 2724 F: (066) 947 2725 E: aoriordan@skdp.net W: www.southkerry.ie C: Ann O'Riordan

Southside Partnership Ltd, The Old Post Office, 7 Rock Hill, Main Street, Blackrock, Co Dublin T: (01) 209 0610 F: (01) 275 5729 E: info@sspship.ie W: www.southsidepartnership.ie C: Marie Carroll, Manager

SPADE Enterprise Centre, North King Street, Dublin 7 T: (01) 617 4800 F: (01) 677 1558 E: mailbox@spade.ie W: www.spade.ie C: Susan Richardson, Centre Manager

Synergy Enterprise Programme, Synergy Centre, ITT Dublin, Tallaght, Dublin 24 T: (01) 404 2000 / 404 2376 F: (01) 404 2700 E: nicola.mountford@ittdublin.ie W: www.m50-enterprise.ie C: Jos Evertsen

Tallaght Partnership, Killinarden Enterprise Park, Tallaght, Dublin 24 T: (01) 466 4280 F: (01) 466 4288 E: anna.lee@tallpart.com W: www.tallpart.com C: Anna Lee, Manager

Teagasc - The Agriculture Food & Development Authority, Oak Park, Carlow, Co. Carlow T: (059) 917 0200 F: (059) 918 2097 E: info@teagasc.ie W: www.teagasc.ie C: PR & Information: Eric Donald; Advisory Services: Pat Boyle

Telework Ireland, Ballaghana, Mountnugent, Co Cavan T: 1800 421 426, (049) 854 0416 W: www.telework.ie C: Siobhán Duffy, Riona Carroll

Terenure Enterprise Centre, 17 Rathfarnham Road, Terenure, Dublin 6W T: (01) 490 3237 F: (01) 490 3238 E: info@tereneure-enterprise.ie W: www.terenure-enterprise.ie C: Michelle Hannon

Tipperary Institute, Nenagh Road, Thurles, Co Tipperary T: (0504) 28000 F: (0504) 28001 E: info@tippinst.ie W: www.tippinst.ie Also at Cashel Court, Clonmel, Co Tipperary T: (0504) 28000 F: (0504) 28001

Tipperary North County Enterprise Board, Connolly Street, Nenagh, Co Tipperary T: (067) 33086 F: (067) 33605 E: info@ tnceb.ie W: www.tnceb.ie C: Rita Guinan, CEO

Tipperary South Riding County Enterprise Board, 1 Gladstone Street, Clonmel, Co Tipperary T: (052) 612 9466 F: (052) 612 6512 E: ceb@southtippcoco.ie C: Thomas Hayes, CEO

Tolka Area Partnership, Rosehill House, Finglas Road, Dublin 11 T: (01) 836 1666 F: (01) 864 0211 E: info@fcp.ie W: www.fcp.ie C: David Orford

TVC Holdings plc, Beech House, Beech Hill Office Campus, Clonskeagh, Dublin 4 T: (01) 205 7700 F: (01) 205 7701 E: info@tvc.com W: www.trinity-vc.ie C: John Tracey, CEO

Tyndall National Institute, Lee Maltings, Prospect Row, Cork T: (021) 490 4177 F: (021) 490 4058 E: info@tyndall.ie W: www.tyndall.ie C: Kieran Flynn, Head of Business Development

Údarás na Gaeltachta, Na Forbacha, Gaillimh T: (091) 503100 F: (091) 503101 E: eolas@ udaras.ie W: www. udaras.ie C: Pádraig Ó hAoláin, Chief Executive Also offices in Dingle, Donegal, Cork and Mayo

Ulster Bank, Small Business Office, 33 College Green, Dublin 2 T: (01) 702 5225 F: (01) 702 5350 W: www. ulsterbank.com

University College Cork, Cork T: (021) 490 3000 F: (021) 490 3612 E: t.weaver@ ucc.ie W: www.ucc.ie C: Tony Weaver, Industrial Liaison Officer

University College Dublin, NovaUCD, University College Dublin, Belfield, Dublin 4 T: (01) 716 3707 F: (01) 716 3709 E: nova@ ucd.ie W: www.ucd.ie/nova C: Dr Ciara Leonard, Project Manager - Enterprise Development

University of Dublin, Trinity College, College Green, Dublin 2 T: (01) 677 5655 F: (01) 677 5883 E: bnoone@tcd.ie W: www.tcd.ie C: Bridget Noone, Enterprise Executive

University of Limerick, Limerick T: (061) 202611 F: (061) 330316 E: paul.dillon@ ul.ie W: www.ul.ie C: Paul Dillon, Director of Technology Transfer

Waterford Area Partnership, Westgate Park, Tramore Road, Waterford T: (051) 841740 F: (051) 843153 E: info@wap.ie W: www.wap.ie C: Joe Stokes, CEO

Waterford City Enterprise Board, Enterprise House, New Street Court, Waterford T: (051) 852883 F: (051) 877494 E: info@waterfordceb.com W: www. waterfordceb.com C: Bill Rafter, CEO

Waterford County Enterprise Board, Court House, Dungarvan, Co Waterford T: (058) 44811 F: (058) 44817 E: waterfordceb@cablesurf.com W: www.enterpriseboard.ie C: Gerard Enright, CEO

Waterford Institute of Technology, Industry Services, Room 2.10, Walton IT Building, WIT Cork Road Campus, Waterford T: (051) 302034 F: (051) 378292 E: kkiely@wit.ie W: www.wit.ie C: Kathryn Kiely, Industry Services Manager

Waterford LEADER Partnership Ltd, Teagasc Centre, Lismore, Co Waterford T: (058) 54646 F: (058) 54126 E: info@wlp.ie W: www.wlp.ie C: Julie O'Donnell, LES Co-ordinator; Jimmy Taafe, Manager

WestBIC (Business Innovation Centre, Galway), Galway Technology Centre, Mervue, Galway T: (091) 730 850 F: (091) 730 853 E: mryan@westbic.ie W: www. westbic.ie C: Mary Ryan

West Cork Enterprise Board, 8 Kent Street, Clonakilty, Co Cork T: (023) 883 4700 F: (023) 883 4702 E: enterprise@wceb.ie W: www.wceb.ie C: Michael Hanley, CEO

West Limerick Resources Ltd, St. Mary's Road, Newcastlewest, Co Limerick T: (069) 79114 F: (069) 61870 E: srowley@wlr.ie W: www.wlr.ie C: Suzanne Rowley, Information & Communication Officer

Westmeath Community Development Ltd, Presentation House, Harbour Street, Mullingar, Co Westmeath. T: (044) 934 8571 F: (044) 934 8441 E: info@westcd.ie W: www.westcd.ie C: Joe Potter, CEO

Westmeath County Enterprise Board Ltd, Business Information Centre, Church Avenue, Mullingar, Co Westmeath T: (044) 934 9222 F: (044) 934 9009 E: info@westmeath-enterprise.ie W: www.westmeath-enterprise.ie C: Christine Charlton, CEO

Wexford County Enterprise Board, Unit 1, Ardcavan Business Park, Ardcavan, Wexford. T: (053) 912 2965 F: (053) 912 4944 E: info@wexfordceb.ie W: www.wexfordceb.ie C: Sean Mythen, CEO

Wexford Local Development, Cornmarket, 9 Mallin Street, Wexford. T: (053) 912 3994 F: (053) 912 1024 E: info@wld.ie C: Bernard O'Brien, CEO

Wicklow County Enterprise Board, Wicklow County Campus, Clermont House, Rathnew, Co Wicklow T: (0404) 30800   F: (0404) 30899 E: enterprise@wicklowceb.ie W: www.wicklowceb.ie C: Sheelagh Daly, CEO

Updates to Appendix 1 are available on www.startingabusinessinireland.com

BOOKS

Blink! Malcolm Gladwell, Penguin

Burn Your Business Plan!, David E Gumpert

Could You Be Your Own Boss? Brian O'Kane, Oak Tree Press

Clicking, Faith Popcorn and Lys Marigold, Thorsons

Creativity for Managers, Alan Barker, The Industrial Society

Don't Make Me Think, Steve Krug, New Riders

Enterprise in Action, 3rd edition, James Cunningham & Colm O'Gorman, Oak Tree Press

European Handbook of Management Consultancy, Oak Tree Press

Fire in the Belly, Yanky Fachler, Oak Tree Press

High Tech Start Up, John L Nesheim, Free Press

How to Form a Limited Company, PDF eBook, Brian O'Kane, Oak Tree Press

Managing & Marketing Your Website, Jim Hutchinson, Oak Tree Press

Multipreneuring, Gorman, Fireside Press

Quick Win Digital Marketing, Annmarie Hanlon & Joanna Akins, Oak Tree Press

Quick Win Marketing, Annmarie Hanlon, Oak Tree Press

Simply Brilliant, Fergus O'Connell, Prentice Hall

Starting a Business in Ireland, Brian O'Kane, 6th edition, Oak Tree Press

Starting on a Shoestring — Building a Business without a Bankroll, Goldstein, Ronald Press

TENBizPlan, Ron Immink & Brian O'Kane, Oak Tree Press

The Art of the Start, Guy Kawasaki, Portfolio

The Beermat Entrepreneur, Mike Southon & Chris West, Prentice Hall Business

The Mind of the Strategist, Ken Ohmae, McGraw-Hill

The Plan-As-You-Go Business Plan, Tim Berry, Entrepreneur Press

The SEED Handbook, Lynne Franks, Thorsons

The Spirit of Enterprise, George Gilder, Penguin

The Women's Business Resource Guide, Barbara Littman, Contemporary Books

MAGAZINES

Irish Entreprneeur, Morrissey Media

Owner-Manager, Small Firms Association

Business Plus, www.bizplus.ie

WEB-SITES

www.basis.ie – Business Access to State Information Services, a new Government web-site

www.bizplus.ie – Business Plus magazine

www.businessandleadership.com

www.chambers.ie – Chambers of Commerce

www.cro.ie – Companies Registration Office

www.cso.ie – Central Statistics Office

www.entrepreneurmag.com

www.enterprise-ireland.ie

www.enterpriseboards.com – a central point for access to the County/City Enterprise Boards

www.franchisedirect.com

www.halfaloaf.ie

www.iia.ie – Irish Internet Association

www.irlgov.ie – the Irish Government web-site

www.isme.ie – ISME

www.managementdirect.com

www.morebusiness.com

www.revenue.ie – Revenue Commissioners

www.ros.ie – Revenue Services On-line

www.sbaonline.sba.gov – US Small Business Administration

sbinformation.about.com

www.sfa.ie – Small Firms Association

www.sfediuk.co.uk

www.smallbusinessscan.com

www.startingabusinessinireland.com – where you will find updates for this guide and will be able to download spreadsheets and templates for use with your business plan

www.startups.co.uk